A Practical
Introduction to
PHIGS
and
PHIGS PLUS

A Practical Introduction to

PHIGS
and
PHIGS PLUS

T.L.J. Howard

W.T. Hewitt

R.J. Hubbold

K.M. Wyrwas

ADDISON-WESLEY
PUBLISHING
COMPANY

Wokingham, England • Reading, Massachusetts • Menlo Park, California • New York

Don Mills, Ontario • Amsterdam • Bonn • Sydney • Singapore

Tokyo • Madrid • San Juan • Milan • Paris • Mexico City • Seoul • Taipei

Cover designed by Crayon Design of Henley-on-Thames and printed by The Riverside Printing Co. (Reading) Ltd.
Printed in Great Britain by T.J. Press (Padstow), Cornwall.

First printed in 1991.

British Library Cataloguing in Publication Data
A Practical introduction to PHIGS and PHIGS PLUS.
   1. Microcomputer systems. Graphic displays. Programming
   I. Howard, T.L.J.
   006.66

   ISBN 0-201-41641-7

Library of Congress Cataloging in Publication Data
A Practical introduction to PHIGS and PHIGS PLUS / T.L.J. Howard …[et al.].
     p. cm.
   Includes bibliographical references and index.
   ISBN 0-201-41641-7
   1. Computer Graphics. I. Howard, T.L.J.
T385.P72   1991
006.6–dc20   90-45548
                                                      CIP

To my mother and, in memoriam, to my father.
And to Jane.

T.L.J.H.

To Jan, Mum and Dad, and the safe arrival
of the next generation.

W.T.H.

To Sarah, and my mother and father.

R.J.H.

To my mother and father, and to Richard.

K.M.W.

Preface

This book is about an international standard software system called PHIGS – the Programmer's Hierarchical Interactive Graphics System, and about a set of proposed extensions called PHIGS PLUS – PHIGS Plus Lumière Und Shading.

Surprisingly, the places *not* to look to try and learn about these systems are the documents which actually define them! International standards are written as technical specifications, and definitely not from a tutorial point of view. Our intention in this book is to provide an introduction to PHIGS and PHIGS PLUS, with the application programmer in mind.

It will help – but it is not essential – if the reader is familiar with straightforward Cartesian geometry, and the simple mathematics of vectors and matrices. We assume familiarity with the basic concepts of computer graphics, and with programming languages, including conditional expressions, loops and procedures.

A note about PHIGS PLUS

As this book goes to press (January 1991), the technical specification of PHIGS PLUS is not yet finalized, and it is therefore not possible for us to give a complete description. However, although the details are subject to change, the underlying philosophy is not, and it is from this point of view that we approach PHIGS PLUS in Chapters 13 and 14.

Notation

For compactness and readability, all PHIGS functions, and most of the examples, are presented using an informal **functional notation**. For example, the specification of the function ROTATE X is as follows:

☐ ROTATE X
    parameters:
        in   rotation angle   real
        out error   integer
        out transformation matrix 4×4 real matrix

This indicates that the function has three parameters. There is one input parameter, *rotation angle*, which is a real number, and two output parameters, *error*, which is an integer, and *transformation matrix*, which is a 4×4 matrix of reals. One of the benefits of using this notation is that we do not have to worry about the conventions various programming languages use for describing procedures and their parameters.

PHIGS functions fall into two classes: those which create structure elements, and those which do not. It is very important when programming to keep in mind to which class a function belongs. To help with this, when we give the specification of a function we indicate its class using special icons:

☐E☐ indicates a function which creates a structure element

☐ indicates a function which does not create a structure element

Thus, the ROTATE X function does not create a structure element. The following function, however, does:

☐E☐   POLYLINE 3
    parameters:
       in   points   list of 3D MC points

In addition to C and Fortran, we also present examples using an informal pseudo-code notation. For example:

```
% Create a structure.
OPEN STRUCTURE (box)
% Draw a polyline.
POLYLINE 3 (box points)
CLOSE STUCTURE
```

Here, we ignore programming language conventions, and comments are indicated by the % character.

Typographical conventions

In this book we use a number of typographical conventions, as follows:

- **bold** is used whenever a new concept or technical term is introduced;

- *italics* are used to indicate the names of parameters in functions. Occasionally, italics are also used for emphasis, but it should be clear from the context in what sense they are being used;

- SMALL CAPITALS are used for the names of PHIGS functions and structure elements;

- `typewriter` font is used for C and Fortran program listings.

Acknowledgements

It is a great pleasure for us to have the opportunity to thank all the people who have helped with the production of this book. For their many helpful comments on the manuscript we thank Tony Arnold, R. Daniel Bergeroñ, Peter Bono, Lesley Carpenter, David Duce, Mike French, Jan Hardenbergh, Bob Hopgood, Mike Stapleton and Phil Willis. Steve Larkin read several preliminary versions, and helped us enormously with PHIGS programming. Lin Fenqiang provided many helpful comments on the manuscript. We would also like to thank all our colleagues in the international standardization community.

Appendix G first appeared as 'An annotated PHIGS bibliography' in *Computer Graphics Forum* **8**(3), 1989 (published by Elsevier Science Publishers), and is reproduced here in modified form by kind permission of Eurographics, the European Association for Computer Graphics. Salim Abi-Ezzi, Chris Cartledge, Jon Owen and Clive Ruggles kindly helped with its compilation.

A book about computer graphics would be a dull affair without some nice pictures, and for their assistance in preparing the colour plates our sincere thanks go to Tim Gilligan, Bob McKee and Jane Powell of Sun Microsystems Inc., to Ian Currington of Stardent Computer Ltd, Jim Flatten and Keith Comeford of Digital Equipment Corporation, Mike French of the Rutherford Appleton Laboratories, and to Mike Koiston, our departmental photographer. Phil Williams spent a busy summer grappling with PHIGS making figures for Chapters 3 and 9, and Gareth Williams created pictures for Chapters 1, 5 and 6. Thank you also to Jen Geck Tan for her B-splines.

From our long-suffering publishers, we thank Sarah Mallen in particular for her determination that this book would eventually appear. On the production and editorial side, we could never have managed without the expert care and attention of Stephen Bishop, Sheila Chatten, and Simon Plumtree. For their help in the preparation of the camera-ready manuscript we are grateful to Cliff Jones, David Carlisle and Mario Wolczko for typesetting assistance, and Colin Morgan of the University of Manchester Staff Development Unit for his help with the Linotron phototypesetter. Graham Gough deserves a special thank you for – amazingly – never once losing his patience being our Local Guide to LaTeX and GNUemacs. And we shall be eternally grateful to Mary McDerby, not only for her cheerful typing, editing and all-round secretarial support, but also, of course, for her coffee – service with a smile.

And finally, thank you Jane, Jan, Sarah and Richard for putting up with us above and beyond the call of duty, and to everyone who ever said 'haven't you finished it *yet*?'

Toby Howard
Terry Hewitt
Roger Hubbold
Karen Wyrwas

Manchester and Adelaide, January 1991

Contents

Chapter 1
A whirlwind tour

This chapter takes you on a guided tour of the main features of PHIGS, to give you a flavour of the sorts of things that PHIGS can do, without at this stage being too technical.

PHIGS – the Programmer's Hierarchical Interactive Graphics System – is a system which combines modelling with two- and three-dimensional computer graphics. It gives application programmers the ability to construct models which have a complex logical structure, and then to create pictures of the models with which users can interact. We can broadly summarize the areas which PHIGS is intended to address, as follows:

- dynamic manipulation of graphical application models;

- 2D and 3D device-independent computer graphics;

- interaction with the graphical model;

- real-time manipulation of pictures;

- off-line storage (and retrieval) of pictures and models.

PHIGS is implemented as a function package which can be called from conventional programming languages such as C and Fortran. There are implementations of PHIGS commercially available for a wide range of hardware and operating systems, and because PHIGS is an **international standard**, it is possible – with care – to write programs which are highly **portable** between different devices and installations.

1.1 Where PHIGS fits in

The role of PHIGS is illustrated in Figure 1.1. The information describing the model, which may be a mixture of graphical and other data specific to the application, is stored in a single area called the **Centralized Structure Store** (CSS). The

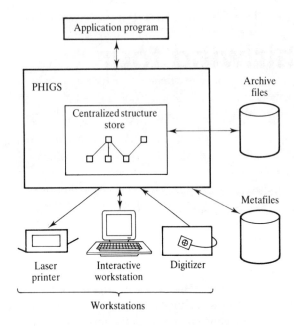

Figure 1.1   Where PHIGS fits in.

application uses graphics devices (called **workstations** in PHIGS terminology) to display and interact with pictures of the model.

At this point, we should mention a possible source of confusion. In computing circles, the term 'workstation' is commonly used to refer to a compact machine, with a keyboard, bit-mapped screen and mouse, which is intended for a single user. In PHIGS, however, the term 'workstation' has a quite different meaning: it is the name given to any combination of hardware and software for providing graphical output and/or graphical input. In fact, it will often be the case that different windows on a single bit-mapped screen will be treated, by PHIGS, as separate workstations.

The activities of **model definition** and **model display** are separate in PHIGS, and we shall look at each in turn. First, the application defines the model. The basic unit of data for storing information is called a **structure element**. Sequences of structure elements are collected into named **structures**. The application can define the logical relationships between different parts of the model by linking different structures together to form **hierarchies**, or **structure networks**. This scheme has a bonus: we can use the hierarchical storage to store only *one copy* of a set of data which occurs several times in the model.

Once the model is defined, the application can create pictures of it on workstations. To do this it must specify which part of the model to display, on which workstations, and an appropriate view of it. PHIGS then reads the definition of the model, extracts the required graphical information, and draws the picture.

This display process is called **traversal**. If the application now **edits** the model, by changing the contents of structures or changing the view, the displayed picture may be automatically updated to reflect the changes.

In the remainder of this chapter we shall take you on a whirlwind tour of the features PHIGS provides for modelling with computer graphics. We begin by listing the main features, and in the following sections we shall describe each feature in more detail:

- **Graphical output**   PHIGS provides a small number of basic types of graphical output called **output primitives**, from which 2D and 3D pictures (the graphical data of models) may be constructed. These include **lines**, **text** and **filled areas**. PHIGS PLUS provides additional primitives such as **triangle strip**, **quadrilateral mesh** and **B-spline curves** and **surfaces**.

- **Attributes**   Describing the **geometry** is only part of the definition of a picture: we must also specify the visual **style**, such as whether a particular line is solid, dashed, or dotted, and so on. The style of graphical output is controlled by data called **attributes**.

- **Creating the model**   Structure elements which define output primitives, attributes and other information are grouped together into lists known as **structures**. Each structure has a name, and structures may be arranged hierarchically to create **structure networks**. This enables the application to create models which have a **hierarchical logical structure**.

- **Displaying the model**   Once the model has been created, it is displayed by calling a function to **post** it to one or more workstations. This causes PHIGS to **traverse** the model, extracting its graphical information for display.

- **Editing the model**   Once a model has been created, it may be repeatedly **edited** – new parts may be added, and existing parts deleted or modified. Changes made to the model are automatically reflected in the displayed picture.

- **Transformations and viewing**   Complex models may be built in terms of simpler components which are defined independently, using convenient local coordinate systems. The individual coordinate systems are called **modelling coordinates**, and are combined together using **modelling transformations** to create the overall picture in **world coordinates** when the model is traversed. Once a 3D model has been defined, we need to create a **view** of it on a graphics device. PHIGS provides a powerful mechanism for this, enabling scenes to be viewed from different viewpoints (as if using a camera to photograph them from different positions), using parallel or perspective projections.

- **Graphical input**   PHIGS is an interactive system. Several different types of graphical input are supported, including the specification of positions, and the selection of structures by name. Input may be supplied in several ways: for example, the program might pause and wait for the operator to do something, or the operator may provide input at arbitrary times, in which case the input will be stored in a queue until it is required by the program.

- **Model and picture files**   Models may be stored on special **archive files**, and pictures on **metafiles**. Each of these types of file is external to PHIGS, and both may be subsequently restored for further processing.

1.2   Graphical output

There are eight different kinds of graphical output primitive:

- **Polyline** for drawing a connected sequence of straight lines.

- **Polymarker** for marking a set of points with symbols.

- **Fill area** for drawing a filled-in area bounded by a set of points.

- **Fill area set** for drawing filled-in areas containing holes.

- **Text** for drawing character strings.

- **Annotation text relative** for annotating pictures with descriptive text, such that if the picture is transformed, the annotation always remains legible.

- **Cell array** for drawing a 2D grid of colours.

- **Generalized drawing primitive (GDP)** for accessing special device features which might be available, such as curves.

Figure 1.2 and Plate 1 show some examples of output primitives. PHIGS provides both 2D and 3D functions to create output primitives. This means that although PHIGS is fundamentally a 3D system, it can be conveniently used by applications which only require 2D graphics. We describe output primitives in Chapter 3.

1.3   Attributes

The appearance of graphical output is determined by two different kinds of data:

- **Geometric information** which specifies the **shape** of the output, such as the path taken by a polyline.

- **Attributes** which specify the **style** of the output, such as whether a polyline is dotted or dashed.

Each type of graphical output has a number of attributes which control its visual appearance; the top left-hand picture in Figure 1.2 illustrates how polylines may be distinguished by drawing them using different attributes. Attributes are described in Chapter 9.

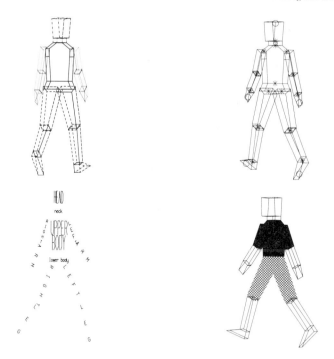

Figure 1.2   Some examples of PHIGS graphical output.

1.4   Creating the model

The basic unit of data is the **structure element**, of which there are several different kinds. There is a structure element for each output primitive (such as polyline or text), and there are also structure elements for setting attributes (such as line style or character height). Structure elements do not exist in isolation – they are collected together into **structures** which are stored in the **Centralized Structure Store** (CSS).

Many pictures exhibit a natural hierarchy. For example, in both molecular modelling and electronic computer-aided design, the picture may contain many repeated parts, such as the molecules in a protein or the integrated circuits in a printed circuit board (Figure 1.3 shows an example). Structures can reference, or **instance**, other structures. In this way, the natural hierarchy which occurs in many models can be represented using collections of linked structures called **structure networks**. Structure instancing is achieved using the **execute structure** element. This has several advantages: it supports models which have a strong logical structure, and it also reduces the amount of storage necessary to describe the model. Instead of repeating the definition of a structure each time it appears in the model, we may have a single master definition, which is instanced a number of times.

PHIGS allows the user to define separate parts of the picture in convenient

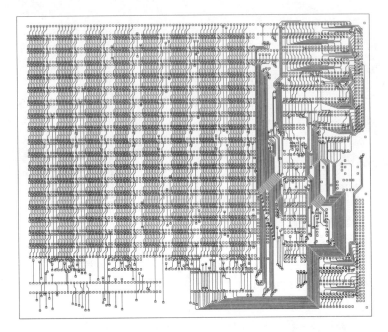

Figure 1.3   Repeated features in a printed circuit board layout.

local coordinate systems, known as **modelling coordinate systems**. **Modelling transformations** are then specified, which combine the parts of the picture together, into a single **world coordinate system**. Modelling transformations are themselves defined by structure elements. There are two kinds of modelling transformation: **local** and **global**, which are combined to form the **composite modelling transformation**. This transformation is applied to all coordinates in a structure. Chapter 4 describes the facilities PHIGS provides for creating models.

We can illustrate the value of hierarchical models and transformations using a simple robot arm, shown in Figure 1.4. The robot is constructed from a number of parts which are mostly instances of basic shapes, such as a cube and a cylinder:

- A cylindrical base (structure Rob).

- An arm pivot, which is a triangular prism (ArmPivot).

- A cylindrical shoulder joint (ShoulderJoint).

- A square section upper arm (UpperArm).

- A cylindrical elbow joint (ElbowJoint).

- A square section lower arm (LowerArm).

- A cylindrical wrist joint (WristJoint).

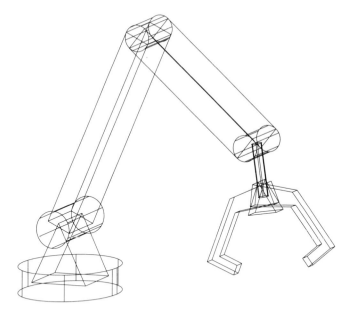

Figure 1.4 A robot arm.

- A circular section wrist (`Wrist`).

- A triangular section gripper pivot (`GripperPivot`).

- A pair of grippers (`Gripper1`, `Gripper2`).

The basic parts are defined to be of unit dimensions and are scaled to the required size by local modelling transformations. Transformations are also employed to position the parts relative to each other. For example, the lower arm is positioned using a local modelling coordinate system whose origin is located at the shoulder joint and whose x axis points along the upper arm. Then when the upper arm is rotated about the shoulder, the coordinate system used to define the lower arm also moves, so that the lower arm itself moves. Similarly, the wrist is positioned relative to the lower arm, and the grippers are positioned relative to the wrist.

In order to animate the robot, we define rotation transformations at each joint. As each transformation is changed the robot moves. Because each part is defined in a relative fashion, moving one part causes all parts further along the structure (lower down the hierarchy) to move appropriately.

With most applications such as this there are several ways in which the PHIGS structures could be defined. Figure 1.5 shows one possibility. There are four basic building blocks which can be instanced, each defined as a structure: `Cylinder`, `Pivot`, `Cube` and `Gripper`. Associated with each structure invocation is a modelling transformation, labelled `M` in the figure, and for each joint which can be manipulated there is a transformation labelled `X`.

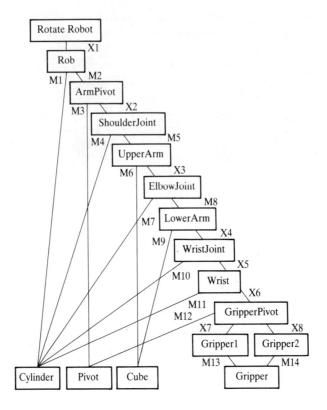

Figure 1.5   Structures and transformations for the robot.

1.5   Displaying the model

Structures are displayed when they are **posted** to a workstation (and the same structure may be posted to several workstations). Posting causes the structure to be **traversed**, generating a picture which is displayed on the workstation. The traversal process visits each element in the structure until the end of the structure is reached. The action taken at each element depends on the nature of the element:

- **Polyline** and other output primitive elements will be drawn on the workstations to which the structure is posted.

- Local or global **modelling transformations** are used to update the current Composite Modelling Transformation (CMT). This is applied to all output primitives encountered during the traversal.

- **Attribute selections** modify the current value of the appropriate attributes. These values are used to determine the appearance of output primitives subsequently generated during the traversal.

- **Execute structure elements** have a special effect on traversal. The current values of all the attributes, and the local and global transformations, are saved on a stack. The executed, or **child**, structure is then traversed. The child structure inherits attributes from the calling, or **parent**, structure. Once the end of the child structure has been reached, the attributes and transformations are reset to those which were in effect before the traversal of the child structure began. Note that the child structure may itself contain execute elements, and so on. By using a stack to save attributes and modelling transformations across references to structures, any changes made to attributes and modelling transformations in a child structure cannot affect the parent structure.

There are also a number of other types of structure element, which cause action to be taken during traversal, and we shall describe these in later chapters.

Once a structure network has been posted to a workstation, traversal may be thought of as a continuous process, so that if any changes are made to the structure definitions the displayed picture is immediately updated to show the changes. Sometimes, however, it may not be appropriate (or efficient) to update the picture after every change – especially when using devices such as plotters which have to redraw the whole picture. For this reason PHIGS gives the application considerable control over exactly *how* and *when* picture updating is performed. This is described in Chapter 8.

1.6   Editing the model

Structures may be **edited**: the elements in a structure are numbered sequentially, and an **element pointer** is used to specify a position within a structure where structure elements are inserted, deleted or replaced. However, it is not always easy to keep track of structure element numbers, particularly when structure elements are deleted or inserted in the middle of a structure, which causes elements further on in the structure to be renumbered automatically. To help solve this problem, there is a special type of structure element to assist in navigating around a structure, called the **label** element. The element pointer can be set to a specified label element, and there is a command to delete all the structure elements between two specified labels. When a structure is traversed for display, label structure elements have no effect.

Since changes to a posted structure network can be immediately reflected at the workstation, we can animate an object by repeatedly editing the structure representing the object in order to change its modelling transformations. PHIGS also has functions for creating, deleting and renaming structures, and for deleting entire structure networks. The facilities for editing the model are described in Chapter 5. Plate 6 shows an example of a PHIGS application for interactively editing a model.

1.7   Transformations and viewing

There are five different coordinate systems used in PHIGS. This may seem overly complicated, but in practice it is a logical approach, and not difficult to understand. We shall look at each coordinate system in turn.

- **Modelling Coordinates (MC)**   Each piece of the model is separately defined in modelling coordinates. This is very convenient, since it allows the application to build up the model in a modular fashion. For each piece, the most suitable coordinate system can be chosen. For example, it might be convenient to define the walls of a house in metres, and the dimensions of the window frames in centimetres.

- **World Coordinates (WC)**   Having defined each part of the model in separate coordinate systems, we now need to combine them all together to compose the complete model, which is defined in world coordinates. To do this, for each modelling coordinate system we define a **modelling transformation** to convert it into world coordinates. In general, this will involve scaling the part to the correct proportions, rotating it to the correct orientation, and translating it to the appropriate position. PHIGS provides a number of utility functions to help the application construct the correct modelling transformations. Plates 2 and 3 show the use of modelling transformations to manipulate a model.

- **View Reference Coordinates (VRC)**   Now we have the complete picture defined in 3D world coordinates, we need to decide how we want it displayed. PHIGS incorporates the idea of photographing the 3D scene with a camera, to produce a flat picture viewed from some position using parallel or perspective projection. 3D viewing can be a tricky subject, and to simplify the definition of views, PHIGS introduces the **view reference coordinate system**, and provides a number of parameters to specify the view position, the position of the plane onto which the view will be projected, and so on. Figure 1.6 shows several different views of a teapot; the distortion of the spout in the upper right-hand picture is due to perspective. Views in PHIGS are defined on a per-workstation basis, which means that you can display different views of the same model on several workstations simultaneously. Each workstation stores a table of view specifications, and the appropriate view is selected using a structure element.

- **Normalized Projection Coordinates (NPC)**   This coordinate system is also used in the specification of a view, and contains the image resulting from the application of the perspective or parallel projection. The application may then select only part of this image for display, if required.

- **Device Coordinates (DC)**   Although PHIGS is, as far as possible, independent of the nature of the graphical devices it uses, it is sometimes necessary to refer directly to positions on the display screen. For viewing,

Figure 1.6   Four different views of the same object.

the application can specify exactly where on the display screen the selected portion of the view is to be placed.

3D viewing is described in Chapter 6.

1.8   Graphical input

With graphical input, PHIGS is faced with essentially the same problems that occur with graphical output: there is a huge range of hardware in use for graphical input, and all hardware is different! It is necessary to have some abstraction for the techniques of input, and therefore PHIGS uses six types of **logical input device**, classified according to the kind of data they return to the application program. They are as follows:

- **Locator** provides an (x, y, z) position in world coordinates. It might be realized using a tablet and puck, or a mouse.

- **Pick** provides the name of a structure on display. A pick device will often be realized using the same hardware as a locator.

- **Choice** provides a single selection from a number of alternatives. For example, a menu or a set of push-buttons.

- **Valuator** provides a single numerical value from a specified range. For example, a dial or a joystick.

- **String** provides a text string. This will usually be a keyboard.

- **Stroke** provides a sequence of (x, y, z) positions in world coordinates. For example, a digitizing tablet.

An input device has a **prompt** which tells the operator that the program is expecting input. The prompt might be the appearance of a special cursor on the screen, or a menu might pop up (see Plate 5). The **echo** of the device is a method of indicating to the operator what the current value of the device is. For example, for a locator device, the echo may be a cursor displayed on the screen which tracks the motion of a mouse; the idea is that the operator looks at the echo on the screen rather than the input device on the desk (Plate 4). There will be several different prompt and echo mechanisms, and you can select the one most appropriate for a particular application.

An application can acquire input in three different styles, called **operating modes**, as follows:

- **Request mode**   When the application requires some data to be input by the operator, it **requests** input from a particular logical device. The program then waits until the operator supplies the required value, or cancels the request.

- **Sample mode**   The application **samples** the current state of a logical input device and receives the current (or most recent) value of the device. The program continues without waiting for the operator to do anything.

- **Event mode**   The operator can generate input without having to wait for the application to ask for it explicitly. Each datum of input generated by the operator is placed on an **input queue**, and the application can interrogate the queue when it actually requires input. If the input queue is empty when the application inspects it, it may optionally wait for a specified time to give input a chance to arrive, before deciding that no input is available.

Input is described in Chapter 7.

1.9   Model and picture files

PHIGS provides functions to save structures and structure networks in **archive files**, which may be read subsequently by other PHIGS programs. This facility is useful for constructing libraries of commonly used models. Alternatively, you can store and retrieve **pictures** of your model (without the hierarchical information) using **metafiles**. It is not mandatory that PHIGS supports metafiles conforming to the international standard **Computer Graphics Metafile**, but most proprietary implementations do so. Metafiles are described in Chapter 8, and the use of archives in Chapter 10.

1.10   PHIGS PLUS

PHIGS PLUS is a proposed set of extensions to provide facilities for more advanced graphical modelling and computer graphics. As this book goes to press (January 1991) PHIGS PLUS is still under development, and its features are still subject to revision. Currently, however, the extensions are as follows:

- **additional output primitives** for curves and surfaces in 2D and 3D;

- functions for defining **sources of illumination**;

- **shading** for controlling the way in which output primitives are rendered;

- **general colour** for more flexible control over the specification of colour.

We describe PHIGS PLUS in detail in Chapters 13 and 14, but we shall briefly cover its features here.

The additional output primitives are as follows:

- **Polyline set with data** for drawing a polyline with additional application specified data which may be used to colour and shade the polyline.

- **Fill area set with data** for drawing a fill area set with additional data such as vertex normals.

- **Set of fill area set with data** for drawing a set of fill area sets.

- **Triangle strip with data** for drawing a collection of connected triangles.

- **Quadrilateral mesh with data** for drawing a mesh of quadrilateral facets.

- **Non-uniform B-spline curve** for drawing curves.

- **Non-uniform B-spline surface** for drawing surfaces, which may be optionally trimmed using **trimming curves**.

- **Cell array plus** for drawing a cell array, specifying cell colours using general colour.

Plates 13 and 20 show some examples. One of the most important features is the introduction of illumination and shading. This enables pictures to be created which have a certain amount of realism. For example, we might model the body of a car using non-uniform B-spline surfaces, and then define some lights which shine on the car. PHIGS PLUS will then compute how each point on the car should be coloured, according to the colour defined for the primitive itself and its distance and orientation to each of the sources of light. The result is an image which looks more solid and convincing than a wireframe picture, as shown in Plate 7.

PHIGS PLUS is not intended to produce images which are indistinguishable from photographs of real scenes (so-called photorealistic images), and there are therefore no facilities for transparency and shadows, or reflections between objects in a scene. Nevertheless, it is possible to create a wide range of shaded images, using the following features:

- **Illumination**   PHIGS PLUS supports four different kinds of illumination: **ambient**, which does not come from any particular direction; a **directional** light source, which shines from a given direction; a **positional** light source, which is located at a particular position; and a **spot** light source, which is a positional light emitting light in a cone, spreading out with distance.

- **Shading**   PHIGS PLUS takes into account the geometry of output primitives and whatever sources of light have been defined, and computes the resulting colours and intensities for all points on an output primitive. There are several types of shading: **none, colour, data, dot** and **normal**.

Chapter 2
Getting started

This chapter looks at the practicalities of using PHIGS. In particular we introduce language bindings, and present some example programs using C.

PHIGS is a library of functions which can be accessed from a variety of programming languages, such as C, Fortran, Pascal and ADA. However, because it is intended to be used in such a wide range of programming environments, PHIGS is defined in purely abstract terms. This definition is known as a functional description, and is the format that we shall use in this book. Details such as conventions for file names or the mechanisms for passing parameters to procedures are not addressed in a functional description. However, to enable application programs to use it, PHIGS must be integrated into a programming language. This is achieved by defining an interface, known as a **language binding**, in which the abstract functionality is expressed in the particular syntax and semantics of the language.

For example, the PHIGS function which connects a list of 3D modelling coordinate points with a sequence of straight lines is called POLYLINE 3, and it has one parameter, which gives the list of points to be connected. Its functional specification is:

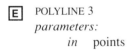 POLYLINE 3
    parameters:
        in   points   list of 3D MC points

Although this definition is precise, in some ways it is quite vague. For instance, it stipulates neither a limit to the number of points which may be specified, nor the number of bits in the binary representation of the real (floating-point) numbers. However, most real programming languages do not support abstractions of this sort, and each language has its own particular syntax and semantics. We therefore need to express PHIGS functions in these terms, and this is the purpose of the language binding. Language bindings are themselves subject to international standardization efforts. As this book goes to press the International Organization for Standardization (ISO) is developing standards for C, Fortran, Pascal and Ada.

15

2.1   The C language binding

In C, POLYLINE 3 becomes the function ppolyline3, which has two parameters. The first gives the number of points, and the second is a pointer to an array containing them. The specification of ppolyline3 is:

```
void ppolyline3(numberofpoints, points)
        Pint numberofpoints;
        Ppoint3 *points;
```

This makes use of a number of data types, which are defined as follows:

```
typedef float Pfloat;
typedef int Pint;
typedef struct {
        Pfloat x;
        Pfloat y;
        Pfloat z;
} Ppoint3;
```

It is not necessary for an application to define all these types explicitly; they will be provided in a header (.h) file, which is incorporated into a program using the #include mechanism.

2.2   The Fortran language binding

In Fortran, POLYLINE 3 is a subroutine called PPL3, and instead of the single list of points used in the functional definition, there are three REAL arrays, one for each of the x, y and z coordinates of the points. The number of points is given by the argument N:

```
SUBROUTINE PPL3(N, PX, PY, PZ)
INTEGER N
REAL PX(N), PY(N), PZ(N)
```

Appendix D describes the Fortran binding in more detail, and gives example programs.

2.3   The *Local Guide*

There will be some local dependencies that cannot be avoided, for example conventions for file names. For simplicity, we shall assume that all the information necessary to create and run PHIGS programs at your particular installation is given in a document called the *Local Guide to PHIGS* – although in practice this will probably be a number of separate documents including manufacturers' manuals. Typically, the *Local Guide* will include information such as the types and capabilities of the graphics devices available, local conventions for file names, and so on. It should also give details of the procedures for compiling and running PHIGS programs, and details of the language bindings available at your site.

2.4   Example 1: a box

We shall start with the following simple program which displays a box. Here, we give each PHIGS function without worrying about programming language binding conventions.

1. OPEN PHIGS (error file, memory)
2. OPEN WORKSTATION (workstation identifier, connection, type)
3. OPEN STRUCTURE (*box*)
4. POLYLINE 3 (box points)
5. CLOSE STRUCTURE
6. POST STRUCTURE (workstation identifier, *box*, priority)
7. sleep (60)
8. CLOSE WORKSTATION (workstation identifier)
9. CLOSE PHIGS

We shall examine the program line by line:

1. PHIGS must be initialized before you can access its functions. This is done using the OPEN PHIGS function. The values of the *error file* and *memory* parameters and how they are interpreted will vary between systems and installations, and you should consult your *Local Guide*.

2. Graphical input–output devices are called workstations in PHIGS. The purpose of the OPEN WORKSTATION function is to make a graphics device ready for use. You choose a number, *workstation identifier*, with which to refer to a particular workstation, and select the device by using two parameters – *connection* and *type* – which are specific to your installation. Your *Local Guide* will give lists of the graphics devices available, and what parameters to specify in the OPEN WORKSTATION function in order to gain access to particular devices.

3. Graphical data defined by the application is stored in structures. The OPEN STRUCTURE function creates a new structure, called *box*, which is initially empty.

4. The POLYLINE 3 function creates a structure element which draws a connected sequence of straight lines. The path taken by the lines is defined by the parameter *box points*, which is a list of 3D points. This structure element is then automatically inserted into the currently open structure, *box*.

5. The definition of the *box* structure is now finished, and the structure is closed.

6. Although we have created a structure to define the box, we have not yet drawn a picture; in PHIGS defining the model and drawing a picture of it are separate operations. To cause a structure to be displayed, it must be posted to a particular workstation. This is done using the POST STRUCTURE function. The first parameter, *workstation identifier*, specifies the workstation on which to draw the picture, and the second parameter, *box*, gives the name of the structure to be drawn. The third parameter, *priority*, gives the structure a priority on the screen, which enables the application to control whether a structure gets drawn on top of anything already on the screen, or whether what is already there has higher priority.

7. Now the program waits for 60 seconds, so that we can view the picture. The 'sleep' function is not provided by PHIGS, but it is easily programmed, using a loop or by calling an operating system function.

8. Now that we have finished drawing the picture, we close down the workstation which frees the graphics device specified by *workstation identifier* parameter for use by another application.

9. Finally, we release PHIGS, and the program is finished.

We might program this in C as follows:

```
/* Access the PHIGS C binding. */
/* The next line is implementation dependent. */
#include <phigs.h>

#define WS 1
#define NUM_PTS 5
#define BOX 1

Ppoint3 box_pts[] =                    /* Define the data
                                          for the box. */

   {{0.2,0.3,0.0}, {0.4,0.3,0.0},
    {0.4,0.5,0.0}, {0.2,0.5,0.0},
    {0.2,0.3,0.0}};

main()
   {
   popenphigs(0, 0);                  /* Open PHIGS. */
   popenws(WS, 0, 0);                 /* Open a workstation. */

   popenstruct(BOX);                  /* Define the box structure. */
   ppolyline3(NUM_PTS, box_pts);      /* Insert a polyline 3 element
                                          to draw the box. */
   pclosestruct();                    /* Close the structure. */

   ppoststruct(WS, BOX, 1.0);         /* Post the structure. */

   sleep(60);                         /* Sleep for 60 seconds. */
```

```
    pclosews(WS);              /* Close the workstation. */
    pclosephigs();             /* Close PHIGS. */
}
```

It is likely that this program will need some modifications before it will run correctly with your implementation. The following checklist should help:

1. Become familiar with the basic procedures for editing, compiling and running programs in the language you are using.

2. Locate and familiarize yourself with your *Local Guide.*

3. Refer to your *Local Guide* to:
   (a) access the appropriate language binding;
   (b) determine the parameters to use in the OPEN PHIGS function;
   (c) find the 'workstation type' of a suitable workstation at your installation;
   (d) find what 'connection identifier' to use.

4. The program will need to access the appropriate language binding. Find out how to link this in with your compiled program.

5. Compile the program, and run it!

2.5   Opening and closing PHIGS

In the preceding example, we used a number of PHIGS functions, and here we present their functional specifications. OPEN PHIGS must be called to initialize PHIGS for use. Its specification is:

☐   OPEN PHIGS
    parameters:
        in   error file   file name
        in   buffer memory size   integer

The *error file* parameter gives the name of a file to which PHIGS writes any error messages that it produces. The second parameter, *buffer memory size*, determines the size of an internal storage area. The use of each of these parameters varies between implementations, and your *Local Guide* will give the appropriate values to use.

At the end of an application, PHIGS must be closed down using:

☐   CLOSE PHIGS
    parameters: none

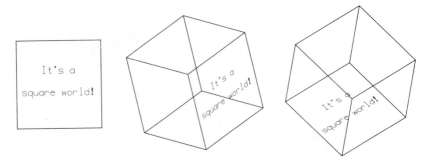

Figure 2.1   Three snapshots of the cube as it rotates.

2.6   Opening and closing workstations

We open a workstation using:

☐ OPEN WORKSTATION
parameters:
       in   workstation identifier   integer
       in   workstation connection   connection type
       in   workstation type   workstation type

Workstation identifier is a name (an integer) chosen by the application to refer to the workstation. You can choose any suitable name for the workstation, so long as there is a unique name for each different workstation in use. *Workstation connection* specifies the correspondence between the PHIGS abstract workstation, and the particular physical devices it refers to. The precise interpretation of this parameter is implementation dependent, and details will be given in your *Local Guide*. *Workstation type* is the type of workstation required, selected from the list of available types listed in the *Local Guide*.
    A workstation is released using:

☐ CLOSE WORKSTATION
parameters:
       in   workstation identifier   integer

2.7   Example 2: a rotating cube

This example displays a 3D cube, and then rotates the cube about its centre. Figure 2.1 shows three snapshots of the picture produced by the program as it runs. The cube is a structure, and the rotation is achieved by repeatedly editing the structure to replace a modelling transformation; the picture is updated automatically, as soon as an edit occurs. The effect is that the cube spins about its centre, the point $(0.5, 0.5, 0.5)$. First we give the program functionally, then in C (the Fortran version is given in Appendix D).

```
OPEN PHIGS (error, memory)
OPEN WORKSTATION (workstation identifier, connection, type)

OPEN STRUCTURE (cube)
% Insert a local modelling transformation
% which will later be edited to rotate the cube.

SET LOCAL TRANSFORMATION 3

POLYLINE 3 (front face)
POLYLINE 3 (back face)
POLYLINE 3 (link between face corner)
POLYLINE 3 (link between face corner)
POLYLINE 3 (link between face corner)
POLYLINE 3 (link between face corner)

SET TEXT ALIGNMENT (CENTRE, NORMAL)
SET CHARACTER HEIGHT (0.015)
TEXT 3 (position, (1,0,0), (0,1,0), "It's a")
TEXT 3 (position, (1,0,0), (0,1,0), "square world!")
CLOSE STRUCTURE

SET DISPLAY UPDATE STATE (workstation identifier, ASAP, UQUM)
POST STRUCTURE (workstation identifier, cube, priority)

% Now open the cube for editing
OPEN STRUCTURE (cube)
SET EDIT MODE (REPLACE)

% Set the element pointer to
% the local modelling transformation.
SET ELEMENT POINTER (1)

for angle := 1 to 360 do
  begin
  % Compute transformation to rotate by 'angle' in x,y and z.
  SET LOCAL TRANSFORMATION 3 (transformation, REPLACE)
  end

CLOSE STRUCTURE

CLOSE WORKSTATION (workstation identifier)
CLOSE PHIGS
```

For convenience, we shall code this program in C using two modules. The first contains the procedure MakeCube, which creates the cube structure.

```
#include <phigs.h>
void MakeCube()
{
/* Creates the cube structure. */
#define CUBE 1
#define CMIN 0.3
#define CMAX 0.7

    Ppoint3 front_face[] = {
            {CMIN, CMIN, CMAX}, {CMIN, CMAX, CMAX},
            {CMAX, CMAX, CMAX}, {CMAX, CMIN, CMAX},
            {CMIN,CMIN,CMAX}};

    Ppoint3 back_face[] = {
            {CMIN, CMIN, CMIN}, {CMIN, CMAX, CMIN},
            {CMAX, CMAX, CMIN}, {CMAX, CMIN, CMIN},
    {CMIN,CMIN,CMIN}};

    Ppoint3 link1[] = {{CMIN, CMIN, CMIN}, {CMIN, CMIN, CMAX}};
    Ppoint3 link2[] = {{CMIN, CMAX, CMIN}, {CMIN, CMAX, CMAX}};
    Ppoint3 link3[] = {{CMAX, CMAX, CMIN}, {CMAX, CMAX, CMAX}};
    Ppoint3 link4[] = {{CMAX, CMIN, CMIN}, {CMAX, CMIN, CMAX}};

    static Ppoint3  origin = {0.5,0.5,0.5};
    static Pvector3 shift = {0.0,0.0,0.0};
    static Pvector3 scale = {1,1,1};

    static Ppoint3 textloc1 = {0.5,0.6,0.7};
    static Ppoint3 textloc2 = {0.5,0.5,0.7};

    static Pvector3 textdir[2]= {1.0,0.0,0.0, 0.0,1.0,0.0};
    static Pchar text1[6] = "It's a";
    static Pchar text2[13] = "square world!";

    static Ptxalign txalign = {PTH_CENTRE, PAV_NORMAL};

    float angle;
    Pint err;
    Pmatrix3 transform;

    popenstruct(CUBE);
    angle = 0;
    pbuildtran3(&origin, &shift, angle,angle,angle,
                &scale, &err, transform);
    psetlocaltran3(transform, PREPLACE);

    ppolyline3(5, front_face);
    ppolyline3(5, back_face);
    ppolyline3(2, link1);
    ppolyline3(2, link2);
```

```
        ppolyline3(2, link3);
        ppolyline3(2, link4);
        psettextalign(&txalign);
        psetcharheight(0.015);
        ptext3(&textloc1, textdir, text1);
        ptext3(&textloc2, textdir, text2);
        pclosestruct();
}
```

The following program edits the cube structure to rotate it.

```
    #include <phigs.h>

    #define CUBE 1
    #define WS 1
    #define PRIORITY 1
    #define PI 3.141592654

    #include "makecube.c"

    main()
    {
        static Ppoint3 origin = {0.5,0.5,0.5};
        static Pvector3 shift = {0.0,0.0,0.0};
        static Pvector3 scale = {1,1,1};

        Pint err, i;
        Pmatrix3 transform;
        float angle;

        popenphigs(0, 0);                       /* Open PHIGS. */
        popenws(WS, 0, 0);                      /* Open a workstation. */

        MakeCube();                             /* Create the cube. */

        psetdisplayupdatest(WS, PASAP, PUQUM);
        ppoststruct(WS, CUBE, PRIORITY);        /* Post the structure. */

        popenstruct(CUBE);                      /* Open the structure. */
        pseteditmode(PEDIT_REPLACE);            /* Select REPLACE mode. */
        psetelemptr(1);
        for (i=0; i<361; i++){                  /* Edit the modelling */
            angle = i*PI/180;                   /* transformation. */
            pbuildtran3(&origin, &shift, angle,angle,angle,
                        &scale, &err, transform);
            psetlocaltran3(transform, PREPLACE);
        }
        pclosews(WS);                           /* Close the workstation. */
        pclosephigs();                          /* Close PHIGS. */
    }
```

Chapter 3
Graphical output

*This chapter describes the eight types of graphical **output primitive** which are the basic building-blocks for describing the graphical data of the model. We also introduce the ways in which **attributes** may be used to control the visual style of output primitives.*

Pictures displayed on a graphics device are constructed from the basic drawing instructions of the device. For example, on a calligraphic (vector) display or a pen plotter the basic drawing primitive may be a line. However, on a raster-scan device, pictures are built up from collections of pixels. A graphics system would not be very convenient to use if it provided only lines or pixels for the construction of pictures, and for this reason PHIGS provides a set of 'higher level' drawing elements known as **output primitives**, which correspond more closely to the ways we think of creating pictures, rather than the ways they will be ultimately realized on graphics devices. There are eight kinds of graphical output primitive, as follows:

- **Polyline** for drawing a connected sequence of straight lines.

- **Polymarker** for marking a set of data points with symbols.

- **Fill area** for drawing a filled-in area bounded by a set of data points.

- **Fill area set** for drawing a collection of filled areas.

- **Text** for drawing a character string.

- **Annotation text relative** for annotating a picture with descriptive text.

- **Cell array** for drawing a two-dimensional grid of coloured areas.

- **Generalized drawing primitive** for accessing special implementation-dependent device features, such as curve drawing.

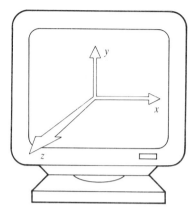

Figure 3.1   A right-handed Cartesian coordinate system.

3.1   Coordinate systems

In PHIGS all coordinates are expressed using **Cartesian coordinate systems**. In two dimensions, a point is described by two numbers – its x and y coordinates. In three dimensions, there is a third number – the z coordinate – which is measured along the z axis, perpendicular to both the x and y axes. A 3D coordinate system has a *handedness*: in a **right-handed** coordinate system, the z axis comes out of the screen as z increases. This is shown in Figure 3.1. If the z axis were to go *into* the screen, the system would be called **left-handed**, and would be the mirror image of a right-handed system. However, all the 3D coordinate systems used in PHIGS are right-handed.

It is important to note that in PHIGS points are represented using **column vector** notation. This is therefore the convention we use in this book, and it is described in detail in Appendix C.

You can draw in whatever units you like – from nanometres to light years, for example – and you can draw at any scale. You will normally need to tell PHIGS the size of your picture, so that it can arrange to fit the picture on a graphics display, but if you do not, it assumes that the coordinates will be in the default range 0 to 1 in each of x, y and z. The coordinates in which you describe the graphical data of the model are called **Modelling Coordinates** (**MC**). Some applications may wish to use other systems, such as polar, cylindrical or spherical coordinates. If this is the case, it is the responsibility of the application to first transform its coordinates into right-handed Cartesian coordinates. Coordinate systems are discussed in detail in Chapter 4.

For convenience, output primitives may either be specified in two dimensions (x and y information) or in three dimensions (x, y and z information). In the two-dimensional case, the z coordinate is assumed to be zero.

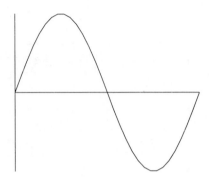

Figure 3.2   Displaying a sine curve using a polyline.

3.2   Polyline

The output primitive for drawing lines is called polyline. This joins a list of
points with a connected sequence of straight lines. If there are *n* points, *n* − 1 line
segments are drawn. We draw a polyline using the function:

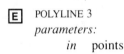 POLYLINE 3
parameters:
   in   points   list of 3D MC points

Plates 1, 9 and 26 illustrate some examples of polyline. It may seem strange that
a *poly* line primitive is provided, rather than a *line* primitive which draws one
line at a time. The reason is really one of convenience: in practice, lists of points
tend to occur more frequently than pairs of points.

Since PHIGS does not provide a facility for drawing curves (although PHIGS
PLUS does, as we shall see in Chapter 13), a curve must be approximated by
a series of small line segments. We can then represent the whole curve using a
single polyline. For example, we could generate an approximation of a sine curve
in terms of straight lines, and use polyline to draw it. This is shown in Figure 3.2,
where we have used another two polylines to draw the *x* and *y* axes. A program
to draw this picture using polylines is as follows:

```
OPEN PHIGS (error, memory)

OPEN WORKSTATION (ws, connection, type)

OPEN STRUCTURE (sine)
POLYLINE 3 (horizontal axis)
POLYLINE 3 (vertical axis)
% Compute points for sine curve.
POLYLINE 3 (points for sine curve)
CLOSE STRUCTURE
```

```
POST STRUCTURE (ws, sine, priority)
CLOSE WORKSTATION (ws)
CLOSE PHIGS
```

This is how we might code it in C:

```c
#include <phigs.h>
#include <math.h>

#define PI 3.141592654
#define MAXPOINT 32
#define WS 1
#define SINE 1
#define PRIORITY 1

static Ppoint3 yaxis[2] = {{0,1,0}, {0,-1,0}}; /* x axis. */
static Ppoint3 xaxis[2] = {{0,0,0}, {1,0,0}};  /* y axis. */

Ppoint3 curve[MAXPOINT];
Ppoint3 graph[MAXPOINT];
Ppoint3 axis[MAXPOINT];
int i;

main(){
  popenphigs(0,0);                  /* Implementation dependent. */
  popenws(WS,0,0);                  /* Implementation dependent. */

  popenstruct(SINE);                /* Open a structure. */

  transform(2, yaxis, axis);        /* Draw the x and y axes. */
  ppolyline3(2, axis);

  transform(2, xaxis, axis);
  ppolyline3(2, axis);

  for (i = 0;i <= 30 ;i++) {        /* Set up the points. */
    graph[i].x = i/30.0;
    graph[i].y = sin(2*PI*i/30.0);
    graph[i].z = 0.0;
  }

  transform(31, graph, curve);      /* Transform into [0,1]. */
  ppolyline3(31, curve);            /* Draw the curve. */

  pclosestruct();                   /* Close the structure. */

  psetdisplayupdatest(WS, PASAP, PUQUM);

  ppoststruct(WS, SINE, PRIORITY); /* Post the structure. */
```

```
    sleep(60);                          /* Wait for 60 seconds. */

    pclosews(WS);                       /* Close the workstation. */
    pclosephigs();                      /* Close PHIGS. */
}

transform(num, arry, a)

/* Takes the sine curve and scales and shifts it to
   fit into the range [0,1]. */

    int num;
    Ppoint3 arry[];
    Ppoint3 a[];

    {
    Pfloat xscale = 0.8;  Pfloat yscale = 0.3;
    Pfloat xshift = 0.1;  Pfloat yshift = 0.5;
    int i;

    for (i = 0; i < num; i++) {
        a[i].x = arry[i].x  * xscale + xshift;
        a[i].y = arry[i].y  * yscale + yshift;
        a[i].z = arry[i].z;
    }
}
```

There is one feature of this example which we must mention before we continue. By default all drawing is expected to be performed in the coordinate range [0, 1] in the x, y and z directions. However, because the sine curve covers 0 to 2π in the x direction, and oscillates between -1 and $+1$ in y, we need to scale the points into the range [0, 1] before we use them in the POLYLINE 3 function. If we did not do this, parts of the picture which lie outside the [0, 1] range would be removed (this is an example of **clipping**). Similarly, we need to shift the intersection of the x and y axes to centre the picture. This scaling and shifting is performed in the example program by the `transform` procedure. In Chapter 4 we will see that there are more convenient ways to cope with this situation, using modelling transformations.

3.3   Styles of output

If we wished to draw a second curve in the sine example, it would be useful to be able to distinguish it from the first by making it look different in some way, such as drawing it in a different colour, or using a thicker line. The visual appearance of graphical output is determined by extra data called **attributes**. Polyline has three attributes, as follows:

Attribute	Effect
linetype	line style (dotted, dashed …)
linewidth scale factor	line thickness (normal, thick, thin …)
polyline colour index	line colour (black, blue …)

There are two alternative methods of specifying attributes: **individual control** and **bundled control**.

With individual control, there is a separate function to set the value of each attribute. With bundled control, the style of a polyline is selected by a single function, which selects a **bundle** of the three attributes from a table of bundles stored in a workstation. In this book we shall use the individual method for controlling attributes. We describe styles of output in detail in Chapter 9.

There are default settings for all the attributes, and these were used for the polylines in the previous example. To change the appearance of polylines, we change the value of the appropriate polyline attribute, and this value will refer to all subsequent polylines, until we change the value again. The functions for controlling the attributes of polyline are:

E SET LINEWIDTH SCALE FACTOR
parameters:
     in   linewidth scale factor   real

E SET LINETYPE
parameters:
     in   linetype   integer

E SET POLYLINE COLOUR INDEX
parameters:
     in   colour index   integer

We can now add another sine curve to our picture, using a different line thickness:

```
POLYLINE 3 (curve1)
SET LINEWIDTH SCALE FACTOR (5.0)
POLYLINE 3 (curve2)
```

Figure 3.3 shows the result.

3.4 Polymarker

Given a set of data points, it is not always appropriate to join them using lines. We often want to display the data by marking the position of each point with a marker symbol. For this we use the **polymarker** output primitive:

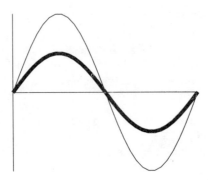

Figure 3.3   Two polylines distinguished using linewidth scale factor.

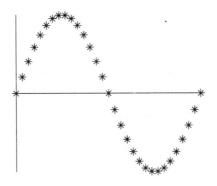

Figure 3.4   Drawing the sine curve with polymarker.

E POLYMARKER 3
parameters:
  in points   list of 3D MC points

Because it has exactly the same parameters as polyline, polymarker can be used interchangeably with polyline. We control the appearance of polymarkers using three attributes, as follows:

Attribute	*Effect*
marker type	dot, cross, ...
marker size scale factor	marker size
polymarker colour index	marker colour

If we change the call to polyline in the sine program to a call to polymarker, we can draw a graph of the sine curve, as shown in Figure 3.4:

SET MARKER TYPE (3)

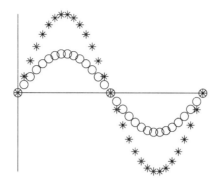

Figure 3.5   Two polymarkers distinguished using marker type.

POLYMARKER 3 (curve 1)

We can add the second curve and set the marker type to graph them both, as shown in Figure 3.5:

SET MARKER TYPE (3)
POLYMARKER 3 (curve 1)
SET MARKER TYPE (4)
POLYMARKER 3 (curve2)

The attribute settings apply to the polymarker primitive as a whole: each individual marker of a polymarker is the same symbol.

3.5   Fill area

Another way of drawing a shape defined by a list of points is to treat the data as a boundary defining a region, and to fill in the interior of the region with a colour or pattern. This is the purpose of the **fill area** output primitive:

E   FILL AREA 3
parameters:
      in   points   list of 3D MC points

Fill area has a number of attributes, some of which are:

Attribute	Effect
interior style	HOLLOW, SOLID, HATCH, ...
interior style index	hatch style
interior colour index	interior colour

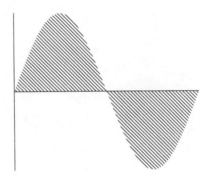

Figure 3.6   Drawing the sine curve using fill area.

(It is also possible to fill an area with a repeating pattern, and this is described in Section 9.4). Because the function is defined in the same way as polyline and polymarker, and we can easily draw a filled-in sine curve, as shown in Figure 3.6:

    SET INTERIOR STYLE (HATCH)
    FILL AREA 3 (curve1)

Although the list of points is the same as we used for polyline and polymarker, PHIGS assumes that the points define a *closed* area, and automatically joins the last point back up to the first. This means that the boundary of the sine curve intersects itself, to create a kind of 'figure of eight'. However, the shape is filled as we would expect. PHIGS uses a fixed rule to determine which points lie inside the area, and which do not. This is described in the next section. Figure 3.7 shows the results of drawing the two sine curves using different interior styles:

    SET INTERIOR STYLE (HATCH)
    FILL AREA 3 (curve1)
    SET INTERIOR STYLE (SOLID)
    FILL AREA 3 (curve2)

These facilities for controlling the ways in which filled areas are drawn are covered in detail in Section 9.4. Another example of fill area is shown in Plate 2.

3.5.1   Insides and outsides

When filling an area defined by a set of data points, we must be precise about which set of points constitutes the 'inside' of the area, and which the 'outside'. For simple shapes it is obvious which points are inside the polygon, and which are not. However, in the case of the sine curve, the outline of the shape intersects itself, and we are faced with a problem in distinguishing the outside from the inside. PHIGS provides a solution to this problem, by applying the 'even–odd' rule. To determine whether a particular point is inside or outside a polygon, draw an imaginary straight line starting at the point and extending out through the edges

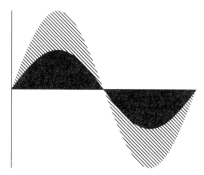

Figure 3.7 Distinguishing between fill areas using interior style.

of the polygon to infinity, as shown in Figure 3.8. The direction of the line is not important, as long as its course takes it beyond the boundaries of the area. Count each intersection the test line makes with the edges of the polygon. (If a test line passes through a vertex tangentially, it is not counted as an intersection.) If the total number of intersections is *odd*, the point is on the inside of the fill area; if the count is *even* (or zero), the point is on the outside. Figure 3.8 shows a self-intersecting area filled using the even–odd rule.

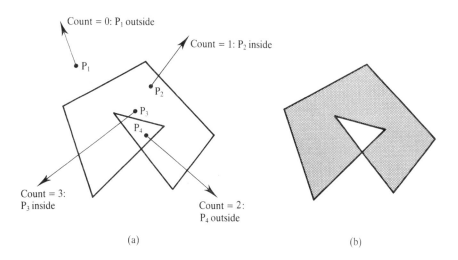

Figure 3.8 The even–odd rule.

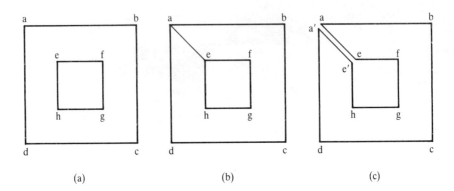

(a)   (b)   (c)

Figure 3.9   Defining a square torus with fill area.

3.6   Fill area set

Although fill area can cope with shapes which have self-intersecting boundaries (such as the sine curve example), it can be awkward to use for defining complex areas which contain a number of holes.

Consider the 'square torus' shown in Figure 3.9(a). To define this shape using fill area we must use a trick, by introducing a dummy edge ae, as shown in Figure 3.9(b), and then unfolding the shape to create an area which can be defined by a single list of points, some of which will be coincident (a, a' and e, e'). Figure 3.9(c) shows the unfolded shape, with the edges ae and a'e' separated for clarity. We can draw this shape using fill area by specifying the list of perimeter points, as follows:

FILL AREA 3 ([a, b, c, d, a', e', h, g, f, e])

In simple cases such as this, we can unfold the shape without too much trouble, but for more complex shapes with several holes the technique soon becomes unworkable. To overcome this difficulty, there is a more general output primitive for drawing filled areas called **fill area set**, which enables complicated shapes to be defined easily:

E   FILL AREA SET 3
    parameters:
        in   points   list of lists of 3D MC points

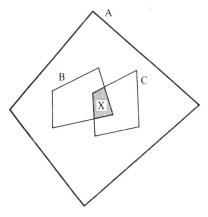

Figure 3.10   Overlapping holes in a fill area set.

With this primitive, a shape is defined as a collection of disjoint subareas to be filled, and the collection is treated as a single entity. We can therefore use fill area set to define the square torus as a single output primitive, by specifying each of its subareas in turn, as follows (the points that make up each subarea are listed in square brackets):

FILL AREA SET 3 ([a, b, c, d], [e, f, g, h])

PHIGS assumes that each subarea of the set is implicitly closed (by joining the last point up to the first). It also keeps track of all the subareas to ensure that the shape is correctly filled, using the even–odd rule. One consequence of this is that within the same shape, holes should not overlap one another. If they do, strange effects can occur. This is illustrated in Figure 3.10, which shows a fill area set comprising three subareas A, B and C. Although B and C are intended to be holes in the main area A, the even–odd rule will decide that the region where they overlap, X, should be filled.

Each of the subareas in a fill area set should be planar, but this is the responsibility of the application: if non-planar areas are defined, the effect will be implementation dependent. Fill area set has the same attributes as fill area, with one significant addition: fill area set offers control over the display of edges, whereas fill area does not.

The attributes of fill area set are described in Section 9.5. For a note on the effects of clipping on fill area set, see Section 9.5.2.

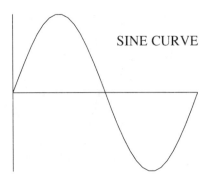

Figure 3.11   Drawing text.

3.7   Text

We often need to draw text on pictures, and for this the **text** output primitive is used:

E   TEXT 3
   parameters:
        in   text point   3D MC point
        in   text direction vectors   two 3D MC vectors
        in   text   character string

This draws a string of characters at a specified position. For example, we can add the label "SINE CURVE" to the sine curve at position $(0.6, 0.6, 0)$ as follows:

   TEXT 3 ((0.6,0.6,0), (1,0,0), (0,1,0), "SINE CURVE")

The result is shown in Figure 3.11.

Text is a planar primitive: each character lies in a 2D plane called the **text plane**. The orientation of this plane in 3D is specified using the *text point* and two *text direction vectors*, as shown in Figure 3.12. Usually the two vectors will be at right angles, but to cater for the general case where they are not, the first vector is used to set the direction of the x axis, and the y axis is perpendicular to it. This defines a new coordinate system, called the **Text Local Coordinate system** (**TLC**), which has its origin at the text point, and which has the same scale as modelling coordinates. In the 2D version of text, the text plane is simply the xy plane of modelling coordinates.

Text has far more attributes that the output primitives we have met so far. We shall explain them in detail in Chapter 9, but we can summarize them as follows:

Attribute	*Effect*
character height	height of characters
text font	font
character up vector	orientation
text precision	quality of text
text path	(UP, DOWN, LEFT, RIGHT)
character expansion factor	aspect ratio
text alignment	positioning of text
character spacing	space between characters
text colour index	colour

A common way to distinguish text is to use different fonts, and we can do this using the SET TEXT FONT function, as follows:

```
SET TEXT FONT (1)
TEXT 3 ((0.6,0.6,0), (1,0,0), (0,1,0), "SINE")
SET TEXT FONT (2)
TEXT 3 ((0.6,0.4,0), (1,0,0), (0,1,0), "CURVE")
```

Figure 3.13 illustrates the result.

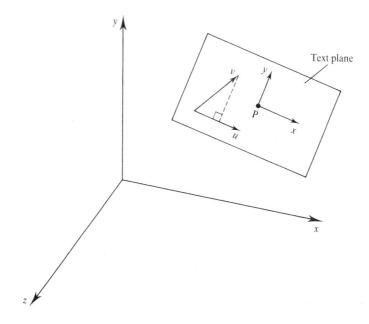

Figure 3.12 Defining the text plane.

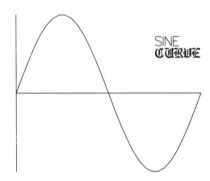

Figure 3.13   Distinguishing text using text font.

3.8   Annotation text relative

In addition to text, there is another primitive for drawing character strings, called
annotation text relative, which is designed specifically for adding descriptive
annotation to pictures. For example, if we are modelling a 3D object, we might
wish to rotate the object on the screen dynamically in x, y and z, to help the user
understand its geometry. Suppose also that the picture includes some text ("It's
a square world!"), as illustrated in Figure 3.14(a). If we consider this text to
be part of the model itself, and we change the orientation of the model, all the
text will be affected, as Figure 3.14(b) shows. In some circumstances, however,
we want to use text to annotate features of the model ("vertex") and keep the
annotation legible, regardless of how the model itself is transformed, as shown in
Figure 3.14(c). This is the purpose of annotation text relative, which is specified
as:

E	ANNOTATION TEXT RELATIVE 3

parameters:

in	reference point	3D MC point
in	annotation offset	3D NPC vector
in	text	character string

To avoid any distortions that might arise from accumulated viewing transformations, annotation text is drawn on a plane parallel to the display surface of the
workstation, which ensures that the text is always displayed legibly. However,
since it is intended to annotate a part of the model, it must be anchored to a specified point in modelling coordinates; otherwise, the annotation might become de-
tached from the model, which would defeat the purpose. *Reference point* is the
location in MC to which the annotation text refers, and *annotation offset* is a
vector which specifies where the annotation text will be drawn relative to the reference point. This parameter is provided for convenience, since annotation text
is often drawn slightly away from the part being annotated, so as not to obscure

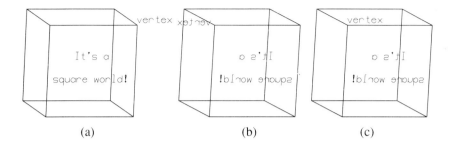

(a)   (b)   (c)

Figure 3.14   Annotation text relative.

geometrical detail. The offset is measured in normalized projection coordinates, NPC (described in Chapter 6), and the location at which the annotation is drawn is determined by first transforming the reference point from MC to NPC, and then adding the annotation offset. Thus, all transformations affect the reference point, but only the workstation transformation affects the characters of the annotation text itself. The attributes of annotation text are described in Section 9.6.

3.9   Cell array

Cell array is an output primitive for drawing a 2D array of cells, each of which is filled with a specified colour. The definition is:

☐ E   CELL ARRAY 3
       parameters:

in	cell parallelogram (A, B, C)	three 3D MC points
in	rows	integer
in	cols	integer
in	array of colour indices	array of integers

The array of cells is defined as a parallelogram, specified by the three points A, B and C, as shown in Figure 3.15. The parallelogram is divided into a grid of identical cells, with *rows* cells in one direction and *cols* in the other. Each cell is assigned a colour using an array of colour indices of dimensions *rows* and *cols*.

Specifying the cells in this way means that they may be arbitrarily sized parallelograms, although applications will usually define a grid of square or rectangular cells. Since the definition is in MC, the cell array will be transformed by the viewing pipeline, which may cause the shapes of the cells to distort. Once the cell array is mapped to DC, a simple rule is used to determine how it maps to pixels: if the centre of a pixel lies within the quadrilateral of a transformed cell, the pixel is set to the colour associated with the cell. This is called **point sampling**, and is the simplest method of mapping cells to pixels (more complex

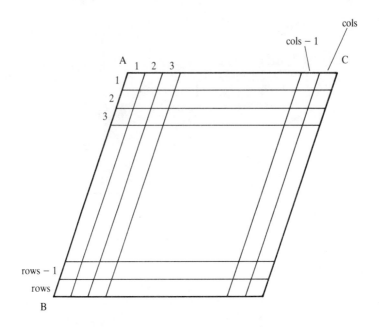

Figure 3.15   The cell array parallelogram.

techniques such as area sampling or filtering are not supported). If the centre of the pixel lies exactly on the boundary of a cell, it is implementation dependent which of the adjacent cells is used to determine the colour of the pixel. In fact, an implementation need not draw each cell at all. The minimum requirement (which is adopted by many implementations) is to draw a line around the transformed boundary of the entire cell array.

The following is an example of the definition of a cell array, defined for simplicity in the $z = 0$ plane, and shown in Figure 3.16. Colour indices 0 and 1 are assumed to be black and white respectively.

A := (0.2, 0.7, 0)   B := (0.2, 0.3, 0)   C := (0.8, 0.7, 0)
rows := 3   cols := 5
colours := (1, 0, 0, 0, 1), (0, 1, 0, 1, 0), (1, 0, 1, 0, 1)
CELL ARRAY 3 (A, B, C, rows, cols, colours)

3.10   Generalized drawing primitive

Many graphics hardware systems can generate more complex kinds of graphical output than the basic primitives of PHIGS, such as circles, arcs, ellipses and spline curves. Figure 3.17 shows some examples. To enable an application to take full advantage of hardware features such as these (which would otherwise have to be simulated using output primitives such as polylines) there is a special kind of

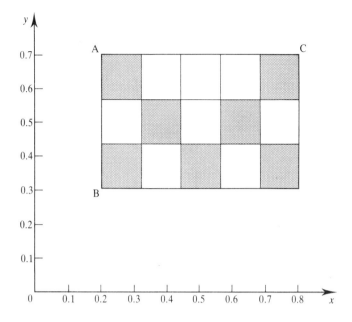

Figure 3.16   An example cell array.

structure element called **Generalized Drawing Primitive (GDP)**:

E   GENERALIZED DRAWING PRIMITIVE 3
  parameters:
      in   points   list of 3D MC points
      in   GDP identifier   integer
      in   GDP data   data record

GDP identifier specifies which of the special workstation output primitives is to be
selected. The geometry is described by *points*, but how they are interpreted will
depend on the GDP. For example, for a circle they might give the centre and the
radius; for a spline curve they may be a set of control points for the curve. Some
GDPs may require additional information (such as chord tolerance for a spline
curve), and this may be supplied using the *GDP data* parameter. When a GDP is
encountered during traversal, its identifier and data are extracted and transmitted
to the workstation, where they are interpreted in a workstation-dependent way.

Using GDPs reduces the portability of a program, because of the reliance on
features that not all graphics devices are likely to provide. However, if a workstation does not support a particular kind of GDP, no error occurs – at least the
standard parts of the program should always work, and the program should not
fail, although where the GDP should appear in the picture there may be blank
spaces! Additionally, all GDPs must obey two rules, so that they behave as far as

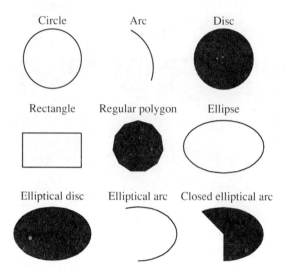

Figure 3.17   Examples of GDPs.

possible like ordinary output primitives. The first rule is that the coordinate data specified for the GDP shall undergo transformation by the viewing pipeline before display, in just the same way as the standard output primitives. For example, specifying a circle GDP when the current composite modelling transformation produces differential scaling for the coordinate axes will result in an ellipse being drawn. The second rule is that GDPs must be be drawn subject to clipping. If a particular workstation is unable to obey these rules, the GDP must not be generated at all. The attributes which affect the style of GDPs are described in Section 9.7.

Chapter 4
Creating the model

One of the strengths of PHIGS is the ability to create models which have a logical structure. In this chapter we describe how to do this using **structure elements**, **structures** *and* **structure networks**.

There is more to graphical modelling than simply creating a model from a collection of output primitives. Generally, a model represents something. It might be a physical structure such as a machine, or a collection of molecules, or a simulation process, but whatever the nature of the model we will usually want to identify particular parts as separate from others. Figure 4.1 shows pictures of a desk lamp created using PHIGS. The lamp comprises a number of separate pieces, such as lower and upper arms, base and lampshade, and there are a number of relation-

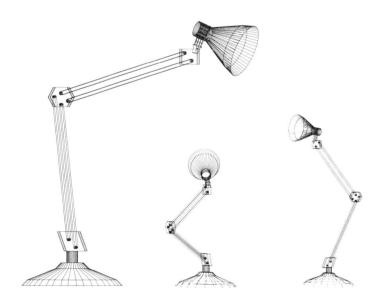

Figure 4.1   A desk lamp drawn using PHIGS.

43

ships between the pieces. For example, if we were to shift the base left or right, we would expect the rest of the lamp to move with it, because the parts are connected. Similarly, we would expect to be able to move the lampshade without affecting the base. From this point of view, the model of the lamp is more than just a collection of polylines. It is a collection of separate parts, each of which has a name, and the parts are connected.

With PHIGS we create models from **structures**, which contain **structure elements** defining the graphical and other information. Usually, we define a separate structure for each of the basic components of the model, which permits us to:

- *name* pieces of the model;

- manipulate pieces *independently* of others;

- *group* pieces together.

Having a separate structure for each part of the model also enables us to use the technique of **instancing**: parts which appear repeatedly in the model may each have a single master definition, which is used in conjunction with **modelling transformations** to create instances of the part in the model. We shall consider this in detail in Section 4.5.

4.1   Simple modelling: a diode

To illustrate how structures are used, we shall model a diode, as shown in Figure 4.2. It is made from four pieces: left wire, cathode, anode and right wire. The coordinate axes in the figure are drawn for reference only, and we shall not include them in the model.

As we saw in Chapter 2, to create a structure we *open* it, using the function:

☐   OPEN STRUCTURE
    parameters:
        in   structure identifier   integer

Once we have an open structure, we can insert structure elements into it to describe the model. We create the diode by reading its coordinates from Figure 4.2, and use polyline and fill area to draw the different parts, as follows:

```
OPEN STRUCTURE (diode)
POLYLINE 3 ( (−0.5, 0, 0), (−0.2, 0, 0) )                    % Left wire.
POLYLINE 3 ( (−0.2, −0.2, 0), (−0.2, 0.2, 0) )              % Cathode.
FILL AREA 3 ( (−0.2, 0, 0), (0.1, 0.2, 0), (0.1, −0.2, 0) )  % Anode.
POLYLINE 3 ( (0.1, 0, 0), (0.4, 0, 0) )                      % Right wire.
CLOSE STRUCTURE
```

When the definition of the structure is complete, we close it using:

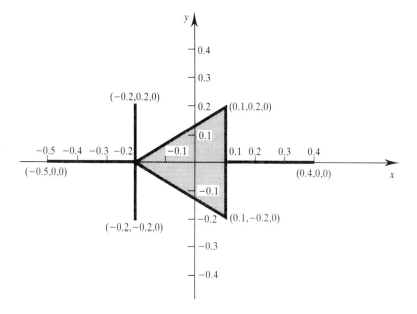

Figure 4.2 Modelling a diode.

☐ CLOSE STRUCTURE
parameters: none

We have now created a structure comprising a list of structure elements, which we shall represent as follows:

diode structure	0
POLYLINE 3 ((−0.5, 0, 0), (−0.2, 0, 0))	1
POLYLINE 3 ((−0.2, −0.2, 0), (−0.2, 0.2, 0))	2
FILL AREA 3 ((−0.2, 0, 0), (0.1, 0.2, 0), (0.1, −0.2, 0))	3
POLYLINE 3 ((0.1, 0, 0), (0.4, 0, 0))	4

Each element has a sequence number (shown on the right of the above diagram). This is used for editing the structure, which we shall describe in Chapter 5.

4.2 Displaying the model: traversal

Creating the model – as we have just done – and displaying a picture of it, are two completely separate operations. To create a picture of a model, we must **post** it to a workstation, using:

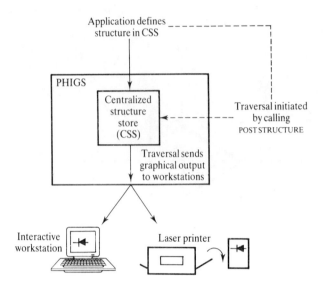

Figure 4.3   Traversal.

☐   POST STRUCTURE
parameters:

in	workstation identifier	integer
in	structure identifier	integer
in	display priority	real

This causes *structure identifier* to be displayed on the workstation selected by *workstation identifier*. We shall ignore the *display priority* parameter for now, and return to it in Section 4.8. We post the diode structure to workstation 1:

POST STRUCTURE (1, diode, 1.0)

This causes the diode structure to be interpreted, sending graphical output to the workstation. This is called **traversal**, and is illustrated in Figure 4.3. It works as follows. PHIGS locates the diode structure in the CSS, and processes each of its elements in their numbered sequence, starting with element 1. The first element in *diode* is the polyline to draw the left wire; its coordinates are extracted and the appropriate instructions are issued to workstation, which draws the polyline. Then the next element is processed, and so on until the end of the structure is reached. At this point, the picture of the diode has been drawn. Once a structure has been posted to a workstation, traversal is conceptually a *continuous* process, so that if we change the contents of a structure (as we shall see in the next chapter), the picture is automatically brought up to date.

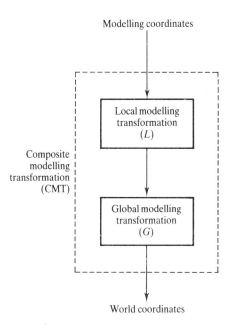

Modelling coordinates

Figure 4.4   The coordinates of output primitives are transformed by *G* and *L*.

4.3   The composite modelling transformation

We have said that when a structure is traversed, its output primitives are displayed on the workstation. In fact, the situation is a little more complicated. Before an output primitive is displayed, its coordinates are automatically changed by a transformation called the **Composite Modelling Transformation (CMT)**. The CMT always exists during traversal, and is *always* applied. The effect is that a point *p* is transformed by the CMT during traversal to become a new point p', as follows:

$$p' \leftarrow CMT \cdot p$$

The CMT is actually made from a combination of two transformations, the **local transformation** (*L*), and **global modelling transformation** (*G*), such that *L* is applied *before* *G*. So, when *p* is transformed by the CMT, it actually undergoes two separate transformations, as follows:

$$p' \leftarrow G \cdot L \cdot p$$

This is illustrated in Figure 4.4. By default, both *G* and *L* are the identity transformation, which has the effect of leaving the coordinates unchanged. We shall describe the use of *G* in Section 4.6, and for now consider only the local transformation *L*.

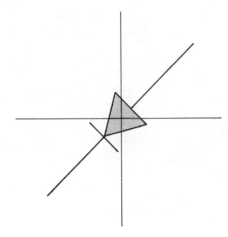

Figure 4.5   Transforming the diode with SET LOCAL TRANSFORMATION 3.

4.4   The local transformation

We can change the value of the local transformation during traversal, by using a structure element to specify a new transformation. This is the SET LOCAL TRANS-FORMATION 3 structure element, and we create it using:

| E | SET LOCAL TRANSFORMATION 3 |

SET LOCAL TRANSFORMATION 3
parameters:
      in   transformation matrix 4×4 real matrix
      in   composition type   (PRECONCATENATE,
                                           POSTCONCATENATE, REPLACE)

If we create a SET LOCAL TRANSFORMATION 3 element as follows:

SET LOCAL TRANSFORMATION 3 (T, REPLACE)

the effect, during traversal, is that the current value of L is *replaced* by T. Because it is applied automatically to all coordinates, we can use the local transformation to alter the position, scale and orientation of the diode, without having to alter the coordinates of each of its polyline and fill area elements.

For example, we can create a transformation matrix T which has the effect of rotating coordinates by $45°$, and apply it to the diode by including a SET LOCAL TRANSFORMATION 3 element in the diode structure, *before* the polyline and fill area elements (Figure 4.5).

diode structure	0
SET LOCAL TRANSFORMATION 3 (*T*, REPLACE)	1
POLYLINE 3 ((−0.5, 0, 0), (−0.2, 0, 0))	2
POLYLINE 3 ((−0.2, −0.2, 0), (−0.2, 0.2, 0))	3
FILL AREA 3 ((−0.2, 0, 0), (0.1, 0.2, 0), (0.1, −0.2, 0))	4
POLYLINE 3 ((0.1, 0, 0), (0.4, 0, 0))	5

This provides a flexible method for creating models: we can take any structure and use *L* to apply a transformation to change its scale, position and orientation, without having to change the coordinates of output primitives.

It is often useful to apply a number of transformations in sequence, such as first scaling a structure, and then rotating it *after* the scale, and so on. PHIGS provides a method for this, using the *composition type* parameter of SET LOCAL TRANSFORMATION 3. This controls how *L* is changed by a new transformation. The following table shows the effect of a SET LOCAL TRANSFORMATION 3 element with a transformation *T*, using the different composition types:

Composition type	Effect on L	
REPLACE	$L \leftarrow T$	(*T replaces L*)
PRECONCATENATE	$L \leftarrow L \cdot T$	(*T* applied *before L*)
POSTCONCATENATE	$L \leftarrow T \cdot L$	(*T* applied *after L*)

Plates 2 and 3 show the use of the local modelling transformation to change the model.

4.4.1 Defining modelling transformations

We have not said anything about how to determine what the actual values for the modelling transformation matrices should be. PHIGS uses homogeneous coordinate transformations, where a 3D transformation is expressed as a 4×4 matrix, and a 2D transformation as a 3×3 matrix. The mathematics of these formulations is described in Appendix C, but it is quite possible to use transformations in practice without understanding the internal detail.

PHIGS provides a number of utility functions to help you to specify matrices in a natural way. The first group of functions take translation, scaling or rotation terms and return the appropriate transformation matrix:

☐ TRANSLATE 3
parameters:

in	translation vector	3D vector
out	error	integer
out	transformation matrix	4×4 real matrix

☐   SCALE 3
parameters:

in	x, y and z scale factors	3 reals
out	error	integer
out	transformation matrix	4×4 real matrix

There are three separate functions for computing rotations: ROTATE X, ROTATE Y and ROTATE Z, for rotations about the x, y and z axes respectively. Each function has the same parameters, and the following illustrates the general form:

☐   ROTATE X
parameters:

in	angle in radians	real
out	error	integer
out	transformation matrix	4×4 real matrix

Often, we shall want to define a sequence of scales, rotations and translations, and we can do this using:

☐   BUILD TRANSFORMATION MATRIX 3
parameters:

in	fixed point	3D point
in	shift vector	3D vector
in	rotation about x	real
in	rotation about y	real
in	rotation about z	real
in	x, y, z scale factors	3 reals
out	error	integer
out	transformation matrix	4×4 real matrix

If we define:

T_{sh}	as the translation by the shift vector
T_{fp}	as the translation by the fixed point
R_x, R_y, R_z	as the x, y and z rotations
S	as the scale transformation
T_{-fp}	as the translation by minus the fixed point

then the function returns a matrix which is equivalent to:

$$T_{sh} \cdot T_{fp} \cdot R_z \cdot R_y \cdot R_x \cdot S \cdot T_{-fp}$$

The effect of applying this sequence of transformations to a point p is to transform it to a new point p' as follows:

$$p' = T_{sh} \cdot T_{fp} \cdot R_z \cdot R_y \cdot R_x \cdot S \cdot T_{-fp} \cdot p$$

Here, the transformation T_{-fp} is the first to be applied, and T_{sh} is the last.

Another common requirement is to take a number of transformation matrices and compose them to form a single equivalent matrix. We can do this using the following function, which accepts two matrices M_1 and M_2 as input, and returns their product, the matrix $M_1 \cdot M_2$:

☐ COMPOSE MATRIX 3

parameters:

in	transformation matrix M_1	4×4 real matrix
in	transformation matrix M_2	4×4 real matrix
out	error	integer
out	composed transformation matrix	4×4 real matrix

Another utility function, COMPOSE TRANSFORMATION MATRIX 3, combines the effect of the previous two functions. It accepts a matrix M as input, together with scale, rotate and shift terms, and returns a matrix M' which has the effect of first applying M and then the scale, rotate and shift parameters:

☐ COMPOSE TRANSFORMATION MATRIX 3

parameters:

in	transformation matrix	4×4 real matrix
in	fixed point	3D point
in	shift vector	3D vector
in	rotation about x	real
in	rotation about y	real
in	rotation about z	real
in	x, y, z scale factors	3 reals
out	error	integer
out	transformation matrix	4×4 real matrix

There is also a function which transforms a point by a given matrix, and returns the new value:

☐ TRANSFORM POINT 3

parameters:

in	point	3D point
in	transformation matrix	4×4 real matrix
out	error	integer
out	transformed point	3D point

4.5 Instancing

Suppose now we wish to model a rectifier, as shown in Figure 4.6. There are several approaches we could take. The first is to forget all about the diode we have just created, and create a single structure called *rectifier*, defining the model by reading off the coordinates for each of the polylines and fill areas. Or, we could

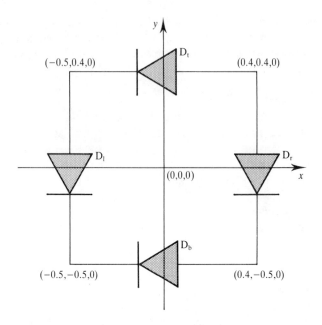

Figure 4.6   Using the diode to model a rectifier.

create four separate structures called *bottom diode*, *top diode*, *left diode* and *right diode*, each of which defines the diode in the appropriate location and orientation, and then post each of them to the workstation. A much better approach is to recognize that the rectifier actually comprises four copies of the diode structure we already have, but that each copy occurs in different locations and/or orientations. This is the approach we shall explore.

Consider the bottom diode of the rectifier, D_b. It differs from the diode structure we have already in that the y coordinates of its fill area and polylines are 0.5 units lower. All the x and z coordinates, however, are the same. We could obtain the coordinates for the bottom diode by taking the coordinates of the diode we have already defined, and transforming them before we draw the diode such that each point (x, y, z) becomes a different point (x', y', z'), as follows:

$$x' \leftarrow x$$
$$y' \leftarrow y - 0.5$$
$$z' \leftarrow z$$

We will call this coordinate transformation T_b, since it refers to the *bottom diode*. We can now begin to model the rectifier in terms of the existing diode structure. We shall create a new structure, called *rectifier*, as follows:

```
OPEN STRUCTURE (rectifier)
SET LOCAL TRANSFORMATION 3 (T_b, REPLACE)
EXECUTE STRUCTURE (diode)
```

CLOSE STRUCTURE

This creates the following structure:

rectifier structure	0
SET LOCAL TRANSFORMATION 3 (T_b, REPLACE)	1
EXECUTE STRUCTURE (diode)	2

Here, we have introduced a new type of structure element, EXECUTE STRUCTURE:

E   EXECUTE STRUCTURE
parameters:
        in   structure identifier   integer

This effect of this element during the traversal of the rectifier is to cause the traversal to be temporarily halted, and for the diode structure to be traversed. When this traversal is complete, traversal of the rectifier resumes. We now describe what happens when the rectifier structure is posted to the workstation. When traversal begins, L is automatically set to the identity transformation (I). Since by default G is also I, the overall effect is that the CMT is I, and so points are transformed onto themselves. The first element to be processed is element 1 of the rectifier structure, SET LOCAL TRANSFORMATION 3 (T_b, REPLACE). At this point L becomes T_b, and therefore the CMT becomes T_b. Now, all the coordinates of any output primitives subsequently encountered during the traversal will be automatically transformed by T_b before being drawn. The next element of *rectifier* is EXECUTE STRUCTURE (diode). When this element is processed, three things happen:

- the current values of L and G are saved on a stack.

- PHIGS records how far in the traversal of *rectifier* it has reached, and it extracts the name *diode* from the EXECUTE STRUCTURE element.

- PHIGS starts to traverse the *diode* structure.

The CMT in effect is still T_b, so the coordinates of the polylines and fill area of the diode will be transformed by T_b before being drawn. The effect is that the diode is not displayed in its original location: it is shifted in y by -0.5, and we have drawn the bottom diode of the rectifier. The bottom diode D_b is called an **instance** of the diode structure. When traversal of *diode* is complete, PHIGS returns to the *rectifier* structure, and because there are no more elements, traversal stops.

Referring again to Figure 4.6, we can determine what the transformations T_l, T_t and T_r should be for the left (D_l), top (D_t) and right (D_r) instances of diode respectively:

    T_l rotate by $90°$ anticlockwise, shift by $(-0.5, 0, 0)$
    T_t shift by $(0, 0.4, 0)$
    T_r rotate by $90°$ anticlockwise, shift by $(0.5, 0, 0)$

We can now extend the definition of the rectifier structure by adding new elements to set up other values for L (and thus the CMT) so that we can create the left, top and right diodes:

rectifier structure	0
SET LOCAL TRANSFORMATION 3 (T_b, REPLACE)	1
EXECUTE STRUCTURE (diode)	2
SET LOCAL TRANSFORMATION 3 (T_l, REPLACE)	3
EXECUTE STRUCTURE (diode)	4
SET LOCAL TRANSFORMATION 3 (T_t, REPLACE)	5
EXECUTE STRUCTURE (diode)	6
SET LOCAL TRANSFORMATION 3 (T_r, REPLACE)	7
EXECUTE STRUCTURE (diode)	8

The effect of traversal is exactly the same as we have described above. When traversal returns from the diode via element 2 of *rectifier*, there are now more elements to be processed in *rectifier*. The value of L is still T_b, but element 3 replaces it with T_l. At element 4, traversal of *rectifier* is again temporarily suspended, and PHIGS returns to the diode, transforming all its points this time by T_l, producing the left diode in the rectifier. The process continues in this way until the end of the rectifier is reached.

The beauty of this scheme is that we only actually need to have one definition of the diode, and we rely on dynamic traversal to instance it with the appropriate modelling transformations. The process of traversal is fundamental, and – in conjunction with hierarchy – is the key to the versatility of PHIGS for modelling.

We can now treat the *rectifier* structure itself as a building block, and create instances of it. Rectifiers are usually drawn rotated, so we will create a new structure *rotated rectifier*, which will use a transformation T_{rot} to rotate the rectifier structure, as shown in Figure 4.7:

```
OPEN STRUCTURE (rotated rectifier)
SET LOCAL TRANSFORMATION 3 (Trot, REPLACE)
EXECUTE STRUCTURE (rectifier)
CLOSE STRUCTURE
```

This defines a structure as follows:

rotated rectifier structure	0
SET LOCAL TRANSFORMATION 3 (T_{rot}, REPLACE)	1
EXECUTE STRUCTURE (rectifier)	2

Now we post the rotated rectifier structure:

POST STRUCTURE (ws, rotated rectifier, priority)

The effect of element 1 of *rotated rectifier* is to set L to T_{rot}. Therefore the current value of the CMT becomes:

$$CMT = G \cdot T_{rot}$$

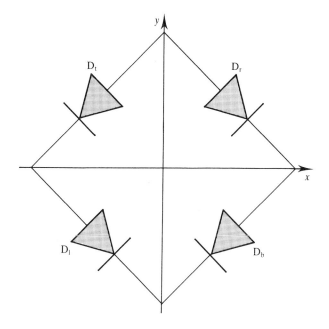

Figure 4.7   Rotating the rectifier.

and since $G = I$, the CMT is effectively T_{rot}. When the EXECUTE STRUCTURE (rectifier) element is processed, PHIGS saves G and L on the stack. It then suspends traversal of *rotated rectifier*, and begins traversing *rectifier*. But first, it changes the values of G and L, as follows:

$$G \leftarrow G \cdot L$$
$$L \leftarrow I$$

The new values in effect are therefore:

$$G = T_{rot}$$
$$L = I$$
$$\text{CMT} = G \cdot L = T_{rot}$$

Notice that although the values of G and L have changed, the overall value of the CMT has not.

The traversal of the rectifier structure begins. The first element is SET LOCAL TRANSFORMATION 3 (T_b, REPLACE). This sets L to T_b, and the CMT is therefore now $T_{rot} \cdot T_b$. At element 2 of *rectifier* PHIGS breaks off traversing *rectifier* to traverse *diode*. Again, the values of G and L are saved on a stack, and again G and L take new values according to:

$$G \leftarrow G \cdot L$$
$$L \leftarrow I$$

which sets G and L and the CMT as follows:

$$G = T_{rot} \cdot T_b$$
$$L = I$$
$$CMT = G \cdot L = T_{rot} \cdot T_b$$

The CMT that transforms the coordinates of the diode is therefore $T_{rot} \cdot T_b$. In other words, a point p on the diode is first transformed by T_b, to give the corresponding point p' in the rectifier. p' is then transformed by T_{rot}, to give the corresponding point p'' in the rotated rectifier. This is exactly the effect we require. We have:

$$p' = T_b \cdot p$$
$$p'' = T_{rot} \cdot p'$$
$$p'' = T_{rot} \cdot T_b \cdot p$$

When traversal of *diode* is complete, PHIGS returns to the rectifier structure, and restores the values of G and L that it saved, making them once again:

$$G = T_{rot}$$
$$L = I$$
$$CMT = G \cdot L = T_{rot}$$

The same process occurs for the other three instances of the diode structure. When the traversal of *diode* is complete, the values of G and L which were in effect before the EXECUTE STRUCTURE (rectifier) element in *rotated rectifier* are restored from the stack. It is important to take care with the use of modelling transformations, since incorrect values can cause very unexpected results. It is often useful to build software tools on top of PHIGS to help with this, and Plate 6 shows a PHIGS application program developed by the authors for interactively designing and manipulating structure networks.

4.6   The global transformation

We can also set the value of the global modelling transformation (G) during traversal, using the function:

E   SET GLOBAL TRANSFORMATION 3
parameters:
        in   transformation matrix 4×4 real matrix

Here, we do not have the ability to *compose* a new matrix with G: it always *replaces* G. The global modelling transformation is useful for applying a transformation to an entire structure network, because it takes effect *after* the local modelling transformation L. Another application is to override the accumulated CMT during traversal, in order to place an output primitive at a specific position.

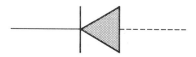

Figure 4.8   Making the right wire DASHED.

4.7   Attributes and inheritance

During traversal PHIGS keeps a data structure called the **traversal state list**, (**TSL**). It is in the TSL that the values of the local and global modelling trans-formations are kept. The current values of primitive attributes (such as linetype) are also kept in the TSL, and it is these values which control the appearance of output primitives when they are drawn.

Before a structure specified in an EXECUTE ELEMENT is traversed, the entire TSL is stacked; on return from the structure, the TSL is unstacked. This has the effect that structures lower down the hierarchy can never affect structures higher up. For example, modelling transformations only pass *down* the hierarchy, never up. The effect of the way in which PHIGS handles the local and global modelling transformations when processing EXECUTE STRUCTURE elements is that child structures inherit the modelling transformations in effect in their parents. For example, in the rotated rectifier example, each of the instances of *diode* inherited the rotation of their parent, the rectifier. Exactly the same mechanism occurs with the attributes of output primitives.

To illustrate the way attributes work during traversal, we shall modify the diode structure slightly, so that the right wire is drawn using a dashed line:

diode structure	0
POLYLINE 3 ((−0.5, 0, 0), (−0.2, 0, 0))	1
POLYLINE 3 ((−0.2, −0.2, 0), (−0.2, 0.2, 0))	2
FILL AREA 3 ((−0.2, 0, 0), (0.1, 0.2, 0), (0.1, −0.2, 0))	3
SET LINETYPE (DASHED)	4
POLYLINE 3 ((0.1, 0, 0), (0.4, 0, 0))	5

If we post this structure, the diode will be drawn as shown in Figure 4.8. The SET LINETYPE element only has an effect on *subsequent* elements in the structure. Let us now instance the diode using a structure which changes linetype to be DOTTED:

dotty diode structure	0
SET LINETYPE (DOTTED)	1
EXECUTE STRUCTURE (diode)	2

When *dotty diode* is posted, the effect is that when *diode* is traversed (via the EXECUTE STRUCTURE element, it inherits all the primitive attributes currently in

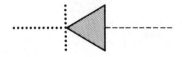

Figure 4.9 *Diode* inherits DOTTED linetype.

effect, including linetype DOTTED. Figure 4.9 shows the result; the first two poly-lines have inherited the DOTTED linetype, and are therefore drawn dotted. The right wire, however, remains DASHED, because the linetype attribute is is set to its new value within *diode*.

Finally, let us add another element to *dotty diode*, to draw a box around the instanced diode:

dotty diode structure	0
SET LINETYPE (DOTTED)	1
EXECUTE STRUCTURE (diode)	2
POLYLINE 3 (box points)	3

The effect is that the box is drawn with the current linetype in effect when *dotty diode* is traversed, as shown in Figure 4.10. Because the TSL is stacked and unstacked around the traversal of *diode*, the change of linetype that occurs in *diode* does not remain in effect when traversal of *dotty diode* resumes.

Going through this example at such a level of detail might make the mechanism appear complicated. But it is really very simple, if you remember that any changes which are made to transformations and attributes are passed *down* the hierarchy, and never *up*. This means that that a child structure inherits the transformations and attributes of its parents.

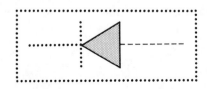

Figure 4.10 DASHED LINES are local to *diode*.

4.8   Controlling the posting of structure networks

To cause a structure network to be displayed, it must be **posted** to a workstation. It is important to realize that the operations of posting and unposting refer only to structure networks. It is not possible to single out particular structures for posting an unposting, such that their descendents are not affected. We post a structure network using the POST STRUCTURE function:

☐ POST STRUCTURE
  parameters:
in	workstation identifier	integer
in	structure identifier	integer
in	display priority	real

Subject to the display update state of the workstation (see Sections 8.5.1 and 8.5.2), the structure network is traversed and displayed. Traversal is conceptually a continuous process: once a structure has been posted, you can think of it as being continually traversed, so that if you make any changes to the structure, they will be reflected in the displayed image automatically. Any output primitives generated will be assigned the specified *display priority*, a real number in the range [0, 1]. If two or more primitives (or parts of them) happen to occupy the same position on the display, the primitive with the highest priority will be displayed. In the case where the priorities are the same, the primitives originating from whichever structure network was most recently posted are visible.

As well as posting structures networks, we need a way to remove structure networks which are displayed, and there are two functions for this. The first is UNPOST STRUCTURE, and it operates on a single structure:

☐ UNPOST STRUCTURE
  parameters:
  | *in* | workstation identifier | integer |
  | *in* | structure identifier | integer |

This function removes the structure network with the specified root from the list of posted structures in the workstation state list of the specified workstation. This will cause the display to be updated, and the image of the structure network removed. Note that the structure network is not itself deleted from the CSS, and it may be later re-posted for display. If the specified structure does not exist, no action is taken. We can remove all the structure networks from display using the UNPOST ALL STRUCTURES function:

☐ UNPOST ALL STRUCTURES
  parameters:
  | *in* | workstation identifier | integer |

All the structure networks which are currently posted to the specified workstation

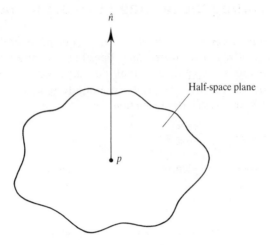

Figure 4.11   Defining a half-space.

are unposted. Note again that while they are removed from the workstation they are not deleted from the CSS.

4.9   Modelling clipping

PHIGS provides a mechanism for removing parts of an object to reveal internal detail, called **modelling clipping**. The application defines a volume in space called the **modelling clipping volume** and only those parts of output primitives which lie within this volume are drawn. This technique can be used for drawing cross-sections of objects, or creating cutaway drawings.

The volume is defined by the intersections of a set of infinite planes, or **half-spaces**. A half-space is defined by a point p in modelling coordinates, and a normal vector $\hat{n}$, which gives the orientation of the half-space plane passing through the point, as shown in Figure 4.11. The plane divides space into two regions. The region in the direction of the normal is inside the modelling clipping volume, and the other region is outside the volume. The current modelling clipping volume in held in the TSL during traversal. It is initially the whole of WC space, so that no parts of the model are clipped. The volume is defined using a structure element, which specifies a collection of half-spaces, and an *operator*:

E	SET MODELLING CLIPPING VOLUME 3

    parameters:

	in	operator	integer
	in	half-spaces	list of 3D MC half-spaces

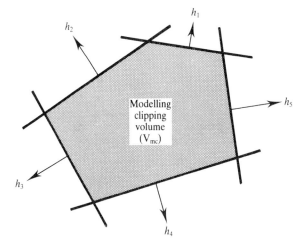

Figure 4.12   Five half-spaces defining a modelling clipping volume.

The effect of this element is that each of the half-spaces is first transformed to WC using the current CMT, and then intersected to produce a volume. We can define this formally as follows. Let the current modelling clipping volume be V_{mc}. If the structure element specifies n half-planes $h_1, h_2 \ldots h_n$, the volume V_h created by their intersection is:

$$V_h = h_1 \cap h_2 \ldots \cap h_n$$

V_h is then used to modify the current modelling clipping volume, according to *operator*:

- *operator* = 1   The current modelling clipping volume is *replaced* by V_h. That is:

$$V_{mc} \leftarrow V_h$$

- *operator* = 2   The current modelling clipping volume becomes the volume obtained by intersecting V_h with the V_{mc}:

$$V_{mc} \leftarrow V_{mc} \cap V_h$$

This definition means that only convex clipping volumes may be defined. Figure 4.12 shows an example.

Since the modelling clipping volume may be changed during traversal of a structure, it is sometimes useful to be able to reset it to the value in effect when the traversal of the structure began. This is done using a structure element:

$\boxed{\text{E}}$ RESTORE MODELLING CLIPPING VOLUME
  parameters: none

Whether or not modelling clipping is applied depends on the setting of a global modelling clipping indicator (held in the TSL), which is controlled using a structure element:

☐E☐   SET MODELLING CLIPPING INDICATOR
parameters:
      in   indicator   (CLIP, NOCLIP)

The default action is that modelling clipping is disabled.

Chapter 5
Editing the model

*In many applications, models are not static: they may change, perhaps to reflect the results of a simulation, or as a response to graphical input. In this chapter we describe how to **edit** structures and structure networks to reflect changes in the model.*

Associated with the open structure is the **element pointer**, which indicates the position of an element in the structure at which element insertion and deletion will occur. If a structure contains n elements, the element pointer may take any of the values

$0 \leq$ element pointer $\leq n$

There is only one element pointer in PHIGS, and it only exists when a structure is open. We open a structure for editing using the OPEN STRUCTURE function. If a structure is opened and it does not already exist, it is automatically created, and the element pointer is set to 0. If, however, a structure which already exists is opened, the element pointer is set to the last element in the structure.

To describe structure editing, we shall return to the example from Chapter 2, which draws the cube. We can represent the structure schematically as follows (for clarity, we omit the SET TEXT ALIGNMENT and SET CHARACTER HEIGHT elements):

cube structure	0
SET LOCAL TRANSFORMATION 3	1
POLYLINE 3 front face	2
POLYLINE 3 back face	3
POLYLINE 3 link 1	4
POLYLINE 3 link 2	5
POLYLINE 3 link 3	6
POLYLINE 3 link 4	7
TEXT 3 "It's a"	8
TEXT 3 "square world!"	9

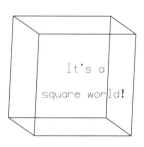

This shows each element in the structure, together with its number. Note that we have included element position 0, although the first element is numbered 1. The

significance of this will be described later. If we now open the structure, using:

OPEN STRUCTURE (cube)

the element pointer will be set to the last element in the structure, element number 9. We shall mark the position of the element pointer with ←EP, as follows:

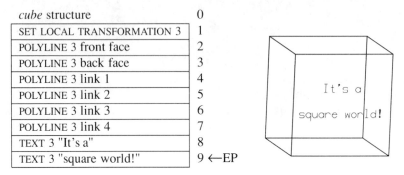

cube structure	0
SET LOCAL TRANSFORMATION 3	1
POLYLINE 3 front face	2
POLYLINE 3 back face	3
POLYLINE 3 link 1	4
POLYLINE 3 link 2	5
POLYLINE 3 link 3	6
POLYLINE 3 link 4	7
TEXT 3 "It's a"	8
TEXT 3 "square world!"	9 ←EP

5.1   Positioning the element pointer

We need to be able to move the element pointer around in the open structure, and there are several functions for doing this. The most straightforward function sets the pointer to a particular position in a structure:

☐   SET ELEMENT POINTER
parameters:
      in   position   integer

We can use this function to set the element pointer to the third element in the cube structure:

SET ELEMENT POINTER (3)

which gives:

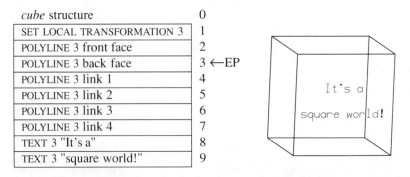

cube structure	0
SET LOCAL TRANSFORMATION 3	1
POLYLINE 3 front face	2
POLYLINE 3 back face	3 ←EP
POLYLINE 3 link 1	4
POLYLINE 3 link 2	5
POLYLINE 3 link 3	6
POLYLINE 3 link 4	7
TEXT 3 "It's a"	8
TEXT 3 "square world!"	9

This function never generates an error. If we specify an element position less than

0, the element pointer is set to 0; if we specify a position greater than the number of elements in the structure, the element pointer is set to the last element in the structure.

It is often convenient to move the element pointer relative to its current position, and we can do this using:

☐ OFFSET ELEMENT POINTER
    parameters:
        in   offset   integer

This adjusts the position of the element pointer by adding *offset* to the current position, and moves the element pointer accordingly. For example:

OFFSET ELEMENT POINTER (1)

moves the element pointer one element forward, to element 4:

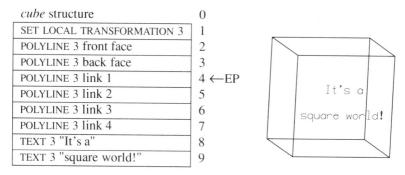

cube structure	0
SET LOCAL TRANSFORMATION 3	1
POLYLINE 3 front face	2
POLYLINE 3 back face	3
POLYLINE 3 link 1	4 ←EP
POLYLINE 3 link 2	5
POLYLINE 3 link 3	6
POLYLINE 3 link 4	7
TEXT 3 "It's a"	8
TEXT 3 "square world!"	9

To enable the element pointer to be moved towards the end or the beginning of the structure, *offset* may be correspondingly positive or negative. For example:

OFFSET ELEMENT POINTER (−2)

moves the element pointer back by two elements to element 2.

5.2 Inserting elements

Whenever the application inserts a new element into a structure, one of two possible actions occurs, depending on the current **edit mode**. It is set using:

☐ SET EDIT MODE
    parameters:
        in   edit mode   (INSERT, REPLACE)

The edit mode applies to the entire CSS: there is no separate edit mode per structure. If the edit mode is INSERT, the new element is inserted into the position immediately following the element pointer, which is then updated to point to the new element. (This is why the element pointer may be set to 0: so that structure elements may be inserted at the beginning of a structure.)

We can make all the lines in the cube dashed-dotted by inserting a new structure element before the polyline elements, as follows:

```
SET EDIT MODE (INSERT)
SET ELEMENT POINTER (1)
SET LINETYPE (DASHED-DOTTED)
```

Here, we first set the element pointer to 1, so that the new element is inserted into position 2. The element pointer is then automatically updated to point to the new element:

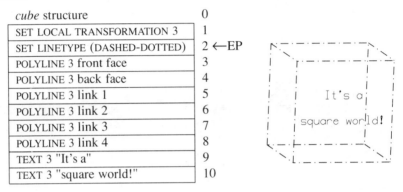

cube structure	0
SET LOCAL TRANSFORMATION 3	1
SET LINETYPE (DASHED-DOTTED)	2 ←EP
POLYLINE 3 front face	3
POLYLINE 3 back face	4
POLYLINE 3 link 1	5
POLYLINE 3 link 2	6
POLYLINE 3 link 3	7
POLYLINE 3 link 4	8
TEXT 3 "It's a"	9
TEXT 3 "square world!"	10

An important consequence of this insertion is that all the remaining elements in the structure have been automatically renumbered. Although we explicitly set the edit mode in this example, by default it is already set to INSERT, and we relied on this fact when we were defining the *diode, rectifier* and *rotated rectifier* structures in Chapter 4.

5.3   Replacing elements

If we set the edit mode to REPLACE, the new element directly replaces the existing element at the element pointer, and the position of the element pointer is not changed. We can use REPLACE mode editing to change from dashed-dotted to dashed lines using:

```
SET EDIT MODE (REPLACE)
SET ELEMENT POINTER (2)
SET LINETYPE (DASHED)
```

The SET LINETYPE function will create a new element which will *overwrite* the element already at position 2, to give:

cube structure	0
SET LOCAL TRANSFORMATION 3	1
SET LINETYPE (DASHED)	2 ←EP
POLYLINE 3 front face	3
POLYLINE 3 back face	4
POLYLINE 3 link 1	5
POLYLINE 3 link 2	6
POLYLINE 3 link 3	7
POLYLINE 3 link 4	8
TEXT 3 "It's a"	9
TEXT 3 "square world!"	10

Note that the position of the element pointer has not changed.

If the element pointer is 0 when we attempt to replace an element, the effect is that the element is inserted into the structure immediately before element 1, and the element pointer is set to 1. This will cause any subsequent elements in the structure to be implicitly renumbered.

Some care is required to use the edit mode correctly. A common source of errors is to have the wrong edit mode in effect, which can lead to very unexpected results. A useful approach is to have a convention of choosing either INSERT or REPLACE to be the working default for a particular application, and to keep any changes to the edit mode as localized as possible. Whenever it is necessary to change the edit mode, it is good practice to first inquire the current mode, make the change and perform the edit, and then reset the mode to its previous state. The function to inquire the current edit mode is:

☐ INQUIRE EDIT MODE
parameters:
      out error   integer
      out edit mode   (INSERT, REPLACE)

5.4   Deleting elements

We can delete the element at the element pointer using:

☐ DELETE ELEMENT
parameters: none

This effect of this function is to remove the element from the structure, and then to move the element pointer to the preceding element. For example, we can delete some text from the cube as follows. First we set the element pointer at the first text element:

SET ELEMENT POINTER (9)

to give:

cube structure	0
SET LOCAL TRANSFORMATION 3	1
SET LINETYPE (DASHED)	2
POLYLINE 3 front face	3
POLYLINE 3 back face	4
POLYLINE 3 link 1	5
POLYLINE 3 link 2	6
POLYLINE 3 link 3	7
POLYLINE 3 link 4	8
TEXT 3 "It's a"	9 ←EP
TEXT 3 "square world!"	10

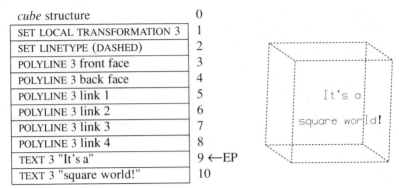

If we now delete the element:

DELETE ELEMENT

the result is:

cube structure	0
SET LOCAL TRANSFORMATION 3	1
SET LINETYPE (DASHED)	2
POLYLINE 3 front face	3
POLYLINE 3 back face	4
POLYLINE 3 link 1	5
POLYLINE 3 link 2	6
POLYLINE 3 link 3	7
POLYLINE 3 link 4	8 ←EP
TEXT 3 "square world!"	9

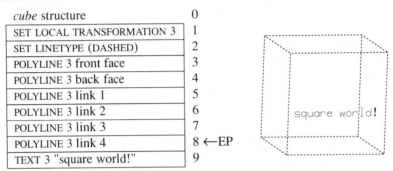

The TEXT 3 element "It's a" has been removed. Note that an implicit renumbering has occurred; for example, the "square world!" TEXT 3 element is now number 9. Attempting to delete element 0 of a structure has no effect, and does not generate an error.

We can also remove a continuous range of elements, using the DELETE EL-EMENT RANGE function, which deletes all the elements between and including two specified element positions:

☐ DELETE ELEMENT RANGE
parameters:
    in   first position   integer
    in   second position   integer

For example, we can delete the links between the front and back faces of the cube (elements 5, 6, 7 and 8) with:

DELETE ELEMENT RANGE (5, 8)

which gives:

cube structure	0
SET LOCAL TRANSFORMATION 3	1
SET LINETYPE (DASHED)	2
POLYLINE 3 front face	3
POLYLINE 3 back face	4 ←EP
TEXT 3 "square world!"	5

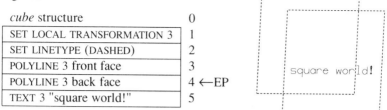

This leaves the element pointer at the element immediately before the first element in the deleted range.

For convenience, there is also a function for deleting all the elements from a structure:

☐ EMPTY STRUCTURE
parameters:
    in   structure identifier   integer

The effect is that all the elements are removed, and although it is now empty, the structure still exists. Note that this function is different from the other element deletion functions, in that the structure does not have to be open for the operation to take place. If, however, the structure is open, after emptying the structure the element pointer is set to 0.

5.5   The label element

As we have seen, when elements are inserted or deleted, the positions of elements which occur later in the structure than the edit position may change, and this makes referring to elements directly using their numbers awkward and error prone. Mismanaging element numbers within a structure is a common source of errors.

For this reason, the **label** structure element is provided, which serves as a convenient place marker in a structure, and has no effect during traversal. A label element is created using:

[E] LABEL
parameters:
    in   label identifier   integer

We can improve the readability of a structure by using labels to mark its different parts. Label identifiers are integers, and it is good practice to use symbolic constants wherever possible. For example, if we restore the original (unedited) cube structure, we can insert label elements to mark the transformation, front face, back face, links and text parts, as follows:

cube structure	0
LABEL *transformation*	1
SET LOCAL TRANSFORMATION 3	2
LABEL *front face*	3
POLYLINE 3 front face	4
LABEL *back face*	5
POLYLINE 3 back face	6
LABEL *links*	7
POLYLINE 3 link 1	8
POLYLINE 3 link 2	9
POLYLINE 3 link 3	10
POLYLINE 3 link 4	11
LABEL *text*	12
TEXT 3 "It's a"	13
TEXT 3 "square world!"	14

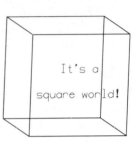

Often, applications will create structures according to particular conventions. For example, a CAD application might construct a model by always preceding a POLY-LINE 3 with a LABEL describing its purpose. It is far safer to position the element pointer in terms of labels than by referring to explicit element positions, since the latter may change because of editing. We can set the element pointer to the next occurrence in the structure of a particular label with the function:

◻ SET ELEMENT POINTER AT LABEL
    parameters:
        in   label identifier   integer

For example, if the element pointer is at position 1, the following call will set the element pointer to the next occurrence of the *front face* label (element 3):

    SET ELEMENT POINTER AT LABEL (*front face*)

Note that this function searches for labels in a structure only in the forward direction. If an attempt is made to set the element pointer at a label which does not occur between the current position of the pointer and the end of the structure, an error is generated and the element pointer is not moved. In some circumstances this behaviour can be somewhat awkward, and if you want to be sure of always setting the element pointer successfully to a label, it is necessary to first set the element pointer to some position (or label) *before* the required label. The simplest solution is to set the element pointer to 0.

It is quite permissible to have several labels with the same identifier in a particular structure. If the element pointer is already positioned at an occurrence of a particular label, and SET ELEMENT POINTER AT LABEL is called specifying the same label identifier, PHIGS will search for the *next* occurrence of the label in the structure. As before, if this label is not found before the end of the structure is reached, an error is reported, and the element pointer is not moved.

As we have seen, label elements are often used to improve the management of complex structures, by marking groups of logically related structure elements. We can also delete all the elements between two specified labels (but retaining the labels), using the function:

☐ DELETE ELEMENTS BETWEEN LABELS
   parameters:
         in   first label identifier   integer
         in   second label identifier   integer

We can use this function to remove the elements which draw the front and back faces, as follows:

DELETE ELEMENTS BETWEEN LABELS (*front face*, *links*)

which leaves

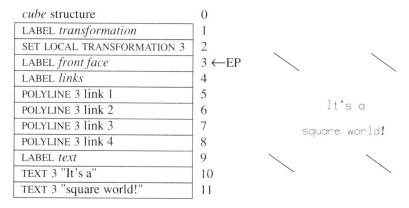

cube structure	0
LABEL *transformation*	1
SET LOCAL TRANSFORMATION 3	2
LABEL *front face*	3 ←EP
LABEL *links*	4
POLYLINE 3 link 1	5
POLYLINE 3 link 2	6
POLYLINE 3 link 3	7
POLYLINE 3 link 4	8
LABEL *text*	9
TEXT 3 "It's a"	10
TEXT 3 "square world!"	11

The element pointer is left positioned at the element immediately preceding the group of elements deleted. PHIGS attempts to locate the labels using the same rules as for the SET ELEMENT POINTER AT LABEL function: if either of the specified labels is not located between the position of the element pointer and the end of the structure, an error is generated and the function has no effect.

5.6 An example of structure editing

We now give an example of a common use of structure editing – to change the values of modelling transformations. In the case of the cube, we can make it rotate by repeatedly changing its SET LOCAL TRANSFORMATION 3 element. To do this, we need to replace this element repeatedly with another containing a different transformation matrix. First, we need to know which element is to be replaced, and we can see that the appropriate modelling transformation is element 2:

cube structure	0
LABEL *transformation*	1
SET LOCAL TRANSFORMATION 3	2
LABEL *front face*	3
POLYLINE 3 front face	4
LABEL *back face*	5
POLYLINE 3 back face	6
LABEL *links*	7
POLYLINE 3 link 1	8
POLYLINE 3 link 2	9
POLYLINE 3 link 3	10
POLYLINE 3 link 4	11
LABEL *text*	12
TEXT 3 "It's a"	13
TEXT 3 "square world!"	14

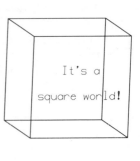

As we have said, rather than using an explicit element number (which may change if the structure is edited), it is better to ensure that the transformation is always accompanied by its preceding label, and then to locate the element by referring to the label. We can set the element pointer at the label using SET ELEMENT POINTER AT LABEL, and then move it on one place to point to the transformation using OFFSET ELEMENT POINTER. Now (using REPLACE mode editing), we can replace the transformation, and because the structure is posted, the picture will be automatically redrawn. The editing sequence is therefore:

```
POST STRUCTURE (workstation, cube, priority)
SET EDIT MODE (REPLACE)

OPEN STRUCTURE (cube)
SET ELEMENT POINTER AT LABEL (transformation)
OFFSET ELEMENT POINTER (1)
repeat
   % Compute a new transformation T to rotate the cube.
   SET LOCAL TRANSFORMATION 3 (T, REPLACE)
until finished

CLOSE STRUCTURE
```

5.7   Copying elements between structures

It is sometimes convenient to copy elements from one structure into another, and there is a function for this purpose:

□   COPY ALL ELEMENTS FROM STRUCTURE
parameters:
      in   structure identifier   integer

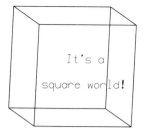

Figure 5.1   An application of COPY ALL ELEMENTS FROM STRUCTURE.

This copies all the elements from the specified structure into the currently open structure, inserting the elements immediately after the element pointer, which is updated to point to the last element inserted. For this function, edit mode is ignored: elements are always *inserted*. If the structure from which the elements are being copied does not exist, or is empty, the function is ignored. If the specified structure happens to be the open structure, its contents are copied into itself.

We can illustrate the use of this function with the following example. Suppose we wish to create the picture in Figure 5.1, where we have two cubes, which are the same except for the text on their front faces. A simple way to do this is to have a separate structure for each cube, and then to execute these structures using modelling transformations to position them correctly. Since we already have the *cube* structure, we shall copy its elements into a new *altered cube* structure, which we shall then edit to change the text, as follows:

```
SET EDIT MODE (REPLACE)

OPEN STRUCTURE (altered cube)            % Create a new structure.
COPY ALL ELEMENTS FROM STRUCTURE (cube)  % Make it a copy of cube.
SET ELEMENT POINTER AT LABEL (text)
OFFSET ELEMENT POINTER (2)               % Move to "square world!".
TEXT 3 ("round world!")                  % Replace the text.
CLOSE STRUCTURE
```

Now, we define another structure for the picture of the two cubes:

```
OPEN STRUCTURE (two cubes)
% Compute transformation T_left to position left-hand cube.
SET LOCAL TRANSFORMATION 3 (T_left, REPLACE)
EXECUTE STRUCTURE (cube)
% Compute transformation T_right to position right-hand cube.
SET LOCAL TRANSFORMATION 3 (T_right, REPLACE)
EXECUTE STRUCTURE (altered cube)
CLOSE STRUCTURE
```

This example demonstrates a shortcoming of PHIGS. The only difference between the *cube* and *altered cube* structures is that they have one different TEXT 3 element.

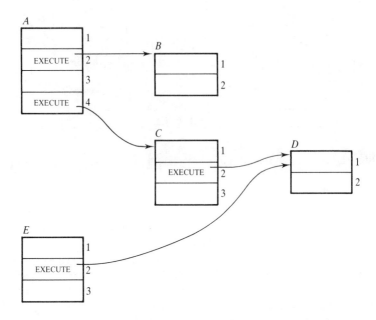

Figure 5.2   Deleting structures and structure networks.

Some systems for hierarchical modelling provide a mechanism for **parametrizing** structures, where additional data may be specified when a structure is executed, causing part of its definition to be modified – in this case, the data in a TEXT 3 element. This is not possible in PHIGS, where we must either make copies of structures and edit them accordingly, or split the structure into other structures which contain the common parts.

5.8   Deleting structures

There are a number of functions for manipulating entire structures and structure networks. We can delete an entire structure using:

☐ DELETE STRUCTURE
   parameters:
        in   structure identifier   integer

As well as completely removing the specified structure and all its contents from the CSS, this function also has a side effect: it removes from all structures in the CSS all EXECUTE STRUCTURE elements which reference the specified structure. For example, referring to Figure 5.2, deleting structure *D* would cause references to it to be removed automatically from structures *C* and *E*.

There is also a function to delete all the structures in the CSS:

☐ DELETE ALL STRUCTURES
parameters: none

5.9 Deleting structure networks

We may also wish to delete an entire structure network, specifying only the root of the network. The function for this is:

☐ DELETE STRUCTURE NETWORK
parameters:
     in   structure identifier   integer
     in   reference handling flag   (DELETE, KEEP)

The action is similar to calling DELETE STRUCTURE for each structure in the specified network, but there is an added complication. Referring to Figure 5.2, suppose that we wish to delete the structure network whose root is A; we would expect each structure in the network to be deleted in turn – A, B, C and D. But, structure D poses a problem: as well as being referenced by C, it is also referenced by E, which is *outside* the structure network whose root is A. Should D be deleted or not? This decision rests with the application, which specifies the required action using the *reference handling flag* parameter If this is DELETE, structures are deleted regardless of whether they are referenced from outside the specified network, and any structures that reference the deleted structure will have the appropriate EXECUTE STRUCTURE elements automatically removed. If, however, the flag is KEEP, a structure will only be deleted if there are no references to it from outside the specified structure network. However, the specified root of the structure network is always deleted, regardless of the setting of the flag.

5.10 Changing structure names

We can change the name of a structure (without affecting its contents) using:

☐ CHANGE STRUCTURE IDENTIFIER
parameters:
     in   old structure identifier   integer
     in   new structure identifier   integer

This changes *old structure identifier* to *new structure identifier*. The detailed operation of this function is actually quite complicated. The basic effect is that after the function is called, the *new* structure will always exist, and – regardless of whether it already existed or not – will be an exact copy of the *old* structure. The *old* structure will no longer exist, unless one or more of the following conditions hold:

- It is already posted to one or more workstations.

- It is the currently open structure.

- There are references to it from other structures.

If any of these conditions are true, the *old* structure will continue to exist, but it will be empty. If the *old* structure is currently open, it will be emptied, and the element pointer set to 0. If the *new* structure is the open structure, it will become an exact copy of the *old* structure, and the element pointer will be set to the last element.

What if the *old* and *new* structure identifiers are the same? There are two cases: if the structure already exists, no action takes place, and no error is reported. If the structure does not exist, it is created (given the name specified by *new*) and it is empty. We did say it was complicated!

5.11   Changing structure references

When editing the CSS, it is often useful to change all references to a particular structure to refer to a different structure, and for this there is the function:

☐ CHANGE STRUCTURE REFERENCES
parameters:
in	old structure identifier	integer
in	new structure identifier	integer

This function operates on all the structures in the CSS. PHIGS searches every structure for EXECUTE STRUCTURE elements which refer to *old* and replaces them with elements which refer to *new*. As with CHANGE STRUCTURE IDENTIFIERS, there are special cases to consider: if there are references to *old* structure, and *new* structure does not exist PHIGS creates an empty structure called *new*. If the *old* structure is posted to one or more workstations, it is unposted, and the *new* structure is posted in its place. There are three circumstances in which the function performs no action:

- if *old* does not exist;

- if there are no references to *old*;

- if *old* and *new* are the same.

For convenience, there is a function which changes both the name of a structure and all references to it:

☐ CHANGE STRUCTURE IDENTIFIER AND REFERENCES
parameters:

in	old structure identifier	integer
in	new structure identifier	integer

The effect is that of first calling CHANGE STRUCTURE IDENTIFIERS and then CHANGE STRUCTURE REFERENCES.

Chapter 6
3D viewing

---

*Viewing is the process of examining a displayed scene. In 3D, this encompasses defining a **viewpoint** and other parameters which describe how a picture is projected – using parallel or perspective projection, for example. In this chapter we examine the comprehensive viewing facilities of PHIGS.*

One of the most powerful features of 3D graphics is the ability to view scenes from different vantage points. An architect might employ this to simulate a 'walkthrough' of a new building design, or a chemist might use it to explore the 3D structures of complex molecules. By selecting a suitable viewpoint we may be able to observe features of a model which are hidden from other positions. PHIGS provides mechanisms for this, and also for **dynamic viewing** – such as displaying a continuously changing view, as if we were flying through the 3D scene.

6.1 The viewing process

There are three stages involved in defining a view of a 3D scene:

- First, we establish the position of the viewer relative to the objects in the scene, and the direction of view. This is known as **view orientation**.

- Next, we specify the type of projection desired. There are two major categories: **parallel projection** and **perspective projection**, although they also have subdivisions, such as one-point or two-point perspective, and orthogonal and oblique projections. This step is called **view mapping**.

- Finally, we define how the projected view of our scene is mapped to a workstation. This is the **workstation transformation**.

Figure 6.1 illustrates these steps. Of course, a typical display contains different kinds of information, which may have different viewing requirements. For example, we would not normally wish to have a 3D perspective view of menus, but equally we may wish to have two alternative views of a single object displayed simultaneously. So, we must be able not only to say what views are required,

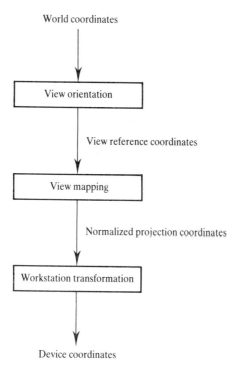

World coordinates

View orientation

View reference coordinates

View mapping

Normalized projection coordinates

Workstation transformation

Device coordinates

Figure 6.1   Stages in defining a 3D view.

but also to specify how these are applied to the different structures which are displayed on a workstation. This is achieved using **view representations**.

The different viewing stages form what is called the **viewing pipeline**. The complete pipeline is quite complicated because there are so many different parameters, and we shall look at each step in turn.

6.2   The view orientation

The first step of the viewing pipeline involves establishing the direction of view relative to the WC system. For example, if we wished to simulate looking at a building from a helicopter we would need some way of defining both the position of the helicopter in space, and the direction we were looking out through its windows. In the real world, the apparent size of the building would depend on how far away from it we were. However, the view orientation step is concerned only with the *direction* of view, so we shall limit ourselves to that for the time being. (The effect of distance on size is a feature of perspective projection, and is controlled by the view mapping stage, described in Section 6.3.)

Defining a view orientation creates a new coordinate system called the **View**

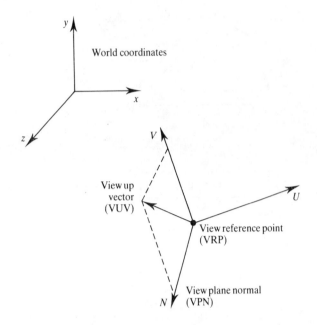

Figure 6.2   The view reference coordinate (VRC) system.

Reference Coordinate system (VRC), with axes labelled U, V and N, as illustrated in Figure 6.2. To define this coordinate system uniquely, we must fix both its position – that is, its origin – and its orientation relative to WC. The origin of the VRC system is called the **View Reference Point (VRP)**, and is given as a point in WC. The orientation of the UV plane is determined uniquely by the direction of the N axis, which we specify by defining a vector parallel to N in WC.

The significance of the UV plane is, as we shall see later, that the view mapping phase defines the **view plane**, which is parallel to the UV plane. In effect, the picture is generated by projecting our 3D scene onto this view plane. In reality, PHIGS does not actually perform a projection, but carries out a series of transformations which produce the same effect, as described in Appendix C. Because the view plane is parallel to UV, the vector which we define parallel to N must also be normal to the view plane, and for this reason it is referred to as the **View Plane Normal (VPN)**.

Returning to our helicopter example, suppose that our WC system was defined such that the ground was the xy plane, and height was represented by z. In order to view the front of the building (the xz plane) we could specify a view plane normal vector of $(0, 1, 0)$. Alternatively, to obtain a view plane which was equally inclined to all three axes we could give a vector of $(1, 1, 1)$.

By defining the view plane normal we have fixed the direction of the N axis, but not the U and V axes. To define our VRC system uniquely, we must supply an

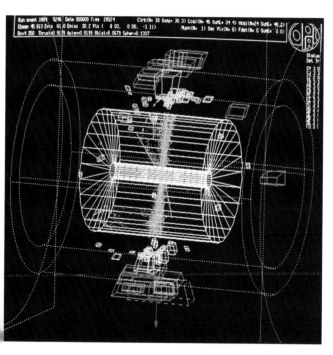

Plate 1 An example of the versatility of polylines, displaying the paths taken by jets of subatomic particles (from the OPAL detector at CERN). (Courtesy of Mike French, Rutherford Appleton Laboratories)

Plate 2 Human figure modelled using fill area with interior style SOLID and diffuse reflections with shading type NONE. (Courtesy of Gareth Williams, Dept. of Computer Science, University of Manchester)

Plate 3 Human figure after changing modelling transformations. (Courtesy of Gareth Williams, Dept. of Computer Science, University of Manchester)

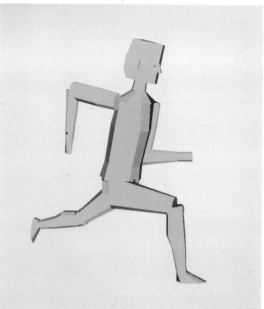

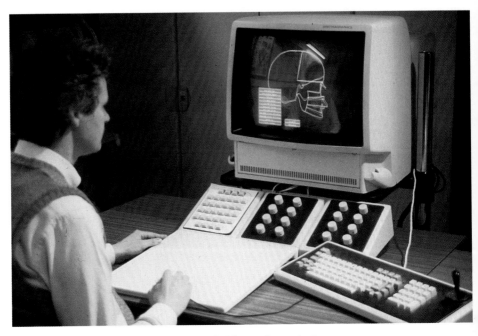

Plate 4 A workstation with a number of different input devices.

Plate 5 An example of a database browsing system implemented using PHIGS, simulating input devices using polylines, fill area and text, and using the pick and locator input devices of PHIGS.

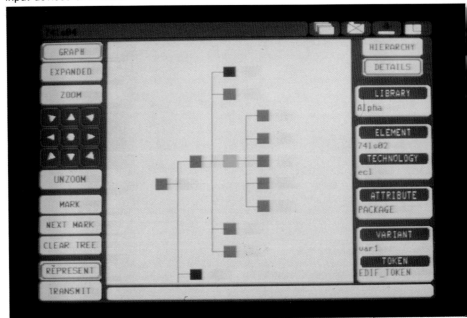

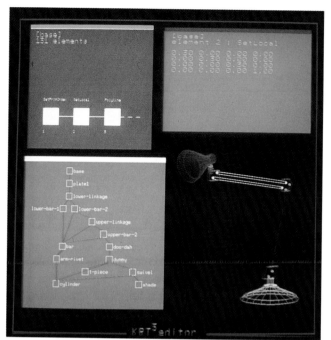

Plate 6 An example of a PHIGS application for interactively designing objects.

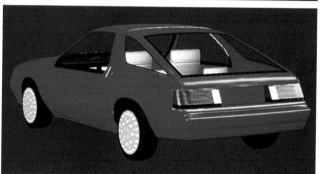

Plate 7 A car modelled using non-uniform rational B-spline surfaces. (Courtesy of Sun Microsystems Inc.)

Plate 8 A McDonnell-Douglas 3D digitizer.

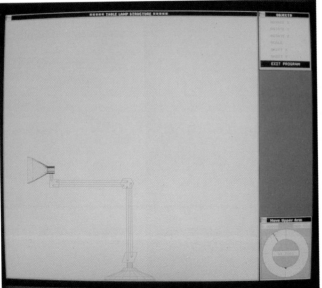

Plate 9 Using a valuator in sample mode to edit a modelling transformation.

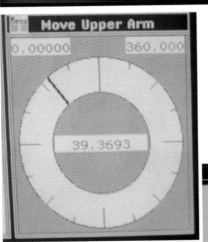

Plate 10 Close-up of the valuator from Plate 9, illustrating a particular prompt and echo type.

Plate 11 The effect on the picture of editing the modelling transformation.

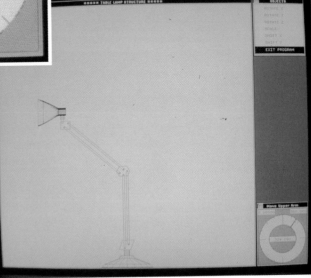

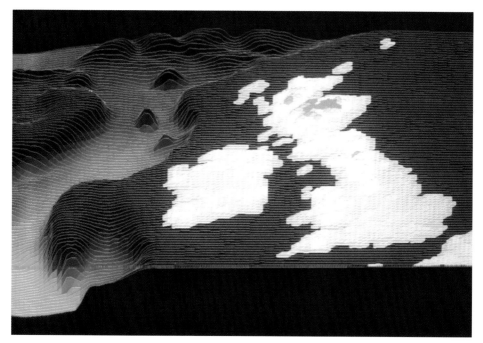

Plate 12 Terrain map displayed using polyline set 3 with data, using colours to show height. (Courtesy of W.T.C. Sowerbutts, Dept. of Geology, University of Manchester)

Plate 13 Quadrilateral mesh with interior style NONE and visible edges.

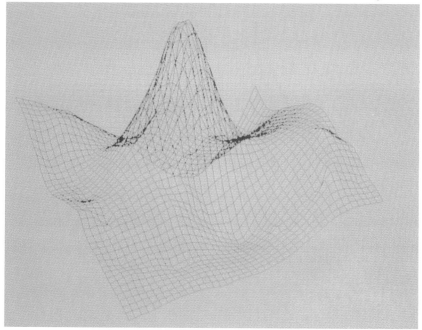

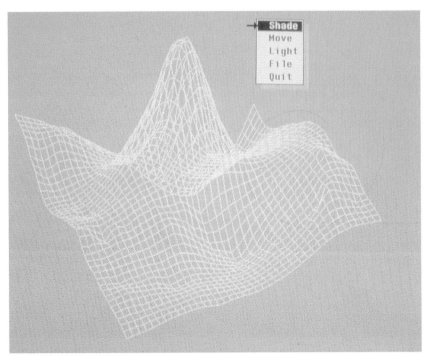

Plate 14 Quadrilateral mesh with interior style NONE and visible edges. A menu (choice input device) is also shown.

Plate 15 Quadrilateral mesh with ambient and diffuse reflections and shading type NONE.

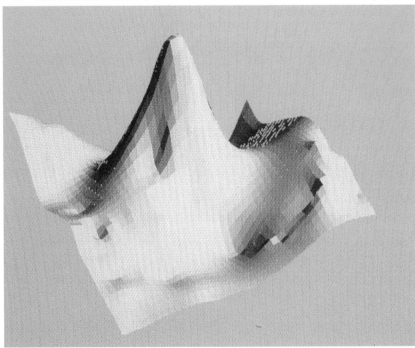

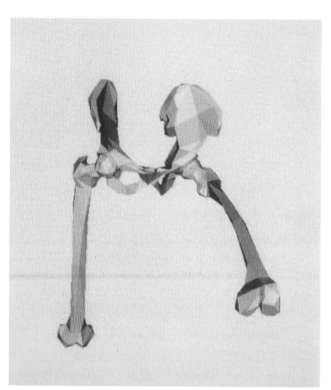

Plate 16 Model of human pelvis and femurs using fill area with interior style SOLID and ambient and diffuse reflections. (Picture courtesy of Gareth Williams, Dept. of Computer Science, University of Manchester; data courtesy of David Delp, Scott Delp and Peter Loan of the V. A. Medical Center, Palo Alto)

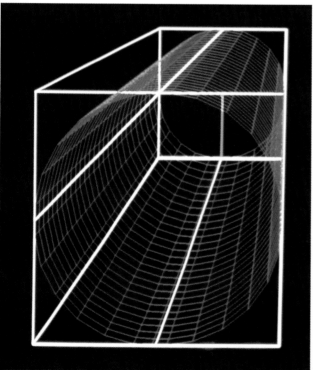

Plate 17 A cylinder modelled using a non-uniform rational B-spline surface.

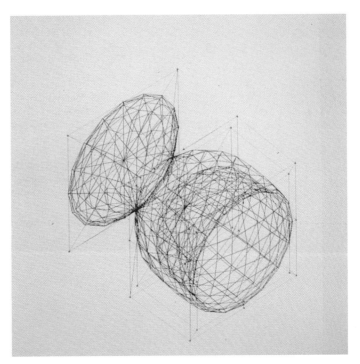

Plate 18 A vase drawn as a non-uniform rational B-spline surface in wireframe. The control points are also shown.

Plate 19 As Plate 18 with shading type NONE and diffuse reflections.

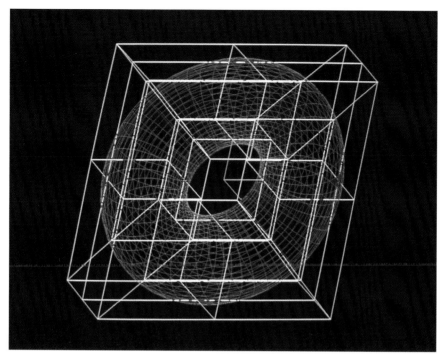

Plate 20 Torus modelled using a non-uniform rational B-spline. The control points are also shown.

Plate 21 As Plate 20 with shading type NONE.

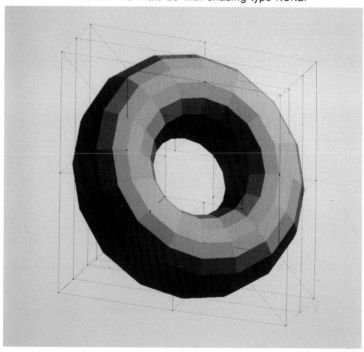

Plate 22 A sphere modelled using a non-uniform rational B-spline surface in wireframe. The control points form a cube.

Plate 23 As Plate 22 with shading type NONE, showing the control points.

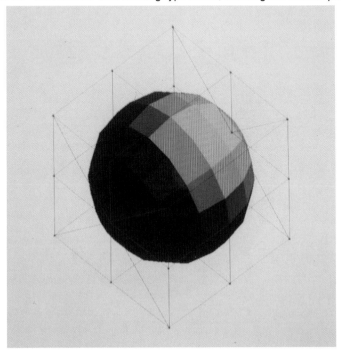

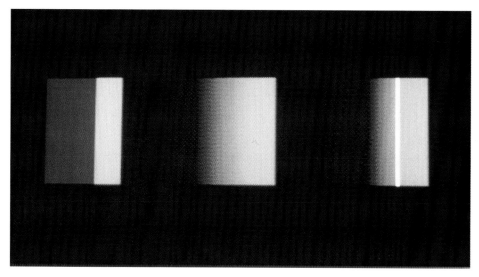

Plate 24   Three cylinders, the left-hand cylinder illustrating shading type NONE, the centre cylinder shading type COLOUR, and the right-hand cylinder shading type NORMAL.

Plate 25   Three spheres, the left-hand sphere with ambient effects only, the centre sphere with ambient and diffuse effects, and the right-hand sphere with ambient, diffuse and specular effects. The same light sources are used in each case.

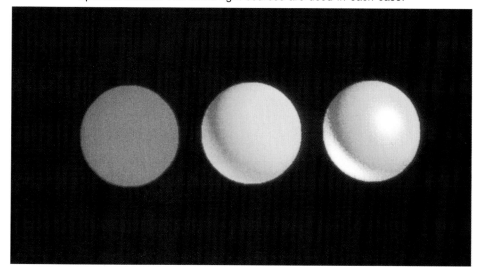

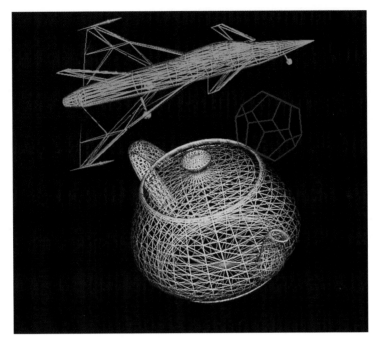

Plate 26 Three objects drawn using polylines. (Courtesy of Digital Equipment Corporation)

Plate 27 As Plate 26, but drawn using a perspective projection. (Courtesy of Digital Equipment Corporation)

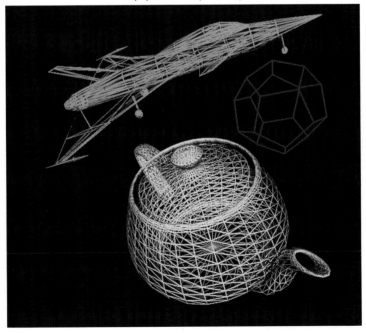

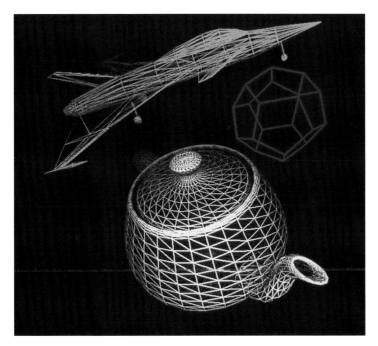

Plate 28 As Plate 27, but including depth cueing. (Courtesy of Digital Equipment Corporation)

Plate 29 As Plate 26, but the objects are drawn using surfaces, with ambient and diffuse lighting, and shading type NONE. (Courtesy of Digital Equipment Corporation)

Plate 30   As Plate 29, but with COLOUR (Gouraud) shading. (Courtesy of Digital Equipment Corporation)

Plate 31   As Plate 30, but with specular lighting added. (Courtesy of Digital Equipment Corporation)

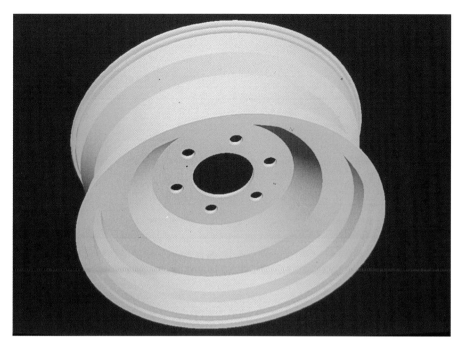

Plate 32 A wheel showing ambient and diffuse reflections. (Courtesy of Sun Microsystems Inc.)

Plate 33 As Plate 32, but with ambient, diffuse and specular reflections. (Courtesy of Sun Microsystems Inc.)

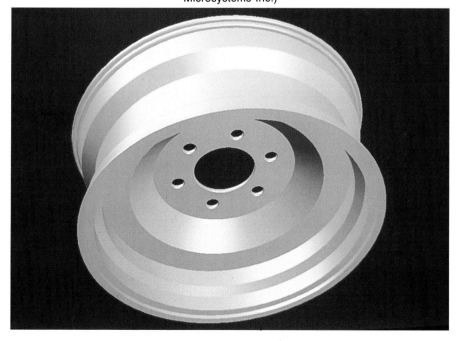

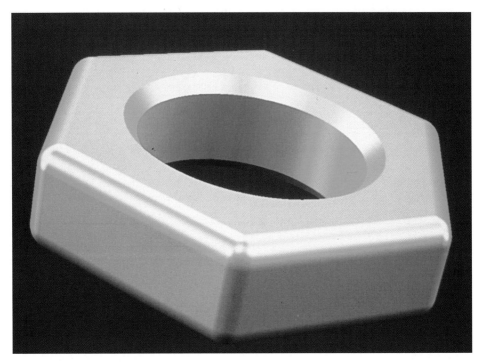

Plate 34 A nut showing shading type NORMAL, with ambient, diffuse and specular reflection. (Courtesy of Sun Microsystems Inc.)

additional piece of information so that the final picture is the right way up. We do this by defining a **View Up Vector (VUV)**. This is another vector, also specified in WC, which defines the 'up' direction of the final projected image. The simplest way to visualize this is to imagine the vector displayed as an arrow. The arrow would appear vertical in the image – that is, parallel to the workstation's y axis, and pointing in its positive direction.

Using the helicopter example again, the VUV can be used to control the yaw angle, assuming we are looking out of the front window. To simulate a view in which the building appears upright, we could give a VUV of $(0, 0, 1)$, since the z axis represents height. If instead we gave an up vector of $(0, 0, -1)$ we would appear to be flying upside down!

The VUV can be any vector which is not parallel to the view plane normal. PHIGS derives the U and V axes from the VUV and the VPN. First, by taking the vector product of VUV and VPN it obtains the U axis (which is at right angles to the other two vectors). Then in a similar manner it derives the V axis from the vector product of the VPN and U. We can see from this why the VPN and the VUV *must not be parallel*, otherwise the final direction of the up vector cannot be correctly calculated.

Internally, PHIGS calculates a transformation matrix from the supplied parameters and uses this to convert from WC into VRC. This matrix is called the **view orientation matrix**. A utility function is provided for calculating the view orientation matrix:

☐ EVALUATE VIEW ORIENTATION MATRIX 3
parameters:

in	view reference point	3D WC point
in	view plane normal	3D WC vector
in	view up vector	3D WC vector
out	error	integer
out	view orientation matrix	4×4 real matrix

The *error* parameter must be tested to ensure that the resulting matrix is valid. A zero-length VPN or VUV will cause an error, as will a VUV which is parallel to the VPN.

6.2.1   A simple example of view orientation

3D viewing is quite a complex phenomenon, and to keep user interfaces simple some easy method must be devised to allow a program's operator to control a viewpoint. One way to do this is to use two angles to control 'latitude' and 'longitude'. Imagine that the scene to be viewed is placed inside a sphere, with the WC origin at its centre. Now think of the sphere as a globe with lines of latitude and longitude upon it. The xy WC plane passes through the equator, and the z axis passes through the North Pole, as shown in Figure 6.3. To establish a viewpoint anywhere above the surface of the globe we need to define a view plane normal which passes through the viewpoint. This is easily calculated from

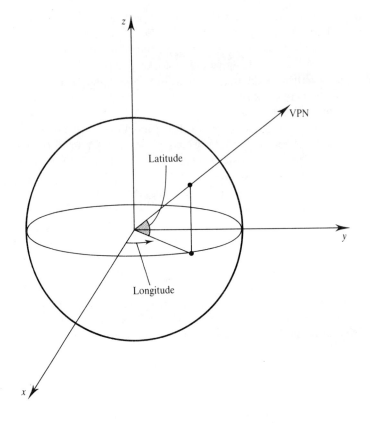

Figure 6.3   Example of view orientation.

the corresponding angles of latitude and longitude:

$vpnx$ = $cosine(latitude)cosine(longitude)$

$vpny$ = $cosine(latitude)sine(longitude)$

$vpnz$ = $sine(latitude)$

Figure 6.4 shows some examples of the use of this technique to simulate flying around a building in a helicopter. The C program which generated these views is given in Appendix A.

There is one precaution we must take here, however. Suppose that we had defined the VUV to be $(0, 0, 1)$, so that the WC z axis, passing through the North Pole, appeared vertical in the final picture. We would have to ensure that we never set the viewpoint exactly over either of the two poles, because the resulting VUV and VPN would then be parallel, making it impossible for PHIGS to establish the correct orientation. In practice, most PHIGS implementations will substitute a default transformation when this situation occurs, causing the picture to 'flip' as the viewpoint passes through the position of the singularity. The helicopter

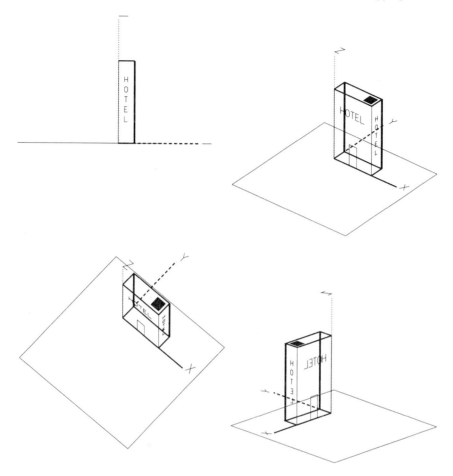

Figure 6.4   Four views from a helicopter.

program in Appendix A does not bother to check for the singularity. The other example program in Appendix B explicitly avoids the problem by preventing views along the z axis.

6.3   The view mapping

We have already mentioned that PHIGS performs transformations which simulate the projection of a 3D scene onto a 2D view plane, which is parallel to the UV plane of the VRC system. Once we have defined the VRC, we can fix the exact position of the view plane by giving its distance along the N axis, known as the **view plane distance**. Its magnitude is expressed in WC, because the VRC system is dimensionally the same as WC.

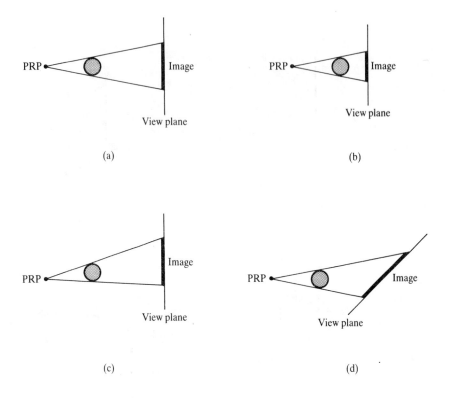

Figure 6.5   Perspective projections of an object onto a view plane.

Figure 6.5 shows a perspective projection of a single 3D object, defined in WC, onto a view plane. We can see that the projected image depends on the relative positions of the **Projection Reference Point (PRP),** the object, and the view plane itself. Moving any of these will cause the projected image to change. In Figure 6.5(a) we see the starting situation. In (b), the view plane has been moved closer to the object, resulting in a smaller image. In (c) the object and view plane are as in (a), but the PRP has been moved, resulting in an oblique projection. Finally, in (d) the PRP and object are fixed, but the view plane has been moved; this yields another oblique projection.

6.3.1   Types of projection

The type of projection – either **parallel** or **perspective** – also affects the way an object is mapped to an image. Plates 26 and 27 respectively show a scene viewed with parallel and perspective projection. In Figure 6.5 we saw some examples of perspective projection, in which the projection lines – known as **projectors** – pass through the projection reference point.

With **parallel projection** the projectors are parallel to each other, as shown

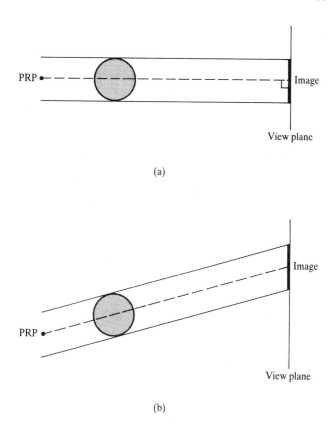

(a)

(b)

Figure 6.6 Parallel projections of an object onto a view plane.

in Figures 6.6(a) and (b). In (a), the projectors are perpendicular to the view plane, yielding an **orthogonal projection**, while in (b) they are not, and the result is an **oblique projection**. By varying these parameters – the PRP, the type of projection, and the view plane distance – we can see that a variety of different pictures can be obtained. These are all different aspects of the view mapping stage of the output pipeline.

Another consideration is how to determine which part of our scene is actually visible. For example, thinking again of our helicopter, our view may be restricted by the sizes of its windows. The first step in this is to define a **view window**, which is a rectangle on the view plane, with sides parallel to the *UV* axes, and defined by its maximum and minimum coordinates in *U* and *V*. This is illustrated in Figure 6.7 for parallel projections, and in Figure 6.8 for perspective projections. In the case of parallel projection, the view window and projectors define a volume of space which is a parallelepiped. The edges of this are parallel to the line formed by joining the PRP to the centre of the view window. We can see from this that it is the relative positions of the PRP and the view window which determine whether

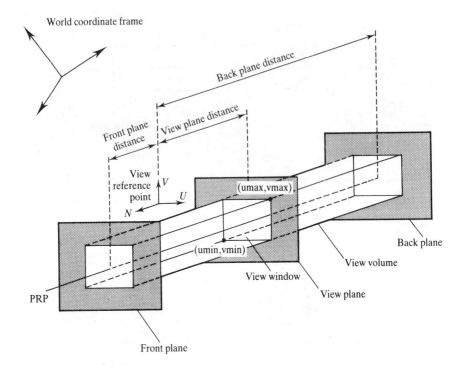

Figure 6.7   Parameters for a parallel view.

the projection is orthogonal or oblique.

For a perspective projection, the projectors passing through the PRP and the corners of the view window define a pyramid. Again, oblique projection effects can be produced by varying the position of the PRP relative to the centre of the view window (or vice versa). In most cases, a simple one-point perspective along the N axis will be required, in which case the line joining the PRP to the centre of the view window should be at right angles to the view plane.

To form a bounded space, we also define a **front plane** and a **back plane** which are parallel to the view plane. Together with the parallelepiped (or pyramid) these form an enclosed space known as the **view volume**. Any parts of the 3D scene which lie within this view volume will be mapped into the final picture (provided that this lies within the workstation viewport). The front and back plane positions are given as the **front plane distance** and **back plane distance**, measured along the N axis in VRC.

There is a utility function for computing a matrix which describes the geometric effects of the view mapping. This is known as the **view mapping matrix**, and the function is:

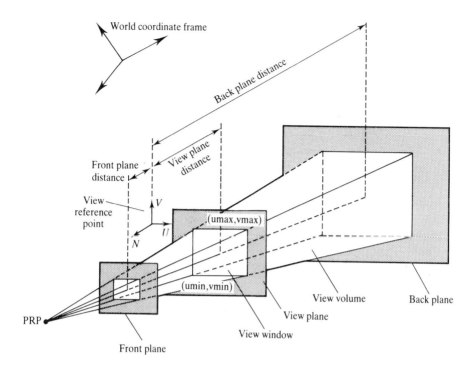

Figure 6.8   Parameters for a perspective view.

☐ EVALUATE VIEW MAPPING MATRIX 3
parameters:

in	window limits	(umin, umax, vmin, vmax (VRC))
in	projection viewport limits	(xmin, xmax, ymin, ymax, zmin, zmax (NPC))
in	projection type	(PARALLEL, PERSPECTIVE)
in	projection reference point	3D VRC point
in	view plane distance	real (VRC)
in	back plane distance	real (VRC)
in	front plane distance	real (VRC)
out	error indicator	integer
out	view mapping matrix	4 × 4 real matrix

This function computes a matrix which can be passed to PHIGS using the function SET VIEW REPRESENTATION 3, described in Section 6.4. The matrix is used to convert from VRC into another coordinate system called **Normalized Projection Coordinates (NPC),** in which the x, y, z axes are parallel to the axes of the workstation's device coordinate system. NPC space is a bounded cube with

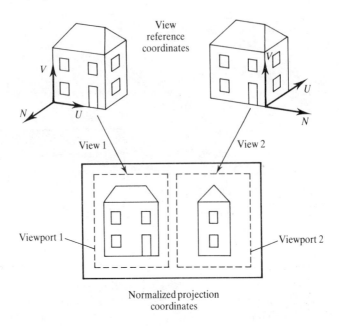

Figure 6.9   Composing views in NPC.

coordinates in each dimension restricted to the range 0 to 1 – hence the term 'normalized'.

6.3.2   Composing pictures in NPC

Normalized projection coordinates are used for composing pictures in 3D space. It is at this point that different views are merged into a single coordinate space. For example, we may have two different views of a 3D scene which we wish to display simultaneously along side each other. Each view would have its own VRC, corresponding to the direction of view.

In order to map VRC into NPC, and to ensure that the different views are correctly assembled, we define a **projection viewport**, in NPC, into which the view volume is mapped. This viewport is given as the parameter *projection viewport limits* to the function EVALUATE VIEW MAPPING MATRIX 3. Figure 6.9 shows how two different views of a house can be obtained and composed in NPC by specifying different projection viewports.

6.4   The view index and view representation

The mechanism used for viewing allows us to refer to a collection of viewing parameters using a single **view index**. The function to set a view index is:

|E| SET VIEW INDEX
parameters:
      in   view index   integer

The view index is used to access a table of view representations stored in each workstation's **view table**. The view information stored in this table is established with the function SET VIEW REPRESENTATION 3, in much the same way that primitive attributes can be grouped into bundles, as described in Section 9.9. Figure 6.10 illustrates how we could use two different view indices to draw two different views of a structure. This example also illustrates that a view index is bound to one or more primitives, rather than to complete structures.

The function for setting an entry in the view table is:

☐ SET VIEW REPRESENTATION 3
parameters:

in	workstation identifier	integer
in	view index	integer
in	view orientation matrix	4×4 real matrix
in	view mapping matrix	4×4 real matrix
in	view clipping limits	(xmin, xmax, ymin, ymax, zmin, zmax (NPC))
in	*xy* clipping indicator	(CLIP, NOCLIP)
in	back clipping indicator	(CLIP, NOCLIP)
in	front clipping indicator	(CLIP, NOCLIP)

The *view orientation matrix* determines the viewing direction, and was described in Section 6.2. The *view mapping matrix* is used to determine the kind of projection required, and was dealt with in Section 6.3. The *view clipping limits* define *x*, *y* and *z* limits to which the picture can optionally be clipped. Usually, these are chosen to match the limits of the view volume.

Because the *workstation identifier* is given as a parameter, we can see that this function not only permits different views to be defined, but also allows the same view index to have different representations on different workstations. Suppose we are developing a flight simulator, where we are dealing with three screens in front of, and to the right and left of a pilot, in order to simulate the views from different windows of a flight deck. We could use a different workstation for each of the three views. Our program to manage this might then look something like this:

```
OPEN WORKSTATION (left, ...)
OPEN WORKSTATION (right, ...)
OPEN WORKSTATION (centre, ...)

OPEN STRUCTURE (scene)

SET VIEW INDEX (1) % Whole scene display as view 1.
% Code to draw trees, runway, mountains.
```

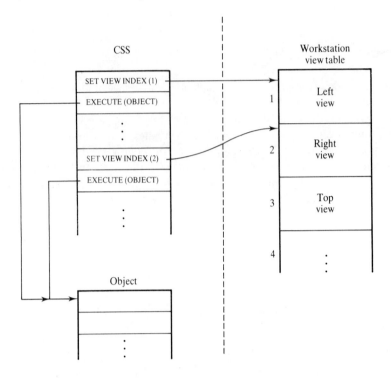

Figure 6.10   View index and view representation.

```
CLOSE STRUCTURE

POST STRUCTURE (left, scene, priority)
POST STRUCTURE (right, scene, priority)
POST STRUCTURE (centre, scene, priority)
```

repeat
    % Update plane's position using input devices.
    % Calculate view parameters for leftview, centreview and rightview.
    SET VIEW REPRESENTATION 3 (left, 1, leftview, ...)
    SET VIEW REPRESENTATION 3 (right, 1, rightview, ...)
    SET VIEW REPRESENTATION 3 (centre, 1, centreview, ...)
until plane crashes.

View index is an integer which must be greater than zero, and less than some
maximum. This maximum may be different on each workstation, and you can
find out the maximum valid value for any particular workstation. using INQUIRE
WORKSTATION STATE TABLE LENGTHS. If you use an invalid number for the index,
view zero will be used by default. View zero is a special case, and its representation cannot be altered by an application program. It maps a unit cube in WC to
the NPC unit cube.

6.5   The workstation transformation

After applying the view orientation and view mapping transformations to WC, the picture is described in NPC. The last step in placing the assembled picture on the workstation's display surface is to define how NPC are mapped to DC. We do this by defining a **workstation window** in NPC and a corresponding **workstation viewport** in DC. The mapping is actually just a scaling, but the same scale factor is applied to each axis to preserve aspect ratios. The scale factor is chosen so that the whole of the workstation window is visible within the defined viewport, with the minimum x, y, z corner of the window mapped to the corresponding minimum corner of the viewport.

The function for defining the workstation window in NPC is:

☐   SET WORKSTATION WINDOW 3
    parameters:
        in   workstation identifier   integer
        in   workstation window limits   (xmin, xmax, ymin, ymax,
                                              zmin, zmax (NPC))

A similar function is provided for defining the workstation viewport in DC:

☐   SET WORKSTATION VIEWPORT 3
    parameters:
        in   workstation identifier   integer
        in   workstation viewport limits   (xmin, xmax, ymin, ymax,
                                              zmin, zmax (DC))

6.6   Summary of the viewing pipeline

Figure 6.11 summarizes the viewing pipeline and the coordinate system used at each stage. There are four transformations:

- the composite modelling transformation

- the view orientation

- the view mapping

- the workstation transformation

If we denote the current modelling transformation as *CMT*, the view orientation matrix as V_o, the view mapping matrix as V_m, and the workstation transformation as W, then the transformation T which must be applied to modelling coordinates to map them to device coordinates is:

$$T = W \cdot V_m \cdot V_o \cdot CMT$$

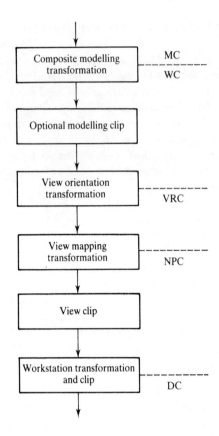

Figure 6.11   The complete viewing pipeline.

Recalling that the *CMT* comprises the local and global modelling transformations *L* and *G*, we obtain the complete sequence of transformations:

$$T = W \cdot V_m \cdot V_o \cdot G \cdot L$$

Note however, that a number of clipping steps are interspersed, so that the actual implementation of the pipeline is rather more complicated than this.

Chapter 7
Graphical input

PHIGS input facilities have to cater for a wide variety of input devices and methods of using them. In this chapter we examine how devices are grouped into **classes**, *and describe ways of using them:* **request**, **sample** *and* **event** *modes.*

Modern graphical user interfaces support a wide variety of interactive techniques. Typical graphical operations include entering points, or sequences of points, in 3D space, pointing at something on a display and having the system recognize the name of the object, accepting input from keyboards and programmable function keys, or manipulating scroll bars which are linked to application-dependent variables. Up-market displays may be equipped with many different kinds of interaction device, such as boxes of buttons, dials for controlling scales and rotation angles (as seen in Plate 4), and even 3D input devices, whereas lower cost workstations are often only supplied with a three-button mouse and a keyboard.

The sheer diversity of input devices creates a problem for PHIGS, which must attempt to define a consistent and device-independent way to control them and receive input. It deals with this by defining a number of abstract devices which cater for the kinds of graphical interaction listed above. A specific PHIGS implementation maps these abstract devices onto the physical devices actually provided by a workstation.

PHIGS devices are divided into six **logical device classes**, each of which can operate in three different **input modes** to cater for different styles of user interface. These input modes are **request**, **sample** and **event**.

7.1 Logical input devices

The six abstract classes of device are: **valuator, choice, locator, stroke, string** and **pick**.

- **Valuator** This is a logical device for controlling a real value. Examples include physical dials and potentiometers, and software sliders and scroll bars. The range values returned by the device can be specified by the ap-

93

plication. For example, if a valuator is to be used to control a rotation, it can be initialized to return values in the range 0 to 2π.

- **Choice** This provides a single selection from a number of alternatives. Examples include physical button boxes, buttons displayed on a screen, and menus. Each possible choice is assigned a positive integer identifier, which is returned to an application when the device is used.

- **Locator** A locator provides a 3D (x, y, z) position in WC and a view index. Actually, PHIGS provides both 2D and 3D locator functions. In practice, these are identical, except that the 2D function returns only the (x, y) values, with the z value being discarded. Physical locator devices include digitizers and mice, which are usually two-dimensional. True 3D locators do exist – such as the McDonnell-Douglas 3D digitizer, shown in Plate 8, and the VPL data glove – but these are fairly rare, so they are often simulated in some way using 2D devices.

- **Stroke** A stroke device is similar to a locator, but generates a sequence of points, in WC, together with a view index. Typical examples are a hand-held stylus with a pressure-sensitive tip switch, used for sketching, and a mouse which is dragged with one of its buttons held down. Such devices can be used for sketching shapes such as curves, and for recognition of hand-drawn characters.

- **String** This is for entering character strings. It is almost always mapped to a physical keyboard, with a defined key – normally the RETURN key – used as the string terminator. As a rule, an associated text area is displayed on the workstation in which typed characters are echoed.

- **Pick** Picking is a technique for identifying a part of a displayed picture by pointing at it. On most workstations, this pointing is performed with a mouse-controlled cursor which the operator positions over, or near, the item to be chosen. This is a powerful feature, and makes the programming of some kinds of interaction very straightforward. For example, it offers a simple method for implementing a menu system, and a neat way of identifying parts of the picture which are to be edited or modified interactively. The pick device returns the name of the structure selected, the **pick identifier** and element position for the selected primitive, and the position of the instance in the hierarchy.

7.2   Measures, triggers, PETs and device numbers

Each device has a current value, which is known as its **measure**. When a device is manipulated by the operator, the measure is updated to reflect the new value. For example, if the operator manipulates a locator, its measure is updated to contain the current (x, y, z) coordinates and view index.

There is also a **trigger** for each device which is used to send the current measure to an application program. For example, when typing a character string on a keyboard the trigger is usually the RETURN key, which causes the typed string to be sent to the application program. However, the precise way in which the measure and trigger are interpreted depends on the input mode, which we will describe later.

So that the operator of a program is aware that a particular device is active, PHIGS arranges for a **prompt** to be displayed. When the prompt appears, the operator knows that the corresponding device is ready to be used.

Feedback, to inform the operator that the system has accepted the input, is provided by **echoing**. Different kinds of input can be echoed in a variety of ways. These can be selected by an application program using predefined **prompt and echo types (PETs)** associated with each device. For example, when entering coordinates with a locator, several different styles of cursor may be available: a filled arrow, cross hairs, a cross, a rubber rectangle, and so on.

The position on a workstation's display where input values are echoed (or where a simulated device is displayed) – known as its **echo volume** – can also be controlled. It is called an echo volume because it applies to 3D. In the case of 2D devices, it becomes an **echo area**. An echo volume is defined by giving its minimum and maximum coordinates for each of x, y and z. These are given in DC to permit full control of the position of the echo volume on a workstation's display surface.

Both the PET and echo volume are specified by calling an initialization function for each device class. Both 2D and 3D versions of the initialization functions are provided so that echo areas/volumes can be specified. Table 7.1 shows examples of typical PETs for each class of device. In addition to these, an implementation may provide several local (implementation-dependent) methods, which will be described in your *Local Guide*.

PHIGS permits more than one physical, or simulated, device in each of the six classes. For example, there may be several physical dials, several software-defined sliders, or several menus, as shown in Plates 4 and 5. These are distinguished by using different **device numbers**. An implementation must support at least one device of each class, although these do not have to be on the same workstation.

7.3   Initializing input devices

It is not essential to initialize devices before use, as there are default values for most of the parameters which will suffice for simple applications. However, initialization functions are provided for each device class in case the default values are not suitable. It is important to note that a device may only be initialized when it is in request mode.

Each type of logical input device has a corresponding initialization function: INITIALIZE XXX, where XXX is one of VALUATOR, CHOICE, LOCATOR 3, STROKE 3,

Table 7.1   Example prompt and echo types.

Valuator	A dial, or thermometer
	A displayed digital value
Choice	Physical lamps associated with buttons
	A menu of alternative strings
	A typed string, selected from a set of valid strings
	Display of an application-defined structure
Locator	A cross-hair cursor
	A small tracking cross
	A rubber-band line
	A rubber rectangle
	A digital display of the coordinates
Stroke	Markers for each point
	A polyline connecting the points
	A digital display of the point coordinates
String	Echo typed characters on the display
Pick	Highlight the selected primitive
	Highlight all primitives with the same pick identifier
	Highlight the structure containing the primitive

STRING or PICK. These functions accept a a 3D echo volume or a 2D echo area. For example, the function to initialize a 3D locator is:

☐   INITIALIZE LOCATOR 3
parameters:

in	workstation identifier	integer
in	locator device number	integer
in	initial view index	integer
in	initial locator position	3D WC point
in	prompt and echo type	integer
in	echo volume	(xmin, xmax, ymin,
		ymax, zmin, zmax (DC))
in	locator data record	record

The parameters of the initialization functions vary slightly, but in general they include the following. The *workstation identifier*, the *device number* of the device to be initialized, and an *initial value* for the device, whose type depends on the particular device being initialized. Supplying an initial value is especially important for sample mode; without it a device may return an undefined or unsuitable value. This may happen because in sample mode it is not necessary for the operator to take any specific action, such as operating a device's trigger, before the measure is returned to the application program.

The other parameters are the *prompt and echo type*, an *echo area/volume*, in which input from the device will be echoed, other device specific parameters, and a *data record* containing any additional, implementation-dependent data required by the device. Examples of the latter are the thickness of lines in a crosshair echo, and the shape and colour of an arrow cursor.

7.4   Input modes

Each input device can be used in one of three input modes, called request, sample and event.

Functions are provided for each class of device in order to set the current input mode: SET CHOICE MODE, SET LOCATOR MODE, SET STROKE MODE, SET STRING MODE, SET VALUATOR MODE and SET PICK MODE. These functions have identical parameters, with the general form:

☐   SET XXX MODE
parameters:

in	workstation identifier	integer
in	device number	integer
in	operating mode	(REQUEST, SAMPLE, EVENT)
in	echo switch	(ECHO, NOECHO)

where XXX is the name of the device class (VALUATOR, CHOICE, LOCATOR, STROKE, STRING, PICK). The *workstation identifier* specifies the workstation whose device is to be set, while the *device number* identifies which device on that workstation is affected. The *operating mode* can take the values REQUEST, SAMPLE or EVENT.

The *echo switch* determines whether the input is to be echoed, according to the current prompt and echo type, and can take the values ECHO or NOECHO. Usually, device echoing will be enabled, but there may be specific cases where it is preferable to turn it off, such as reading a password without echoing characters.

Note that each different device can be switched between modes independently – devices do not all have to be in the same mode. An application program may find out the current operating mode by calling an inquiry function of the form INQUIRE XXX DEVICE STATE, as described in Section 7.14.

7.5   Request mode

With request mode a program calls a function to request input from a particular device. For example, to use a valuator, you would call REQUEST VALUATOR. This

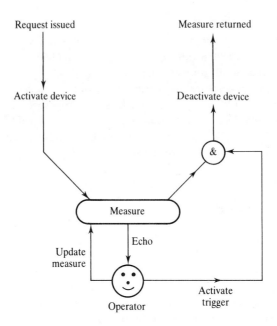

Figure 7.1   Request mode.

causes a prompt to be displayed, to signify to the operator that input is required. Execution of the application program is then suspended until the input request is satisfied. The operator completes the request by entering the required value(s) and operating the device's trigger, as illustrated in Figure 7.1. This behaviour is sometimes referred to as blocking input – further execution or action is blocked until the input request is completed. The blocking behaviour of request mode can be very inconvenient if errors are made, because it is possible for a program to become stuck waiting for input which the operator did not intend to enter. For example, suppose that the operator wrongly selects an option to read a new data file, and the program responds by requesting a string, which will be the name of the file. If REQUEST STRING is called to read the file name, the program's execution will be suspended until the operator enters some input. But the operator does not want to enter a file name, because the previous choice was a mistake! To cater for this, PHIGS provides a **break** facility so that the operator can abort an input request. Each request mode function has a status parameter which should be checked by a program to catch such breaks.

Functions are provided for each type of device to read input in request mode. These have the general form REQUEST XXX, where XXX is one of VALUATOR, CHOICE, LOCATOR 3, STROKE 3, STRING or PICK. The functions have similar parameters: a *workstation identifier*, the *device number* for the device to be used, a *status*, returned by the device to indicate whether the request was satisfied correctly, and a *data record* containing the input value(s) returned by the device.

The data returned depends on the kind of device. *Status* can take the values OK or NONE, where the former indicates that the operator completed the request satisfactorily, and the latter that a *break* of some kind was made and the data returned is invalid. Choice and pick devices may also return the values NOCHOICE and NOPICK respectively to signify that no choice or pick was made by the operator.

As an example, the function to request input from a valuator is:

☐ REQUEST VALUATOR
parameters:

in	workstation identifier	integer
in	valuator device number	integer
out	status	(OK, NONE)
out	value	real

Here is an example which shows how the cube program of Chapter 2 can be amended to use a valuator to control the scale factor for the cube.

```
OPEN PHIGS (error, memory)
OPEN WORKSTATION (workstation identifier, connection, type)

MakeCube                    % Invoke function to create the cube structure.

POST STRUCTURE (cube)       % Display it.

REQUEST VALUATOR (workstation identifier, valuator device, status, value)

if status = OK then         % Check for break.
begin
   OPEN STRUCTURE (cube)    % Now open the cube for editing.

   SET EDIT MODE (REPLACE)  % and set REPLACE mode.

   SET ELEMENT POINTER (1)  % Set the element pointer to
                            % the local modelling transformation.
% Compute transformation to scale by value.
   SET LOCAL TRANSFORMATION 3 (transformation, REPLACE)

   CLOSE STRUCTURE          % Close the structure.
end

CLOSE WORKSTATION (workstation identifier)
CLOSE PHIGS                 % Close PHIGS.
```

The function REQUEST VALUATOR waits for the operator to enter a value and then returns this in the parameter *value*. In this example, we have not initialized the valuator, so the value returned will be the in default range determined by the implementation, which is usually 0 to 1. Provided that the operator completed the request successfully (*status* = OK), the value is used to compute a modelling transformation, which then replaces the one contained in the cube structure.

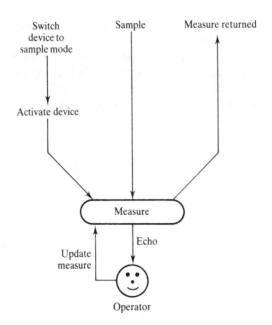

Figure 7.2   Sample mode.

7.6   Sample mode

In sample mode, the measure of an input device can be read immediately by an application program without any need for the operator to activate its trigger. This behaviour, illustrated in Figure 7.2, is sometimes known as polling. It has the advantage that a device's measure can be queried at any time, without any special action by the operator, and a program is guaranteed not to become stuck waiting for such an action. Once a device has been switched to sample mode, as described in Section 7.4, its current measure can be read by calling a function of the form SAMPLE XXX, where, as before, XXX is one of VALUATOR, CHOICE, LOCATOR 3, STROKE 3, STRING or PICK. If the operator has not used the device prior to it being sampled, then it will return an initial value, which may be either a default value or the initial value specified when the device was initialized.

Here is the previous cube example amended to use a valuator in sample mode. The program loops 20 times and resets the scale each time.

```
OPEN PHIGS (error, memory)
OPEN WORKSTATION (workstation identifier, connection, type)

MakeCube                    % Invoke function to create the cube structure.
POST STRUCTURE (cube)

% Switch valuator to sample mode.
SET VALUATOR MODE (workstation identifier, valuator device, SAMPLE, ECHO)
```

```
OPEN STRUCTURE (cube)            % Now open the cube for editing.
SET EDIT MODE (REPLACE)          % and set REPLACE mode.
SET ELEMENT POINTER (1)          % Set the element pointer to
                                 % the local modelling transformation.
for loop := 1 to 20
begin
    SAMPLE VALUATOR (workstation identifier, valuator device, value)
    % Compute transformation to scale by value.
    SET LOCAL TRANSFORMATION 3 (transformation, REPLACE)
end

CLOSE STRUCTURE                  % Close the structure.

CLOSE WORKSTATION (workstation identifier)

CLOSE PHIGS                      % Close PHIGS.
```

Plate 9 shows a desk lamp controlled by a valuator seen in the bottom right-hand corner of the picture. In Plate 10 we see that the valuator is used to control the rotation angle, and here the echo displays the angle in digital and analogue forms. The low and high values of the valuator's range can also be seen. Changing the angle gives the result seen in Plate 11.

7.7 Event mode

This is the most flexible mode of operation, because it allows several devices to be active simultaneously. An operator may use any of the active devices at any time. Operating the trigger of the device causes an **event report**, containing the device's class, number and current measure, to be placed in a time-ordered **event queue**. Functions are provided for examining the event queue and for reading event reports from it. With this approach, operator actions are stored until consumed by the application, and no data will be lost, unless the queue becomes full. The operator's actions and the application program's execution are independent, and can proceed simultaneously – that is, asynchronously. Further discussion of event mode is deferred until Section 7.13.

7.8 Valuator devices

A valuator returns a single real value within a defined range. This range can be specified by giving the low and high values when the device is initialized. In the following example we show the complete cube program, in C, in which a valuator is initialized, switched to sample mode and then used to control the scale of the cube. Note that the data record used for initialization is implementation-dependent; the program shown here uses SunPHIGS.

```c
#include <phigs.h>
#include "makecube.c"
#define CUBE 1                               /* structure id */

main()
{
    Pint        wsid;               /* workstation identifier */
    Pint        valdev = 1;         /* valuator device number */
    Pint        PET = 1;            /* Prompt and echo type */
    Plimit3     echo = {0.0,1152.0,0.0,900.0,0.0,1.0};
                                            /* echo volume */
    Pvalrec     valrecord;                  /* data record */
    Pmatrix3    transform;          /* transformation matrix */
    Pfloat      value;          /* value returned by valuator */
    Ppoint3     origin = {0.5,0.5,0.5};    /* use to compute */
    Pvector3    shift = {0.0, 0.0, 0.0};   /* transformation */
    Pvector3    scale = {1, 1, 1};        /* scale values */
    Pfloat      angle = 30.0             /* rotation angle */
    Pint        err;                    /* error indicator */
    Pfloat      initval = 0.5;          /* initial value */
    int         loop;                   /* loop counter */

    popenphigs(0, 0);
    popenws(wsid, 0, 0);

    MakeCube();                      /* Create the CUBE structure */

    ppoststruct(CUBE);                      /* Display it */
    valrecord.valpet1_datarec.low = 0.0;        /* low value */
    valrecord.valpet1_datarec.high = 0.5;       /* high value */
    pinitval3(wsid, valdev, initval, PET, &echo, &valrecord);
                                /* Initialize the valuator */

    psetvalmode(wsid, valdev, PSAMPLE, PES_ECHO);
                        /* Switch valuator to sample mode */

    popenstruct(CUBE);              /* Open CUBE for editing */
    psetelemptr(1);                         /* at element 1 */
    pseteditmode(PEDIT_REPLACE);      /* using replace mode */
        for (loop=0; loop<100; loop++){ /* Loop 100 times ... */
            psampleval(wsid, valdev, &value);    /* get value */
            scale.x = value; scale.y = value; scale.z = value;
            pbuildtran3(&origin, &shift, angle,angle,angle,
                        &scale, &err, transform);
            psetlocaltran3(transform, PREPLACE);
}

    pclosews(wsid);
    pclosephigs();
}
```

7.9 Choice devices

A choice device returns an integer value. This value represents a single selection from a set of alternatives. For example, with a box of sixteen buttons the value returned might be a number between 1 and 16, depending on which button had been pressed. Another example would be a menu, in which each item in the menu corresponds to a different choice value. Usually, the details of the menu contents would be specified via the initialization data record. For example, if the menu items contained character strings, then the individual strings would be passed via the data record. The following fragment of C shows how this can be achieved with SunPHIGS.

```
Pint WS  = 1;                            /* workstation identifier */
Pint dev = 1;                            /* device number for the menu */
Pchoicerec choicedata;          /* data record for initialization */
Plimit3 echo_vol - {0, 1, 0, 1, 0, 1};            /* echo volume */
Pint pet  = 3;             /* PET 3 is a user-defined pop-up menu */
Pint init = 1;                            /* initial choice value */
Pchoicestatus status = PCH_NOCHOICE;/* initial value for status */

Pchar shade[] = "Shade";            /* define menu item strings */
Pchar move[] =  "Move";
Pchar light[] = "Light";
Pchar file[] =  "File";
Pchar quit[] =  "Quit";

/* define an array of menu items */
Pchar *menu[] = {shade, move, light, file, quit};

/* initialize the data record to contain the relevant data
   for PET 3: number of strings and array of strings */
Pchoicepet0003 cdata = {5, menu};
. . . . .
. . . . .
/* set up the data record */
choicedata.choicepet3_datarec = cdata;

/* and initialize the device */
pinitchoice3(WS, dev, status, init, pet, &echo_vol, &choicedata);
```

7.10 Locator and stroke devices

A locator returns the WC of a point to an application. In order to do this, PHIGS must convert the locator's DC into WC. During output, WC are subjected to a viewing transformation, specified via a view index, which converts WC to NPC, followed by a workstation transformation, which converts NPC to DC. Converting DC back into WC requires the application of the inverse of the workstation and viewing transformations. This is performed internally, saving a substantial amount of work for the application program.

The mapping from DC to WC can only be performed correctly if the coordinate transformations used in the output pipeline have an inverse. This will usually be the case, but cannot be guaranteed because an application program can pass any arbitrary 4×4 viewing transformation matrix to PHIGS. If the utility functions EVALUATE VIEW ORIENTATION MATRIX 3 and EVALUATE VIEW MAPPING MATRIX 3 are used, then invertible view orientation and mapping matrices are guaranteed (unless an error is returned).

7.10.1   Input priority

Because a picture may be constructed with several different viewing transformations, the implementation must determine the correct one to use for this inverse mapping. Each defined view has an associated **view transformation input priority**, and also a set of clipping limits. These are checked to find the highest priority view within whose bounds the locator is positioned. The corresponding view transformation is used for the conversion into WC and its view index is returned to the application.

View transformation input priorities can be set for each view with:

☐   SET VIEW TRANSFORMATION INPUT PRIORITY
parameters:

in	workstation identifier	integer
in	view index	integer
in	reference view index	integer
in	priority	(HIGHER, LOWER)

The priority associated with the specified *view index* is set to be higher or lower than that of the *reference view index*. View 0 is a special case which encompasses the whole of the NPC space, and which cannot be changed by an application program. It is the default view, and input which is not within the clipping bounds of any other view is guaranteed to be in view 0. To obtain input from a particular application-defined view, its input priority must be set higher than the priority of view 0. Forgetting to set the input priority is a common problem which you should guard against. If you do forget, you may wonder why the coordinates are not in the range you expected!

The processing of stroke input is handled in a similar way to a locator. However, a stroke may contain many points and these may lie inside the clipping bounds of different views. The view which PHIGS uses for conversion from DC to WC is the highest priority view which contains the whole of the stroke.

Figure 7.3 illustrates two overlapping views. View 2 has a higher priority than view 1, which in turn is higher than view 0 (the default view). A locator input made at point A would return view index 2. However, a stroke, such as that labelled B, would return a view index value of 0 because part of the stroke lies outside both view 1 and view 2. Note that this is a 2D example; in 3D a similar

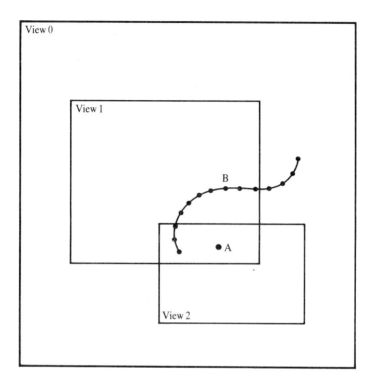

Figure 7.3   View transformation input priority.

check is made, but the 3D limits of the view volumes are used for checking each point. Testing the view index provides a simple method for distinguishing locator or stroke inputs made in different areas of a display, such as menus and drawing areas, provided that a suitable view transformation has been set up for each one. Note that it is not possible to perform any input *outside* the NPC unit cube.

7.10.2   An example – sampling a locator

This example program waits for locator input using request mode, and then switches the locator to sample mode.

```
#define MAXPOINTS 100;
Ppoint3 points[MAXPOINTS];
Pqloc3    locdata1;      /* record for requested locator input */
Ploc3     locdata2;        /* record for sampled locator input */
Pint      wsid = 1;               /* workstation identifier */
Pint      locdev = 1;              /* locator device number */

npts = 0;
preqloc3(wsid, locdev, &locdata1);
```

```
if locdata1.status == PSTAT_NONE printf("Operator break");
else {
  points[npts++] = locdata1.loc.position; /* Store first point */
  psetlocmode(wsid, locdev, PSAMPLE, PES_ECHO);/* Switch modes */
  do {
    psampleloc3(wsid, locdev, &locdata2);       /* Get position */
    points[npts++] = locdata2.position;           /* Store point */
    } while(npts < MAXPOINTS);           /* Stop after MAXPOINTS */
  }
psetlocmode(wsid, locdev, PREQUEST, PES_ECHO); /* Switch modes */
```

It may seem strange that two different types of locator record are used (`locdata1` and `locdata2`.) This results from the way the C language binding is defined.

7.11 String devices

String devices are used for entering text. Most often, they correspond to a physical keyboard, but like other devices this depends on the application. For example, some speech recognition systems can generate ASCII text and could be used to implement a string device.

Most good implementations will provide the usual range of editing keys, allowing a string to be corrected before the trigger is activated. Examples include using the DELETE or BACKSPACE keys to remove erroneous characters from the end of the string, and possibly CTRL-U to erase the whole string.

It may appear odd that it is possible to sample a string device. The effect of this is implementation dependent but one possible interpretation is that the characters typed so far are returned. This allows a program to use sample mode to see whether anything has been typed, but you should check your *Local Guide* before relying on this.

When a string device is initialized, an **initial string** is specified. Any characters typed by the operator overwrite part of this string, or are appended to it. The effect obtained depends on the **initial edit position**. This is an integer value which indicates where the first character typed by the operator should be stored in the input buffer. By setting the initial edit position to the end of the initial string, it is possible to use the initial string as a default string, which will be returned unaltered to the application program if the operator simply activates the trigger. Useful as this may be, it is fraught with problems, as shown by the next example.

7.11.1 An example – reading a string in request mode

The following fragment of code initializes a string device and requests input from it. It should be noted that the initial string is used as a prompt. It is up to the application to interpret the returned string correctly, as it may include the initial string. In some implementations the operator may be able to delete characters from the initial string using the DELETE or BACKSPACE keys. In this case, whether the returned string contains none, some, or all of the initial string will depend on how the operator has edited the input before operating the trigger.

```
Pint wsid      = 1,                    /* workstation identifier */
     stringdev = 1,                    /* string device number */
     pet       = 1;                     /* prompt echo/type */

Pchar initstring[] = "filename: ";          /* initial string */
Plimit3 echovolume  = {0.0,1152.0,0.0,900.0,0.0,1.0};
Pstringrec stringdata = {1000,                  /* buffer size */
                         10};           /* initial edit position */

Pqstring string                /* string data returned here */
     .
     .
     .

pinitstring3(wsid,stringdev,initstring,PET,
             &echovolume,&stringdata);      /* initialize string */

preqstring(wsid,stringdev,&string);      /* request input string */

if string.status == PSTAT_NONE {
                            /* operator performed a break!
                     /* input invalid and cannot be used */
}
else {
    ...                             /* process valid input */
}
```

7.12 Pick devices

A pick device returns information about a primitive selected interactively by an operator. Specifically, the function returns a list defining the **pick path**. Conceptually, picking involves traversing the CSS to locate which instance of a structure the operator has picked. This is illustrated in Figure 7.4. If the operator points at the back wheel of the bicycle, this is an instance of structure *wheel*. The complete path in this case is

< bike, back wheel, wheel >

In this example the order of the pick path shown is TOPFIRST – that is, with the highest level in the hierarchy listed first. It is also possible for the list to be ordered BOTTOMFIRST, which would result in the order

< wheel, back wheel, bike >

This option can be selected with the INITIALIZE PICK function. Each entry in the

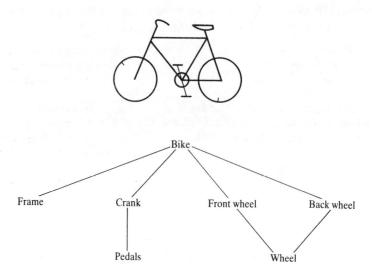

Bike

Frame   Crank   Front wheel   Back wheel

Pedals   Wheel

Figure 7.4   A hierarchical model of a bicycle.

pick path list is a **pick path item** corresponding to a structure in the hierarchy. It contains:

- The *structure identifier*.

- The *pick identifier* associated with the selected primitive. This offers a convenient and relatively cheap mechanism for labelling primitives. The pick identifier is an integer name which is bound to primitives during traversal. Its value can be changed between individual primitives to provide a very fine-grained level of naming. Note, however, that the pick identifier cannot be used to distinguish between different invocations of the same structure. If it is known that only a single instance of a given structure will be used at any one time, then the pick identifier can be used safely; otherwise the use of pick paths will be necessary.

- The *element position* of the chosen primitive. This is especially useful for subsequent editing operations.

The function to set a pick identifier is:

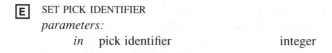

E   SET PICK IDENTIFIER
parameters:
    in   pick identifier   integer

Picking of primitives can also be controlled using the **pick inclusion** and **pick exclusion** filters, which are described in Chapter 11.

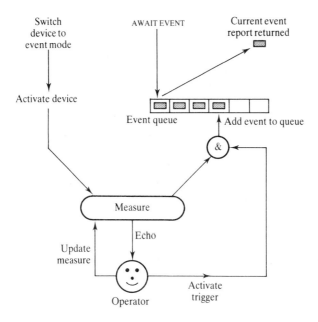

Figure 7.5 Event mode.

7.13   The details of event mode

Devices are switched into event mode using the appropriate SET XXX MODE function, as described in Section 7.4. Once a device has been placed in event mode, activation of its trigger by the operator causes an event report to be placed in the time-ordered event queue. The event report contains the class, device number and measure for the event – that is, it identifies which device was used and its associated value. The queue, and a typical event report, are illustrated in Figure 7.5.

7.13.1   Finding out what events have occurred

An application program can interrogate the input queue by using the function:

AWAIT EVENT
parameters:

in	timeout	real
in	workstation identifier	integer
out	class	(NONE, CHOICE,
		LOCATOR, STROKE,
		STRING, VALUATOR, PICK)
out	device number	integer

Timeout is a time-out value in seconds. If there is some input already waiting in the event queue, then the function returns immediately and the time-out value is ignored. However, if the queue is empty then AWAIT EVENT blocks, either until the specified time period has elapsed, or until a new event occurs, whichever is sooner. By using a time-out value of zero, the event queue can be sampled to see whether it contains anything. One useful application of this is to allow a program to carry on with other processing until some event occurs. To accomplish this the program must check the queue periodically by calling AWAIT EVENT. Alternatively, if a very large time-out is specified then, in effect, AWAIT EVENT will block more or less indefinitely, unless some input is generated.

Workstation identifier is the workstation identifier for the workstation on which the input was generated. Even though several workstations may be active, there is only a single event queue. *Class* is the logical class of device which generated the input. This is needed so that the corresponding measure can be read subsequently by calling an appropriate function. The value NONE is returned for *class* when AWAIT EVENT times out – that is, when the queue is empty. *Device number* is the number of the device which generated the input.

7.13.2   Reading the data from an event

AWAIT EVENT allows a program to wait for an event to happen, and discovers what that event was, but does not read the corresponding measure. The measure can be read by calling an appropriate function corresponding to each device class, as follows:

☐   GET VALUATOR
parameters:
      out value   real

☐   GET CHOICE
parameters:
      out status   (OK, NOCHOICE)
      out choice number   integer

☐   GET LOCATOR 3
parameters:
      out view index   integer
      out locator position   3D WC point

☐   GET STROKE 3
parameters:
      out view index   integer
      out stroke   list of 3D WC points

☐ GET STRING
parameters:
      out character string   string

☐ GET PICK
parameters:
      in   pick path depth   integer
      out status   (OK, NOPICK)
      out pick path   list of pick path elements

These functions should only be called once it has been established (by calling
AWAIT EVENT) that an input of the corresponding type has occurred.

The following example illustrates a typical program structure for processing
data in event mode:

```
Pfloat   timeout = 2.0,      /* timeout period for await event */
Ploat    value;                /* value returned by valuator */
Ploc3    locator;              /* values returned by locator */
Pevent   eventdata;          /* await event returns data here */
int      exit;  /* assumed to be non-zero when we have finished */
  .
  .
  .
do {

  pawaitevent(timeout,&eventdata);

  switch (eventdata.class)

  case PI_VALUATOR: {                  /* Process valuator input */
    pgetval(&value);
    ...
  }

  case PI_LOCATOR: {                   /* Process locator input */
    pgetloc3(&locator);
    ...
  }

} while !exit;
```

Care is needed when event mode is used with a locator. The PHIGS standard
makes it clear that the generation of locator input and its translation into world
coordinates cannot be guaranteed to be an atomic action. In other words, it is
possible for the view to change after the operator has entered a point but before
PHIGS has performed the inverse transformation. Applications should therefore
make sure that view transformations are not changed whilst a locator is in event
mode, otherwise the results cannot be guaranteed to be correct.

7.13.3 Input queue overflow

If a program removes events from the input queue at a slower rate than the operator generates them, then at some point the input queue may overflow. This causes an error to occur when the next attempt is made to access the queue, usually with AWAIT EVENT. There are two ways to handle this: one is to replace the standard error handler by a user-supplied one and to trap the error condition oneself, as described in Chapter 12. The second method is to use an inquiry function to test for queue overflow:

☐ INQUIRE INPUT QUEUE OVERFLOW
　parameters:

out	error	integer
out	workstation identifier	integer
out	class	(CHOICE, LOCATOR, STROKE, STRING, VALUATOR, PICK)
out	device number	integer

If input queue overflow has occurred then the value of *error* will be zero, and details of the device causing the overflow are returned in the other parameters. Otherwise, *error* will be non-zero.

Note that once an overflow has occurred no more events can be added to the queue until *all* previous events have been removed from it. A program can do this by repeatedly calling AWAIT EVENT with a time-out value of zero, or, more drastically, by using FLUSH DEVICE EVENTS (see below) to remove events for each device from the queue.

With programs which perform only simple tasks the chances that the queue will fill up are small, and there is therefore a temptation not to bother with handling queue overflow. Clearly, if an application program takes a long time to process a particular input then there is a greater danger that the input queue will overflow, and so input overflow assumes a greater importance. A well-designed user interface should take action to make the operator aware of the fact that input actions are temporarily being ignored.

7.13.4 Flushing the input queue

Sometimes you may wish to dispose of unwanted input from the queue. This can happen if something goes wrong, or if you want to guarantee that no input of a particular type is in the queue, prior to beginning some interactive sequence.

As an example, suppose that a program wishes to start some activity, and to terminate it when some specific event happens. By flushing the queue of this type of event, it is possible to make sure that the action is not prematurely terminated by old input, which happened to be already in the queue when the action started. Of course, this style of programming results in an interface which precludes the use of techniques like 'mouse-ahead' or 'type-ahead', but sometimes this is useful.

To flush events from the input queue, an application should call:

☐ FLUSH DEVICE EVENTS
parameters:

in	workstation identifier	integer
in	class	(CHOICE, LOCATOR, STROKE, STRING, VALUATOR, PICK)
in	device number	integer

7.13.5   Simultaneous events

It is quite possible in PHIGS to have several logical devices which map to the same physical device. For example, on some workstations, several of the logical devices may be controlled by a mouse. But, what happens if two different devices share the same trigger? In this situation two events are generated, one for each device. The order of these in the input queue is implementation dependent. To find out whether any simultaneous events have occurred, an application may call:

☐ INQUIRE MORE SIMULTANEOUS EVENTS
parameters:

out	error	integer
out	more	(NOMORE, MORE)

If *error* is zero then *more* indicates whether or not there are more simultaneous events in the queue. If *error* is non-zero, then the value of *more* is undefined. Where more events do exist they can be read in the usual way by AWAIT EVENT.

7.13.6   An example use of event mode

This is an adaptation of an earlier example (see Section 7.10.2), which is used to record a number of points entered with a locator. The program uses two locators which are assumed to use the same view transformation, and which therefore return WC in the same range. One of the locators (loc1) is used in sample mode in order to record points. The second locator (loc2) is placed in event mode and is used as a way of terminating the loop. In order to achieve this, the two locators must use different triggers. For example, loc1 might use mouse input triggered by the left mouse button, whilst loc2 uses the same mouse but triggered by the middle button. (Remember, however, that triggers are implementation-dependent – the mouse buttons are used here only as an example.)

As before, the program records points, up to a maximum of MAXPOINTS in number, but now recording can be terminated by pressing the middle mouse button. This is checked by seeing whether a locator event has been generated with loc2. Initially, loc1 is in request mode, but is switched to sample mode once the first point has been entered.

To complete the example, once the points have been entered the program creates a structure containing a polyline.

```
#define MAXPOINTS 1000;                  /*max number of points*/
#define wsid      1;                      /*workstation identifier*/
#define structid  1;                      /*structure identifier*/
#define loc1      1;                      /*first locator number*/
#define loc2      2;                      /*second locator number*/


int     npts;                        /*number of points recorded*/
Ppoint3 points[MAXPOINTS];               /*array of 2D points*/
Pqloc3  locdata1;                /*data record for request mode*/
Ploc3   locdata2;          /*data record for sample/event modes*/
Pevent  eventdata;                       /*event data record*/
  .
  .
  .
npts = 0;

preqloc3(wsid,loc1,&locdata1);            /*wait for first point*/

if locdata1.status == PSTAT_NONE {        /*check for break*/
  ...
}

else {
  points[npts++] = locdata1.loc.position;          /*store point*/
  psetlocmode(wsid,loc1,PSAMPLE,PES_ECHO); /*loc1 to sample mode*/
  psetlocmode(wsid,loc2,PEVENT,PES_ECHO);   /*loc2 to event mode*/

  do {                           /*now loop until finished*/

    psampleloc3(wsid,loc1,&locdata2);           /*sample loc1*/

    points[npts++] = locdata2.position; /*and store its position*/
    pawaitevent(0.0,ws,&eventdata);
  } while (((eventdata.class != PI_LOCATOR)||
          (eventdata.dev != loc2))&&        /*check for loc2*/
          (npts < MAXPOINTS)));             /*or array full*/
}

psetlocmode(wsid,loc1,PREQUEST,PES_ECHO);       /*request mode*/
psetlocmode(wsid,loc2,PREQUEST,PES_ECHO);

popenstruct(structid);                   /*open a structure*/
ppolyline3(npts,points);                 /*draw a polyline*/
pclosestruct();                          /*close the structure*/
```

Appendix B contains a further example of event mode, used in conjunction with other modes.

7.14   Inquiring about the current state of a device

For each device it is possible to find out its current state by calling a function of the form:

    INQUIRE XXX DEVICE STATE
    parameters:

in	workstation identifier	integer
in	XXX device number	integer
in	type of returned values	(SET, REALIZED)
out	error	integer
out	operating mode	(REQUEST, SAMPLE, EVENT)
out	echo switch	(ECHO, NOECHO)
out	prompt and echo type	integer
out	echo volume	(xmin, xmax, ymin, ymax, zmin, zmax (DC))
out	valuator data record	record

Here, XXX may be VALUATOR, LOCATOR, CHOICE, STROKE, STRING or PICK. The *error* parameter returns 0 if the required information is available, otherwise it returns a specific error code. The other parameters give information about the operating mode, prompt and echo type, and so forth. The parameter lists for specific devices vary slightly.

Chapter 8
Workstations

PHIGS shields the application programmer from the details of real graphics devices by operating in terms of idealized devices known as **workstations***. In this chapter we describe the workstation concept, including the* **workstation description table***, the* **workstation state list** *and how* **picture updating** *is controlled.*

As an international standard, PHIGS must be able to support a wide range of graphics hardware. This is achieved using the idea of workstations, which are not physical devices, but idealized versions of real devices. This concept provides a high degree of device independence, and for the most part the application need not be too concerned about the details of each real device. On the other hand, a typical installation will provide a number of devices with very different characteristics, and it is essential that an application can make the best use of whatever hardware is available. The workstation approach is an attempt to reconcile these two seemingly incompatible goals: the general need for device independence, and the requirement that applications can use real devices as effectively as possible.

8.1   The workstation

A workstation is an *abstraction* of one or more physical devices. A bit-mapped display which has a number of input devices such as a dial box, a mouse and a keyboard, may be a single workstation as far as PHIGS is concerned. Alternatively, there may be a one-to-one correspondence between a physical device and a workstation, such as a laser printer. In fact, a workstation may be realized by any combination of hardware and software. Each workstation has a **category**, which broadly summarizes what it can do: whether it can perform graphical output, graphical input or both. There are five categories:

- OUTPUT workstations can only produce graphical output. An OUTPUT workstation has only one area where pictures are displayed, called its **display space**, and has no input devices. Examples are a laser printer and a penplotter.

Table 8.1   An example workstation list from the *Local Guide*.

Workstation	Type	Category	Location
Sun 4/160 'Eve'	36	OUTIN	Room 2-93
Sun 4/160 'Adam'	36	OUTIN	Room 2-103
Sun 4/160 'Cain'	36	OUTIN	Room 2-110
Sun SparcStation	37	OUTIN	Room 2-108
VaxStation 3540	17	OUTIN	Room G-49
A4 Laser printer	51	OUTPUT	Print Room
A3 Laser printer	56	OUTPUT	Print Room
Digitizer	3	INPUT	CAD Laboratory

- INPUT workstations can only provide graphical input, under the control of an operator manipulating one or more input devices, such as a mouse. A digitizer table is an example of an INPUT workstation.

- OUTIN workstations can perform both graphical input and output. A raster display with an attached mouse and tablet would be classed as an OUTIN workstation.

- METAFILE INPUT (MI) and METAFILE OUTPUT (MO) are special categories of workstation which are able to read and write **metafiles** – special files external to PHIGS which contain graphical data.

There are many different kinds graphics device on the market, and classifying a device on the basis of its input and output capabilities is too wide a distinction to be useful. Therefore, as well as a category, a workstation also has a **type**. This is a code which uniquely identifies it in terms its manufacturer and model number. Your *Local Guide* will give details of all the workstations available at your installation, and Table 8.1 shows an example.

To use workstations, we need two kinds of information: what the workstation (and its underlying collection of physical devices) can do, and what the state of the workstation is at a given time. For example, if it is an output workstation, can it update the picture dynamically, or must it redraw the entire picture? A detailed description of what a particular type of workstation can do is stored in a data structure called the **workstation description table (WDT)**.

8.2   The workstation description table

The WDT describes exactly which facilities a particular type of workstation provides. This is a very large amount of information and we shall not list it all here. However, the following should give an idea of the sort of information held in the WDT:

- workstation category (OUTPUT, INPUT, OUTIN, MI, MO);

- type of display (RASTER or VECTOR);

- size of the display area;

- number and list of linetypes available;

- number of display priorities supported;

- number of locator input devices;

- number of colour models supported.

Your *Local Guide* will provide a complete WDT for each type of workstation at your installation. Section 8.10 describes how to inquire about information in the WDT from an application program.

There is one WDT for each different type of workstation, and the information it contains is read-only. You may consult this information by using inquiry functions, or by referring to your *Local Guide*, but you cannot change it.

8.3   How a workstation can react to picture changes

Many applications build and modify models incrementally and iteratively. Not all workstations, however, have the ability to modify parts of a displayed picture *selectively*. On some workstations, such as a laser printer, the only way to bring the picture up to date is to redraw it completely. Redrawing the entire picture in this way is known as an **implicit regeneration**. It is implicit because the redrawing is not *explicitly* requested by the application, which specifies only the incremental changes required to the picture. Implicit regenerations occur under the control of PHIGS.

Information about how a workstation can respond to picture changes is held in its WDT. For example, changing a polyline representation on a workstation means that all polylines currently displayed using that particular representation (on that workstation) must change accordingly. There are a number of operations which have an effect on the appearance of displayed pictures, and they are listed in Table 8.2. For each, there is an entry in the WDT called **dynamic modification accepted**, which describes how the workstation can react to a change in its value. There are three possibilities:

- IRG   The whole picture must be redrawn to reflect the change; that is, an implicit regeneration is required.

- IMM   The change can be performed immediately, without the need to redraw the whole picture.

- CBS   The change can be simulated using a 'quick update method' (see Section 8.5.2).

Table 8.2   Operations affecting visual appearance.

Changing entry in WSL	Structure changes
primitive representation	editing a structure
view representation	posting a structure
colour representation	unposting a structure
workstation transformation	deleting a structure
highlighting filter	changing structure references
invisibility filter	

You can inquire how a workstation can react to each of the workstation and structure operations in Table 8.2 using the following functions:

INQUIRE DYNAMICS OF WORKSTATION ATTRIBUTES
parameters:

in	workstation type	workstation type
out	error	integer
out	polyline representation	(IRG, IMM, CBS)
out	polymarker representation	(IRG, IMM, CBS)
out	text representation	(IRG, IMM, CBS)
out	interior representation	(IRG, IMM, CBS)
out	edge representation	(IRG, IMM, CBS)
out	pattern representation	(IRG, IMM, CBS)
out	colour representation	(IRG, IMM, CBS)
out	view representation	(IRG, IMM, CBS)
out	workstation transformation	(IRG, IMM, CBS)
out	highlighting filter	(IRG, IMM, CBS)
out	invisibility filter	(IRG, IMM, CBS)
out	HLHSR mode	(IRG, IMM, CBS)

and

INQUIRE DYNAMICS OF STRUCTURES
parameters:

in	workstation type	workstation type
out	error	integer
out	structure content modification	(IRG, IMM, CBS)
out	post structure	(IRG, IMM, CBS)
out	unpost structure	(IRG, IMM, CBS)
out	delete structure	(IRG, IMM, CBS)
out	reference modification	(IRG, IMM, CBS)

By using these inquiry functions carefully, it possible to write portable programs

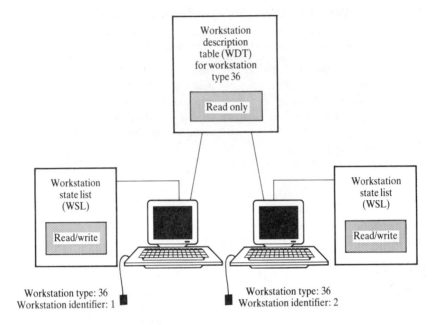

Figure 8.1 WDTs and WSLs.

which can modify their behaviour to make the best use of the workstations available at a particular installation.

8.4   The workstation state list

Although the capabilities of a workstation are fixed, its **operating state** may be constantly changing. For example, structure networks may be posted and unposted, and representations (see Section 9.9) and filters (see Section 11.1) may be changed dynamically. The current operational state of a workstation is recorded in a data structure called the **workstation state list (WSL)**.

There is an important difference between the WDT and the WSL: for a given type of workstation, a WDT always exists which describes its functionality. However, a particular workstation has a WSL only when it is open. For example, Table 8.1 listed three different workstations of type 36. Figure 8.1 shows the situation when two workstations of this type have been opened. Although the same WDT describes their facilities, each open workstation has its own private WSL. This is because each workstation can be independently controlled by the application.

To summarize, there is a WDT for each different type of workstation, and a WSL exists for each open workstation.

8.5 Controlling how the picture is updated

Workstations can be used very flexibly: the application can control *when* visual effects take place on a workstation, and *how* they take place. When they take place is controlled by the **deferral mode** of the workstation, and how they take place is determined by its **modification mode**. The application specifies the deferral mode and the modification mode for a workstation using:

☐ SET DISPLAY UPDATE STATE
parameters:

in	workstation identifier	integer
in	deferral mode	(ASAP, BNIG, BNIL
		ASTI, WAIT)
in	modification mode	(NIVE, UWOR, UQUM)

We shall look at deferral mode and modification mode separately.

8.5.1 Deferral mode

Not all workstations can respond instantly to changes to the picture requested by the application. For example, if the physical interface between the host computer and a workstation is slow, transmitting information to the workstation after every change made to the picture may be extremely inefficient. Instead, the application may wish to buffer picture changes and request the picture to be brought up to date at a convenient time.

The application can control the amount of delay which occurs between making changes to the picture and the changes being visible on a workstation. The speed with which a workstation responds to picture changes is determined by its deferral mode, which has five possible values:

- ASAP (as soon as possible) The picture displayed on the workstation is brought up to date as soon as possible.

- BNIG (before next interaction globally) The workstation display will be brought up to date before an operator starts using an input device on *any* open workstation.

- BNIL (before next interaction locally) The workstation display will be updated when the operator uses an input device on *this* workstation.

- ASTI (at some time) The workstation display will be brought up to date at some time, but it is not possible to predict when this will be.

- WAIT (when the application requests it) All required changes to the picture are recorded, but the picture is brought up to date only when the application explicitly requests it, using UPDATE WORKSTATION or REDRAW ALL STRUCTURES (see Section 8.6), or by changing the deferral mode.

8.5.2   Modification mode

Some workstations have capabilities midway between being able to reflect a change immediately, and having to perform an implicit regeneration. They can signal that some aspect of the picture has changed, by **simulating** the change using a quick updating method, without necessarily making the full effects of the change accurately and immediately visible. For example, the deletion of a displayed structure might be simulated by redrawing it in the background colour of the display. The operator will see that the structure has been deleted, although if it overlapped other parts of the picture there would be gaps, and for an accurate display the whole picture must be regenerated. There are three methods of picture modification:

- NIVE (no immediate visual effects)   In this mode, the picture is not updated at all until the application explicitly requests it.

- UWOR (update without regeneration)   All picture changes that can be performed correctly without the need for a complete regeneration, or the use of simulation, are performed.

- UQUM (use quick update method)   The picture is updated using a quick update method, as described above.

It is often difficult to keep track of whether, at a particular time, the picture displayed on a workstation correctly reflects the current state of the CSS and all the state lists. At any point in time, the display on an OUTPUT or OUTIN workstation is recorded by the **state of visual representation (SVR)** entry in the WSL, which has three states:

- CORRECT   The picture on the display is completely up to date.

- DEFERRED   The picture is not up to date. There are a number of changes which still have to be made to the picture to make it correct. When the changes will occur depends on the deferral and modification modes.

- SIMULATED   The picture is not up to date. One or more of the required changes have been simulated using a quick update technique.

The current state of the picture can be determined by using the function:

☐   INQUIRE DISPLAY UPDATE STATE
parameters:

in	workstation identifier	integer
out	error	integer
out	deferral mode	(ASAP, BNIG, BNIL, ASTI, WAIT)
out	modification mode	(NIVE, UWOR, UQUM)
out	display surface state	(EMPTY, NOT EMPTY)
out	state of picture	(CORRECT, DEFERRED, SIMULATED)

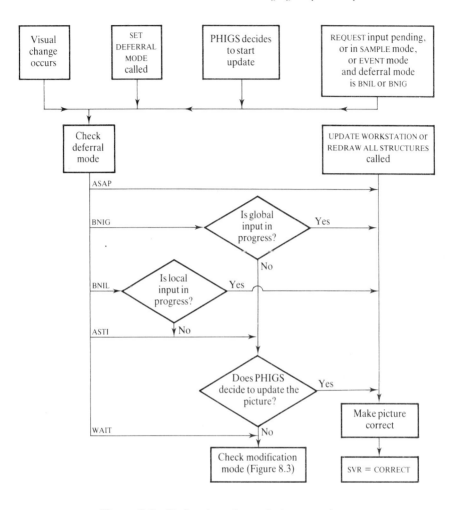

Figure 8.2 Deferral modes and picture updates.

Because of the interactions between deferral mode and modification modes, the detailed control of workstations can be quite involved. Figures 8.2 and 8.3 summarize the rather complicated logic for deferral mode and modification mode respectively.

8.6 Bringing the picture up to date

Sometimes it is necessary to ensure that the picture displayed on a workstation is completely up to date, and reflects the current state of the CSS and all the state lists. The application can make the picture up to date by calling one of

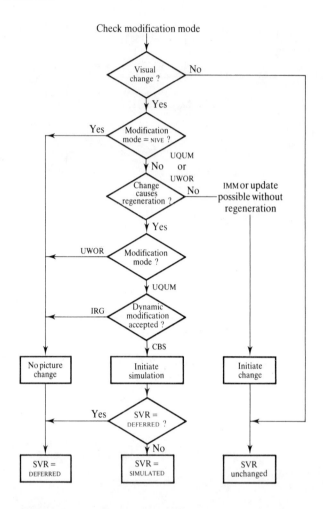

Check modification mode

Figure 8.3   Modification modes and picture updates.

two functions provided for this purpose: UPDATE WORKSTATION and REDRAW ALL STRUCTURES. We shall look at each in turn.

☐ UPDATE WORKSTATION
parameters:
    in   workstation identifier   integer
    in   regeneration flag   (PERFORM, POSTPONE)

If *regeneration flag* is PERFORM, any deferred actions for the workstation are immediately performed. If it is POSTPONE, the effect of the function is to initiate the transmission to the workstation of any data that has been queued. The REDRAW ALL STRUCTURES function is similar:

☐ REDRAW ALL STRUCTURES
  parameters:
in	workstation identifier	integer
in	control flag	(CONDITIONALLY, ALWAYS)

All the structures posted to the workstation are redrawn, and the picture is brought completely up to date. If *control flag* is CONDITIONALLY, the display is only cleared if it is not empty. If *control flag* is ALWAYS, the display surface is always cleared (one possible use of this would be to generate empty frames on a film recorder).

8.7 Sending messages to workstations

Sometimes it is useful to send messages to the operator of a workstation, for example to indicate that a particular file which the application has attempted to open does not exist. This communication is quite distinct from the normal modelling and graphics operations, and there is a special function for displaying such messages:

☐ MESSAGE
  parameters:
in	workstation identifier	integer
in	message text	character string

The effect of the function is to display the specified message on the specified workstation. However, the application has no control over where exactly the message appears; this is determined by the implementation (and will be described in your *Local Guide*). It is quite permissible that the message does not appear on the workstation at all, as long as it does appear on an associated device the operator is likely to be looking at.

8.8 Using more than one workstation

An application may use more than one workstation at a time. A common situation is to use an interactive workstation for editing the model, and then to obtain hardcopy by posting structures to a suitable output workstation such as a laser printer. For example:

OPEN WORKSTATION (1, conn, interactive)   % Open an interactive workstation.

OPEN WORKSTATION (2, conn, printer)   % Open a hardcopy workstation.

POST STRUCTURE (1, model, priority)   % Post to interactive workstation.

```
repeat
    % Interact, using a choice device:
    case choice of
        1: % Change modelling transformation.
        2: % Unpost structure.
        3: % Delete structure.
        4: % Empty structure.
        5: POST STRUCTURE (2, model, priority)    % Make hard copy.
    end
until finished
```

This technique is used in the program in Appendix A to generate the pictures shown in Figure 6.4.

8.9   Hidden line/hidden surface removal

An important consideration when displaying 3D images is that some parts of the image may lie in front of other parts, and thus obscure them. If the image is to look at all realistic, those parts of primitives which are obscured by others should not be drawn. In general, the process of determining which parts of primitives are invisible is called Hidden Line/Hidden Surface Removal (HLHSR). It is implementation dependent whether HLHSR is supported, and what methods are used, although many implementations do provide HLHSR facilities. Recognizing the ubiquity of HLHSR techniques, PHIGS provides a framework to enable their use to be controlled by the application.

HLHSR is a process performed by a workstation, and it is controlled by two factors: HLHSR mode and HLHSR identifier. The former is held in the WSL, and the latter is an output primitive attribute. Partitioning the control of HLHSR between the CSS and the workstation is convenient for two reasons: first, the application may only wish to apply HLHSR to selected parts of the CSS, especially if HLHSR is slow in a particular implementation, and it is known that primitives are more likely to obscure one another in some structure networks than others. Second, a workstation may provide several HLHSR techniques, and it is convenient to be able to switch between them. A workstation's HLHSR mode is set using:

☐   SET HLHSR MODE
    parameters:
           in   workstation identifier   integer
           in   HLHSR mode   integer

This sets an entry in the WSL for the workstation. The WDT records how many HLHSR modes a workstation supports, and what their values are, and this information can be inquired using INQUIRE HLHSR FACILITIES (see Section 8.10). The current HLHSR mode may be determined using INQUIRE HLHSR MODE.

The second attribute, HLHSR identifier, is set with a structure element:

| E | SET HLHSR IDENTIFIER
     parameters:
        in   HLHSR identifier   integer

This is an attribute which becomes bound to output primitives during traversal. The HLHSR identifier selects a particular HLHSR technique on a workstation, and how the selection occurs depends on the workstation's HLHSR mode. For example, a workstation might provide a selection of HLHSR techniques, such as *z*-buffer, scan line and painter's algorithms. In this case the HLHSR identifier might be used to select the appropriate method, and the workstation's HLHSR mode might be used to disable or enable HLHSR processing completely. Alternatively, if we know that only certain parts of the CSS might require HLHSR processing, the HLHSR identifier could be used to group the appropriate output primitives together.

8.10   Inquiring about the WDT

It is often necessary for applications to modify their behaviour to make the best use of workstations, and to do this they need to be able to inquire the information in the WDT. For programs which are intended to be portable, a fundamental requirement is to be able to find out (at run time) what types of workstation are actually available in a particular implementation. This may be done using:

☐   INQUIRE LIST OF AVAILABLE WORKSTATION TYPES
     parameters:
        out error   integer
        out workstation types   list of workstation types

Once we know which types of workstation are available, we can ask questions about the capabilities of each type. Below, we summarize the WDT inquiry functions.

- INQUIRE DEFAULT DISPLAY UPDATE STATE returns the default display update state (see Section 8.5) of the workstation. This value will often be set to make best use of the workstation.

- INQUIRE DISPLAY SPACE SIZE 3 returns the size of the display space of an OUTPUT or OUTIN workstation in DC.

- INQUIRE DYNAMICS OF STRUCTURES describes how a workstation can respond to changes in the CSS. See Section 8.3.

- INQUIRE DYNAMICS OF WORKSTATION ATTRIBUTES describes how a workstation can respond to changes to its WSL. See Section 8.3.

- INQUIRE LIST OF AVAILABLE GENERALIZED DRAWING PRIMITIVES 3 returns a list of all the GDP identifiers supported by a particular workstation type. Generalized drawing primitives are described in Section 3.10.

- INQUIRE LIST OF AVAILABLE GENERALIZED STRUCTURE ELEMENTS returns a list of all the GSE identifiers supported by a particular workstation type. Generalized structure elements are described in Section 11.5.

- INQUIRE WORKSTATION XXX where XXX may be CATEGORY, CLASSIFICATION, or STATE TABLE LENGTHS. These functions enable you to determine the category of a particular workstation type (OUTPUT, OUTIN, ...), its classification (VECTOR, RASTER, OTHER), and the size of each of the bundle tables in the workstation state list of a workstation of this type.

- INQUIRE XXX FACILITIES where XXX may be ANNOTATION, COLOUR, COLOUR MODEL, EDGE, GENERALIZED STRUCTURE ELEMENT, HLHSR, INTERIOR, MODELLING CLIPPING, PATTERN, POLYLINE, POLYMARKER, TEXT, or VIEW. These functions return information about the respective facility on the workstation. For example INQUIRE POLYLINE FACILITIES returns lists of the available linetypes and linewidths, as well as the value of the workstation's nominal linewidth, and the range of linewidths supported.

- INQUIRE NUMBER OF DISPLAY PRIORITIES SUPPORTED returns the number of different display priorities (specified in the POST STRUCTURE function) which the workstation can support.

- INQUIRE PREDEFINED XXX REPRESENTATION where XXX may be COLOUR, EDGE, INTERIOR, PATTERN, POLYLINE, POLYMARKER, TEXT, or VIEW. Each of these functions returns information about the respective predefined representation, whose index is specified by the application.

- INQUIRE LIST OF XXX INDICES where XXX may be COLOUR, EDGE, INTERIOR, PATTERN, POLYLINE, POLYMARKER, TEXT, or VIEW. Each of these functions returns a list of all the supported indices for the respective item.

- INQUIRE NUMBER OF AVAILABLE LOGICAL INPUT DEVICES returns the number of each type of logical input device (LOCATOR, STROKE, ...) supported by an INPUT or OUTIN workstation.

- INQUIRE DEFAULT XXX DEVICE DATA 3 where XXX may be CHOICE, LOCATOR, STROKE, STRING, VALUATOR, or PICK. Each function returns the default device data for specified logical input device on a workstation. For example, INQUIRE DEFAULT LOCATOR DEVICE DATA returns the default initial locator position, a list of the available prompt and echo types, and the default echo volume and locator data record.

8.11 Inquiring about the WSL

The following functions provide information about the WSL of a particular open workstation:

- INQUIRE XXX FILTER where XXX may be HIGHLIGHTING or INVISIBILITY. These functions return the current contents of the workstation filters. To inquire about a pick filter, the function INQUIRE PICK DEVICE STATE 3 is used.

- INQUIRE WORKSTATION CONNECTION AND TYPE returns the connection identifier and type of an open workstation.

- INQUIRE WORKSTATION TRANSFORMATION 3 returns the workstation transformation update state (NOT PENDING or PENDING), and both the values of the workstation window and workstation viewport limits.

- INQUIRE DISPLAY UPDATE STATE returns the display update state of the workstation. This function is described in detail in Section 8.5.2.

- INQUIRE XXX REPRESENTATION where XXX may be COLOUR, EDGE, INTERIOR, PATTERN, POLYLINE, POLYMARKER, TEXT, or VIEW. Each function returns the value of a specified representation from the respective workstation table.

- INQUIRE XXX DEVICE STATE 3 where XXX may be CHOICE, LOCATOR, STROKE, STRING, VALUATOR, or PICK. Each function returns the current state of a specified logical input device on a workstation. For example, INQUIRE LOCATOR DEVICE STATE returns the current operating mode (REQUEST, SAMPLE or EVENT), the echo switch, prompt and echo type, initial values and data record.

- INQUIRE SET OF OPEN WORKSTATIONS returns a list of the currently open workstations.

8.12 Metafile workstations

In Chapter 10 we shall describe the mechanism for storing structures and structure networks in archive files. This technique is specific to PHIGS, and does not address the question of writing graphical data to files which may be moved between applications, some of which may not use PHIGS. For this purpose, there is an interface to a different kind of external file called a **metafile**. There is a fundamental difference between archives and metafiles: archives store structures and structure networks, retaining hierarchical information, whereas metafiles store the 2D *picture* produced by the traversal of one or more structure networks.

A metafile is a sequence of **items**, each of which may be graphical or application data, but PHIGS does not define the format in which data is encoded in an item. However, there is an international standard encoding for metafiles called the **Computer Graphics Metafile (CGM)**, and some implementations are able to read and write CGM-conforming metafiles. For a detailed description of CGM, see [Henderson and Mumford, 1990].

Metafiles are read using workstations of category METAFILE INPUT (MI), and written using workstations of category METAFILE OUTPUT (MO).

8.12.1   Writing a metafile

In many ways, an MO workstation behaves just like an OUTPUT workstation: it may be opened (and connected to an external metafile), and structure networks may be posted to it, causing the resulting output primitives to be written to the metafile. The WDT for an MO workstation is the same as that for an OUTPUT workstation, but it is implementation dependent whether all the information is available.

As well as posting structure networks to an MO workstation, an application may also write arbitrary data to the metafile, using the function:

☐   WRITE ITEM TO METAFILE
parameters:

in	workstation identifier	integer
in	item type	integer
in	item data	record

It is up to the application to manage the use of item types and the precise format of the item data.

8.12.2   Reading a metafile

A metafile is read one item at a time, under the control of the application, using the concept of a **current item**. When an MI workstation is opened, the first item in the metafile becomes the current item. The application can inquire about the current item using the function:

☐   GET ITEM TYPE FROM METAFILE
parameters:

in	workstation identifier	integer
out	item type	integer
out	length of data	integer

This returns the type of the current item, and the length of its associated data record. The following function returns the data of the item:

☐ READ ITEM FROM METAFILE
parameters:

in	workstation identifier	integer
in	maximum data length	integer
out	item data	record

This also makes the next item in the metafile the current item. Once the data has been obtained, it is decoded using:

☐ INTERPRET ITEM
parameters:

in	item type	integer
in	item data	record

The effect of this function depends entirely on the nature of implementation defined mapping between metafiles and PHIGS, which you will find described in your *Local Guide*. However, we can describe what happens in general terms. PHIGS examines *item type* and determines whether or not it can recognize it. If it can, the information in *item data* is interpreted and the appropriate action is taken; otherwise an error is reported. For example, item type p may encode a POLYLINE 3. In this case, there must be a structure open when a type p item is interpreted, and the appropriate POLYLINE 3 element will be inserted at the element pointer.

We can summarize the method of reading a metafile as follows:

```
% Open the workstation.
OPEN WORKSTATION (ws, connection, metafile)

finished := false


while not finished do
% Loop until end of metafile.

  begin
  % Determine the type of the current item.
  GET ITEM TYPE FROM METAFILE (ws, itemtype, itemlength)
  % Now take the appropriate action according to itemtype.
  if itemtype = end-of-metafile then
    finished := true
  else
    begin
    % Obtain the item itself.
    READ ITEM FROM METAFILE (ws, maxlength, itemdata)
    % Process the item.
    INTERPRET ITEM (itemtype, itemdata)
    end
  end
```

Chapter 9
Styles of output

The visual style of output primitives is determined by **attributes**. *This chapter describes the attributes of each output primitive and the* **individual** *and* **bundled** *methods for their control.*

The appearance of an output primitive is completely defined by two kinds of information:

- **Geometry**   For example, for a polyline this is a list of points expressed in modelling coordinates.

- **Attributes**   These determine the style, such as whether a polyline is drawn dashed or dotted.

Attributes are divided into two classes: in the first class are attributes such as character height, which are closely connected with the geometry of a primitive, and are therefore independent of the capabilities of workstations. These are called **global attributes** (or **geometric attributes** or **workstation-independent** attributes). In the second class are those attributes which are not geometrical in nature, such as colour, and which may give different effects on different workstations. These are called **workstation-dependent** attributes (or **non-geometric attributes**).

In the following sections we describe the attributes associated with each kind of output primitive.

9.1   The attributes of polyline

Polyline has three workstation-dependent attributes: **linetype**, **linewidth scale factor** and **polyline colour index** (see Table 9.1). Linetype determines the style of the polyline, and is set using the following function:

[E]   SET LINETYPE
parameters:
        in   linetype   integer

Table 9.1   The attributes of polyline.

Global attributes	*Workstation-dependent attributes*
–	linetype
–	linewidth scale factor
–	polyline colour index

There are four predefined styles:

1   solid
2   dashed
3   dotted
4   dashed-dotted

It may appear strange that as few as four types are defined. The difficulty lies in selecting enough types to be useful, yet easily distinguishable, given that each workstation will have its own different interpretation of exactly what dotted or dashed means. Implementations may provide more linetypes, and these will be listed in your *Local Guide*.

Linewidth scale factor controls the width of lines. It is set using:

|E| SET LINEWIDTH SCALE FACTOR
    parameters:
        in   linewidth scale factor   real

Each workstation has a default linewidth, called its **nominal linewidth**, which is expressed in device coordinates. What the linewidth scale factor attribute speci-fies is the width of lines *relative* to the nominal linewidth of a workstation. For example, setting linewidth scale factor to 2.0 will cause lines to be drawn twice as thick as the nominal width; a value of 0.5 draws lines half as thick as the nominal width, and so on. With a linewidth scale factor less than zero, lines are drawn as thin as possible.

Because linewidth scale factor is a workstation-dependent attribute (it is not defined as part of the geometry of polyline), when a picture is scaled up or down, the widths of the polylines do not change. It is not difficult to think of applications when we would wish line widths to change according to the scale at which the picture is viewed. Modelling a printed circuit board, for example, we might use thick lines to represent the copper tracks in the artwork. If we enlarge a section of the picture for detailed editing, we would expect the whole picture to enlarge consistently – as it would if we were to inspect it with a lens. But, we cannot guarantee that a workstation can accurately display all widths of line, so the pic-ture may not look as expected. The correct approach in this case would be to draw the tracks using fill area or fill area set. On the other hand, we might not want

Table 9.2   The attributes of polymarker.

Global attributes	Workstation-dependent attributes
–	marker type
–	marker size scale factor
–	polymarker colour index

lines to change in thickness as we scale a picture. An artist preparing a layout would typically require to view the picture at various magnifications, and would want the line widths to stay unchanged.

The polyline colour index attribute determines the colour in which lines are drawn, and selects a colour from the workstation's colour table. It is set using:

[E]   SET POLYLINE COLOUR INDEX
parameters:
       in   colour index   integer

9.2   The attributes of polymarker

Polymarker has three workstation-dependent attributes: **marker type, marker size scale factor** and **polymarker colour index** (see Table 9.2). Marker type determines the kind of symbol used to mark each data point. It is set using:

[E]   SET MARKER TYPE
parameters:
       in   marker type   integer

Each kind of marker symbol has a number, and there are five predefined symbols, as follows:

1	dot	.
2	plus sign	+
3	asterisk	*
4	circle	o
5	diagonal cross	×

The marker size scale factor attribute controls the size of marker symbols, and it is specified in a similar way to line thickness:

[E]   SET MARKER SIZE SCALE FACTOR
parameters:
       in   scale factor   real

Table 9.3   The attributes of text.

Global attributes	Workstation-dependent attributes
character height	text font
character up vector	text precision
text path	character expansion factor
text alignment	character spacing
	text colour index

Each workstation has a nominal marker size, and the marker size scale factor selects a multiple of this size. A workstation will map the requested marker size onto the nearest size available. Dot markers, however, are an exception: they are always drawn as small as possible, regardless of the value of the marker size scale factor. The colour in which a polymarker is displayed is selected by the polymarker colour index, which selects a colour from the workstation's colour table. It is set using:

E SET POLYMARKER COLOUR INDEX
parameters:
     in   colour index   integer

9.3   The attributes of text

Of all the kinds of graphical output, text is by far the most complicated. It has both global and workstation-dependent attributes (see Table 9.3). We shall first describe the global attributes: **character height**, **text path**, **text orientation** and **text alignment**.

9.3.1   Character height

We can control the size of the characters used to draw text using:

E SET CHARACTER HEIGHT
parameters:
     in   character height   real

This sets the character height with which subsequent text will be drawn. For example, Figure 9.1 shows the result of the following:

```
SET CHARACTER HEIGHT (0.1)
TEXT 3 ((0.8, 0.3, 0), (1, 0, 0), (0, 1, 0), "SINE")
SET CHARACTER HEIGHT (0.04)
TEXT 3 ((0.8, 0.2, 0), (1, 0, 0), (0, 1, 0), "CURVE")
```

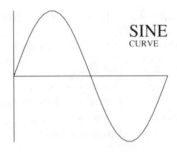

Figure 9.1   Changing character height.

9.3.2   Text path

We can control where successive characters in a string are placed, relative to the previous character, using the **text path** attribute, which can be left, right, up or down:

[E]   SET TEXT PATH
parameters:
         in   text path   (LEFT, RIGHT, UP, DOWN)

Figure 9.2 shows the effect of selecting each of these paths. The text position is marked with an asterisk.

```
                              H
                              T
                              A
                              P

                              P
                              U
                              *

    HTAP TFEL  *              *  RIGHT PATH

                              *
                              D
                              O
                              W
                              N

                              P
                              A
                              T
                              H
```

Figure 9.2   Different text paths.

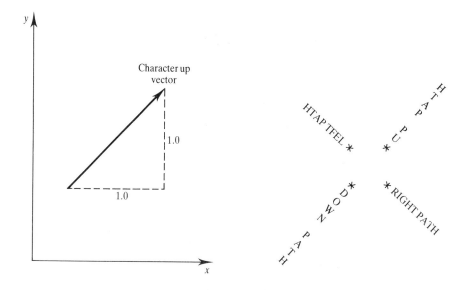

Figure 9.3   The character up vector.

9.3.3   Text orientation

We can control the orientation of text using the **character up vector**, which determines the upright direction of each character in the string. It is set using:

[E]   SET CHARACTER UP VECTOR
    parameters:
        in   character up vector   *x* and *y* components

We can set the character up vector rotated 45° anticlockwise from the *x* axis, as shown in Figure 9.3, using:

    SET CHARACTER UP VECTOR (1.0, 1.0)

The magnitude of the character up vector does not matter, since the vector is used only to specify a direction. Figure 9.3 also shows the effect of the orientation of the character up vector on the writing directions for each of the text paths. Notice that the up direction of each character is parallel to the character up vector, and the effect is that the entire text string is rotated according to the character up vector. A common mistake is to assume that the text string itself is drawn along the character up vector; the character up vector actually defines the orientation of each character.

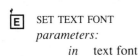

Figure 9.4   Examples of fonts.

9.3.4   Characters and fonts

The workstation-dependent attributes of text are **text font, text precision, character expansion factor, character spacing** and **text colour index**. Before describing these attributes, we shall look at how characters and fonts are defined in PHIGS.

A **font** is a collection of characters with a number of visual features in common: all the characters look as if they belong together. Figure 9.4 shows some examples of fonts. Text font is set using:

☒ | SET TEXT FONT
parameters:
    in   text font   integer

Fonts are workstation-dependent, which means that the font used to display a character string depends entirely on the capabilities of each workstation on which it is displayed. Every workstation must provide at least two different fonts, and in practice most workstations will provide many more (your *Local Guide* will have details). The shape of each character is determined precisely by the font designer as shown in Figure 9.5. Horizontally, a character has three reference lines, **left, centreline** and **right**. Vertically, there are five reference lines: **bottomline, baseline, halfline, capline** and **topline**.

9.3.5   Text alignment

Text alignment controls how a text string is positioned horizontally and vertically with respect to its reference point. It is set using:

☒ | SET TEXT ALIGNMENT
parameters:
    in   horizontal alignment   (NORMAL, LEFT,
                                                        CENTRE, RIGHT)
    in   vertical alignment   (NORMAL, TOP, CAP,
                                                        HALF, BASE, BOTTOM)

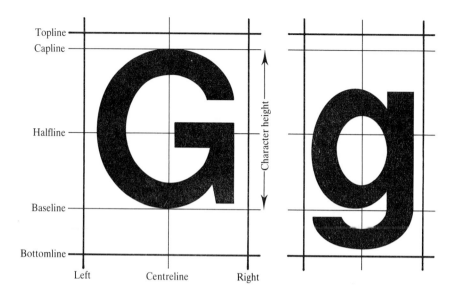

Figure 9.5 Defining a character.

The NORMAL values select default positioning which depends on the text path in effect:

Text path	NORMAL *alignments*
RIGHT	(LEFT, BASE)
LEFT	(RIGHT, BASE)
UP	(CENTRE, BASE)
DOWN	(CENTRE, TOP)

Figure 9.6 shows the result of the following:

```
SET TEXT ALIGNMENT (LEFT, NORMAL)
TEXT 3 ((0.1, 0.5, 0), (1, 0, 0), (0, 1, 0), "THIS TEXT")
TEXT 3 ((0.1, 0.4, 0), (1, 0, 0), (0, 1, 0), "IS")
TEXT 3 ((0.1, 0.3, 0), (1, 0, 0), (0, 1, 0), "LEFT")
TEXT 3 ((0.1, 0.3, 0), (1, 0, 0), (0, 1, 0), "ALIGNED")

SET TEXT ALIGNMENT (RIGHT, NORMAL)
TEXT 3 ((0.3, 0.5, 0), (1, 0, 0), (0, 1, 0), "THIS TEXT")
TEXT 3 ((0.3, 0.4, 0), (1, 0, 0), (0, 1, 0), "IS")
TEXT 3 ((0.3, 0.3, 0), (1, 0, 0), (0, 1, 0), "CENTRE")
TEXT 3 ((0.3, 0.3, 0), (1, 0, 0), (0, 1, 0), "ALIGNED")

SET TEXT ALIGNMENT (RIGHT, NORMAL)
```

THIS TEXT	THIS TEXT	THIS TEXT
IS	IS	IS
LEFT	CENTRE	RIGHT
ALIGNED	ALIGNED	ALIGNED

Figure 9.6   Examples of horizontal text alignment.

TEXT 3 ((0.6, 0.5, 0), (1, 0, 0), (0, 1, 0), "THIS TEXT")
TEXT 3 ((0.6, 0.4, 0), (1, 0, 0), (0, 1, 0), "IS")
TEXT 3 ((0.6, 0.3, 0), (1, 0, 0), (0, 1, 0), "RIGHT")
TEXT 3 ((0.6, 0.3, 0), (1, 0, 0), (0, 1, 0), "ALIGNED")

We can now combine these four text attributes to add some text to the sine curve
example of Chapter 3, as follows. Figure 9.7 shows the result of the following:

SET CHARACTER HEIGHT (0.15)
SET TEXT PATH (DOWN)
TEXT 3 ((0, 0.7, 0), (1, 0, 0), (0, 1, 0), "SINE X")
SET TEXT PATH (RIGHT)
SET CHARACTER UP VECTOR (−0.2, 0.1)
TEXT 3 ((0.2, 0.2, 0), (1, 0, 0), (0, 1, 0), "Going up...")
SET CHARACTER UP VECTOR (0.2, 0.1)
TEXT 3 ((0.5, −0.2, 0), (1, 0, 0), (0, 1, 0), "Going down...")
SET CHARACTER UP VECTOR (0, 1)
TEXT 3 ((0, −1, 0), (1, 0, 0), (0, 1, 0), "−1")
TEXT 3 ((0, 1, 0), (1, 0, 0), (0, 1, 0), "+1")
TEXT 3 ((0.05, 0, 0), (1, 0, 0), (0, 1, 0), "0")
TEXT 3 ((0.5, 0, 0), (1, 0, 0), (0, 1, 0), "PI")
TEXT 3 ((0.9, 0, 0), (1, 0, 0), (0, 1, 0), "2PI")

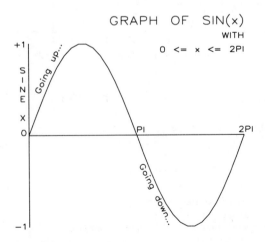

Figure 9.7   An example of the versatility of text.

```
SET CHARACTER HEIGHT (0.2)
SET TEXT ALIGNMENT (RIGHT, NORMAL)
TEXT 3 ((1, 1.2, 0), (1, 0, 0), (0, 1, 0), "GRAPH OF SIN(x)")
SET CHARACTER HEIGHT (0.15)
TEXT 3 ((1, 1, 0), (1, 0, 0), (0, 1, 0), "WITH")
TEXT 3 ((1, 0.8, 0), (1, 0, 0), (0, 1, 0), "0 <= x <= 2PI")
```

9.3.6   Text precision

We now turn to the workstation-dependent attributes of text, beginning with text precision. There are three levels of text precision, which determine how accurately text attributes are reflected in displayed text. In order of increasing fidelity, the levels of precision are STRING, CHAR and STROKE.

- STRING is the lowest level of precision, and is designed for producing text quickly and efficiently. The text string is generated in the specified font and positioned at the specified text position, and the workstation is expected to take into account the character height and character expansion factor as well as it can, but none of the other attributes need to be considered. If part of the string passes through a clipping boundary, the effect is implementation and workstation-dependent.

- CHAR precision produces text more accurately, because each character is processed separately. For each character, character height, character up vector and character expansion factor are evaluated as accurately as possible by the workstation, and character spacing is evaluated exactly. Clipping is performed on a per-character basis.

- STROKE precision has all the character attributes evaluated exactly. The term 'stroke' derives from the common technique of defining high-quality characters using collections of many short vectors. However, there is no requirement that fonts be encoded using vectors; many workstations will use raster font descriptions.

Text precision is set using:

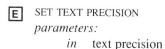

<pre>
E   SET TEXT PRECISION
     parameters:
         in   text precision   (STRING, CHAR, STROKE)
</pre>

Note, however, that it is quite permissible for a workstation to provide a font at a higher precision than you have specified.

9.3.7   Character expansion factor

The font designer specifies the default width-to-height ratio of characters. This can be changed using the character expansion factor attribute, which specifies a deviation from the default value, expressed as a real number:

EXPANSION = 0.5

EXPANSION = 1 (default)

EXPANSION = 1.5

EXPANSION = 2.5

EXPANSION = 3

Figure 9.8   Examples of character expansion.

E   SET CHARACTER EXPANSION FACTOR
parameters:
    in   expansion factor   real

For example, setting the character expansion factor to 2.0 will result in characters which are stretched to be twice as wide as normal, and setting it to 0.5 will squash characters to half their normal width (see Figure 9.8). The default value of the character expansion factor is 1.0, which gives the normal width-to-height ratio.

9.3.8   Character spacing

By default, the characters in a string are placed next to each other with their bodies touching, to give a neat, legible appearance. The character spacing attribute allows additional space to be inserted between character bodies, expressed as a fraction of the character height. It is set using:

E   SET CHARACTER SPACING
parameters:
    in   character spacing   real

With a character spacing of 1.0, adjacent characters will be separated by an additional space equal to the character height; setting it to a negative value will cause characters to overlap (see Figure 9.9). The value for normal spacing is 0.

SPACING = -0.2

SPACING = 0 (default)

S P A C I N G   =   1

S   P   A   C   I   N   G   =   2

S   P   A   C   I   N   G   =   3

Figure 9.9   Examples of character spacing.

9.3.9   Text extent

The **text extent rectangle** is an imaginary rectangle that precisely encloses the text string after taking into account the character height, character expansion factor, text path, character spacing and text font attributes.

When laying out pictures it is often useful to determine the extent rectangle of text before actually drawing it, for example to ensure that it does not overlap other features of the picture. This is done using:

☐   INQUIRE TEXT EXTENT
parameters:

in	workstation type	workstation type
in	text font	integer
in	character expansion factor	real
in	character spacing	real
in	character height	real
in	text path	(RIGHT, LEFT, UP, DOWN)
in	text alignment horizontal	(NORMAL, LEFT, CENTRE, RIGHT)
in	text alignment vertical	(NORMAL, TOP, CAP, HALF, BASE, BOTTOM)
in	character string	string
out	error	integer
out	text extent rectangle	(xmin, ymin, zmin), (xmax, ymax, zmax (TLC))
out	concatenation offset	two TLC vectors

This returns the text extent rectangle in Text Local Coordinates (TLC). To determine its corresponding value in modelling coordinates, it must be transformed to take into account the text position and the character up vector. The function also returns a concatenation offset, to enable the application to concatenate a new text string with an existing string, such that they appear to be a single uniform string. The horizontal and vertical components of text alignment refer to the appropriate parts of the text extent rectangle. Figure 9.10 shows some examples.

Finally, the colour in which text is drawn is determined by the text colour index attribute, set using SET TEXT COLOUR INDEX.

9.4   The attributes of fill area

Fill area has three workstation-dependent attributes – **interior style, interior style index** and **interior colour index** – and three global attributes – **pattern reference point, pattern reference vectors** and **pattern size**, summarized in Table 9.4.

Interior style determines how an area is filled, and is set using:

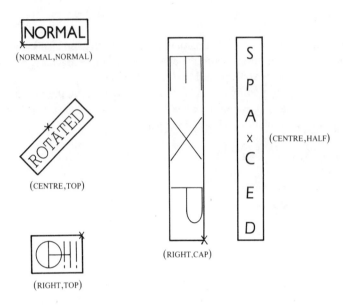

Figure 9.10   Examples of text extent.

E   SET INTERIOR STYLE
parameters:
        in   interior style   (HOLLOW, SOLID, PATTERN,
                                                  HATCH, EMPTY)

With HOLLOW style, the area is not filled at all; rather, the boundary is marked with a line. The colour of the line is determined by the interior colour index (set using SET INTERIOR COLOUR INDEX), which is an index into the workstation's colour table. However, the line used to draw the outline is *not* a polyline, and the application has no control over its thickness or style. With interior style SOLID, the interior of the fill area is filled with a colour, selected from the workstation's colour table by the interior colour index attribute. HATCH style is often used when colour is not available, and the interior is marked using sets of lines, with the hatching style selected by the interior style index (SET INTERIOR STYLE INDEX). With EMPTY, the filled area will not be visible. Table 9.5 summarizes the way the

Table 9.4   The attributes of fill area.

Global attributes	Workstation-dependent attributes
pattern reference point	interior style
pattern reference vectors	interior style index
pattern size	interior colour index

Table 9.5 Use of indices for fill area.

Interior style	Interior colour index	Interior style index
HOLLOW	colour of border	*not used*
SOLID	colour of interior	*not used*
PATTERN	*not used*	selects pattern from pattern table
HATCH	colour of hatching	selects hatch technique from hatch table
EMPTY	*not used*	*not used*

various indices are selected.

PATTERN interior style provides another way to fill an area, using a repeating pattern, and is illustrated in Figure 9.11. The basic unit of the pattern is a box of rectangular cells, which is replicated horizontally and vertically enough times to fill the area completely. The pattern box is defined as a parallelogram in the plane of the fill area. Its shape, and the position of the first instance of the pattern, are set using:

E SET PATTERN REFERENCE POINT AND VECTORS
parameters:
    in   reference point   3D MC point
    in   pattern reference vectors   two 3D MC vectors

The pattern reference vectors V_1 and V_2 are projected normal to the plane of the fill area to give two vectors in the plane, P_w and P_h, which define the shape of the pattern box, as shown in Figure 9.12. The lengths of P_w and P_h, which define the size of the pattern box, are set using the following function:

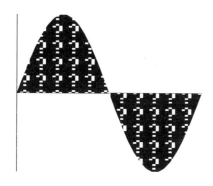

Figure 9.11 An example of PATTERN fill.

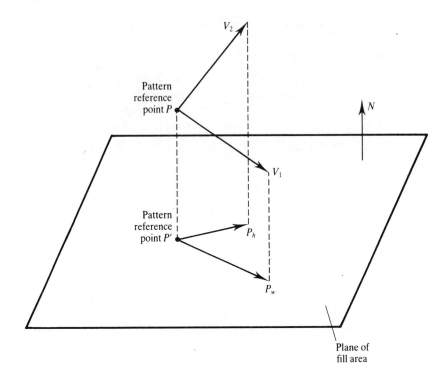

Figure 9.12   Projecting the pattern reference vectors.

E SET PATTERN SIZE
parameters:

in	pattern width	MC
in	pattern height	MC

The geometrical specification of pattern filling is workstation independent. However, the appearance of the pattern itself is defined on a per-workstation basis, using a pattern representation. A workstation has a **pattern table**, each entry of which specifies a grid of cells which will be mapped to the pattern box used to fill an area. Each cell in the grid is assigned a colour by specifying an index into the workstation's colour table. Each pattern box has dx cells horizontally, and dy cells vertically, as shown in Figure 9.13. By convention, cell (1, 1) is at the top left. A pattern is defined using:

☐ SET PATTERN REPRESENTATION
parameters:

in	workstation identifier	integer
in	pattern index	integer
in	pattern colour index array	array of integers

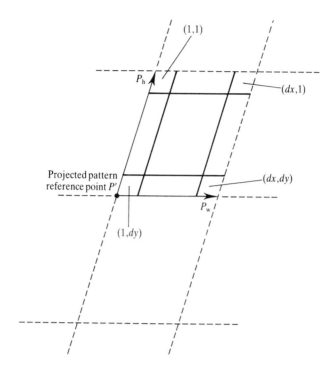

Figure 9.13   Defining the pattern box.

The representation of a pattern is specified independently of any coordinate system. When the pattern is generated, it is scaled to fit the size of the pattern box specified.

9.5   The attributes of fill area set

Fill area set has the same attributes as fill area. However, it is also possible to control how the edges of subareas are drawn, using a number of additional workstation-dependent attributes: **edge flag, edgetype, edgewidth scale factor** and **edge colour index** (see Table 9.6).

Edge flag controls whether or not the edges of the fill area set are drawn, and is set using:

 E   SET EDGE FLAG
       parameters:
              in   edge flag   (ON, OFF)

If the value is ON, the edges are drawn, subject to the edgetype, edgewidth scale

Table 9.6   The attributes of fill area set.

Global attributes	Workstation-dependent attributes
pattern reference point	interior style
pattern reference vectors	interior style index
pattern size	interior colour index
	edge flag
	edgetype
	edgewidth scale factor
	edge colour index

factor and edge colour index attributes. These control the visual appearance of displayed edges, and have the same meanings as the linetype, linewidth scale factor and polyline colour index attributes of polyline. They are set using the functions SET EDGETYPE, SET EDGEWIDTH SCALE FACTOR and SET EDGE COLOUR INDEX.

9.5.1   Interiors and edges

Sometimes, unusual effects are observed when edges are displayed in a fill area set, and it is useful to describe how the concepts of edge and interior are defined. From a mathematical point of view, the boundary of an area is distinct from the interior of the area, and this is reflected in the way PHIGS handles interiors and edges. As we saw in the previous section, interiors and edges have their own separate sets of attributes. However, there are some interactions between the two.

Fill area sets drawn with interior style EMPTY are visible only if the edge flag is ON. However, there is a practical problem of distinguishing precisely between interiors and edges on graphical output devices; for example, given the discreteness of a raster display, how can we decide whether a pixel is part of the interior or part of the edge of a region? To resolve this question, PHIGS defines that edges are drawn *on top of* any region filled as an interior. This can cause strange effects: in the case of a fill area set drawn with interior style HOLLOW, a polyline is drawn to mark the boundary of the interior (in the same way as for fill area). If the interior style is HOLLOW, edges are defined to be visible, and the edgetype is set to something other than solid (such as dashed), the polyline drawn around the boundary of the fill area set may be visible *underneath* the edge.

9.5.2   Fill area set and clipping

Fill area set is subject to clipping in exactly the same way as fill area. However, any new boundaries creating by clipping are not considered to be edges. Figure 9.14 illustrates how a clipped fill area set will be drawn for different values of

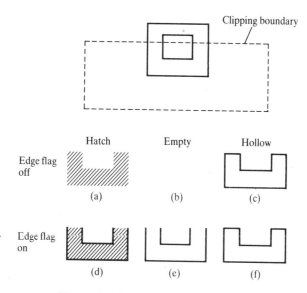

Figure 9.14   Clipping a fill area set.

interior style and edge flag. In Figure 9.14(f), although it is recommended that the bounding polyline includes the new boundaries generated by clipping, this is not mandatory.

9.6   The attributes of annotation text relative

The attributes of annotation text relative are summarized in Table 9.7.

The global attributes are analogous to those of the text primitive, but they refer in this case to the **annotation text local coordinate system**. This has its origin at the annotation point (obtained by adding the annotation offset to the transformed reference point), and its axes parallel to the x and y axes of NPC. The annotation style attribute determines the visual appearance of the annotation text, and is set using:

Table 9.7   The attributes of annotation text.

Global attributes	Workstation-dependent attributes
annotation text character height	text font
annotation text character up vector	text precision
annotation text path	character expansion factor
annotation text alignment	character spacing
annotation style	text colour index

E SET ANNOTATION STYLE
parameters:
        in   annotation style   integer

There are two predefined styles:

- **Style 1**   The annotation reference point is not visually connected to the annotation point.

- **Style 2**   The annotation reference point is connected to the annotation point with a straight line. The visual appearance of the line is determined by the current polyline attributes.

PHIGS does not preclude particular implementations providing additional annotation styles (perhaps involving arrows, or boxed text), but the use of these features will reduce the portability of applications. Annotation text also has a number workstation-dependent attributes, defined similarly to those of text, which are set using the functions SET ANNOTATION TEXT CHARACTER HEIGHT, SET ANNOTATION TEXT CHARACTER UP VECTOR, SET ANNOTATION TEXT PATH and SET ANNOTATION TEXT ALIGNMENT.

9.7   The attributes of GDP

The precise visual appearance of GDPs is left up to the workstation, which will use zero or more of the sets of polyline, polymarker, text, annotation text, fill area and fill area set attributes.

Workstations are expected to associate attributes with GDPs in the most appropriate ways. For example, a spline curve would probably use polyline attributes, and a filled ellipse might use fill area attributes. Exactly which sets of attributes the workstation will use for each GDP it supports are recorded in the WDT, and may be inquired using INQUIRE GENERALIZED DRAWING PRIMITIVE 3.

9.8   Colour

Colours are controlled on a per-workstation basis. Every workstation which can produce graphical output has a **colour table**, each entry of which defines a colour according to a particular set of conventions called a **colour model**. Colours are selected from the table using the appropriate colour index parameter (for polyline this is set using SET POLYLINE COLOUR INDEX), as shown in Figure 9.15. There are several different methods for specifying colours. Every PHIGS implementation must support at least the RGB and CIE LUV models, and others, such as HSV and HLS may be available. The RGB, CIE LUV, HSV and HLS models are described in Appendix F.

We select which colour model to use on a workstation with:

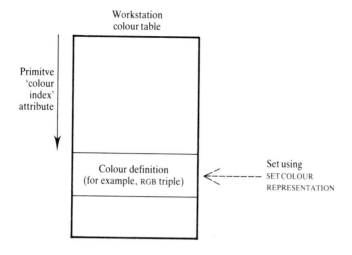

Figure 9.15   Selecting colours.

☐ SET COLOUR MODEL
parameters:
in	workstation identifier	integer
in	colour model	integer

This sets the colour model to be used by a particular workstation, and *colour model* is interpreted as follows:

1   RGB
2   CIE LUV
3   HSV
4   HLS

To set the contents of entry *index* in the colour table on *workstation* we use the SET COLOUR REPRESENTATION function:

☐ SET COLOUR REPRESENTATION
parameters:
in	workstation identifier	integer
in	index	integer
in	colour	colour tuple

The workstation colour table is the only method PHIGS supports for specifying and selecting colours. When an application changes the contents of a workstation's colour table, it will have an immediate effect on any output displayed on the workstation. This is illustrated by the following example, which simulates

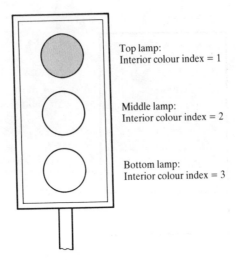

Top lamp:
Interior colour index = 1

Middle lamp:
Interior colour index = 2

Bottom lamp:
Interior colour index = 3

Figure 9.16   Traffic lights (at 'stop').

the operation of (British) traffic lights, as shown in Figure 9.16.

Each lamp is drawn as a fill area with using SOLID interior style, and the interior colour index selects the appropriate colour. If we subsequently change the colour representation on the workstation, the colour of the displayed traffic lights will change accordingly. We use SET INTERIOR COLOUR INDEX to draw each fill area using colour indices 1, 2 and 3 respectively.

```
OPEN STRUCTURE (traffic lights)
SET INTERIOR STYLE (SOLID)
SET INTERIOR COLOUR INDEX (1)      % The top light, colour 1.
FILL AREA 3 (top lamp)
SET INTERIOR COLOUR INDEX (2)      % The middle light, colour 2.
FILL AREA 3 (middle lamp)
SET INTERIOR COLOUR INDEX (3)      % The bottom light, colour 3.
FILL AREA 3 (bottom lamp)
CLOSE STRUCTURE
```

Initially, the lights are at 'stop', so we want the top lamp red and the others off (black). After two seconds, the lights change to red and amber, so we redefine entries 1 and 2 in the colour table accordingly. Finally, after another two seconds, the lights are 'go', so we reset the colours again:

```
SET COLOUR MODEL (ws, 1)                        % Select RGB colour model.
SET COLOUR REPRESENTATION (ws, 1, (1, 0, 0))    % Colour 1 = red.
SET COLOUR REPRESENTATION (ws, 2, (0, 0, 0))    % Colour 2 = black.
SET COLOUR REPRESENTATION (ws, 3, (0, 0, 0))    % Colour 3 = black.

POST STRUCTURE (ws, traffic lights, 1.0)        % Display the traffic lights.
```

```
sleep (2)                                        % Wait, then set red and amber.
SET COLOUR REPRESENTATION (ws, 1, (1, 0, 0))     % Colour 1 = red.
SET COLOUR REPRESENTATION (ws, 2, (1, 0.7, 0))   % Colour 2 = amber.
SET COLOUR REPRESENTATION (ws, 3, (0, 0, 0))     % Colour 3 = black.

sleep (2)                                        % Wait, then set green.
SET COLOUR REPRESENTATION (ws, 1, (0, 0, 0))     % Colour 1 = black.
SET COLOUR REPRESENTATION (ws, 2, (0, 0, 0))     % Colour 2 = black.
SET COLOUR REPRESENTATION (ws, 3, (0, 1, 0))     % Colour 3 = green.
```

Every output workstation must provide at least two colours, but PHIGS sets no maximum limit on the number available. An application can inquire the size of a particular workstation's colour table, and choose an appropriate range of colours to use.

9.9 Bundled attributes

We have actually been rather loose in our description of primitive attributes. To be precise, the visual appearance of an output primitive is determined by data called **aspects**, and we use **attributes** to control their value. Aspects come in two kinds: global and workstation dependent.

Each global aspect, such as character height, is controlled by a corresponding attribute, which is set using a structure element, such as SET CHARACTER HEIGHT. This is the only method of controlling the global aspects of a primitive.

For the workstation-dependent aspects, however, the application has two methods at its disposal:

- **Individual**   The value of the aspect is controlled using an attribute set with a structure element.

- **Bundled**   The value of the aspect is obtained from an entry in a workstation table. The entry is selected by the **primitive index** attribute.

Each workstation that can produce graphical output has a separate table for each primitive, in which is stored a number of **bundles** (or **representations**), comprising each of the workstation-dependent aspects of the primitive. Figure 9.17 illustrates the polyline bundle table. Here, each entry contains a value for linetype, linewidth and polyline colour index. When a workstation is opened, each bundle table is pre-initialized to give a range of different representations. Every output primitive has a **primitive index**, which selects a representation from the primitive's bundle table. This is set using a function of the form SET XXX INDEX, where XXX may be POLYLINE, POLYMARKER, EDGE, INTERIOR or TEXT. For example, two polylines may be drawn using different representations as follows:

```
SET POLYLINE INDEX (1)
POLYLINE 3 (points)
```

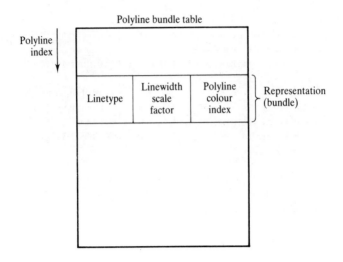

Figure 9.17   Selecting a representation using the primitive index.

```
SET POLYLINE INDEX (2)
POLYLINE 3 (points)
```

A representation is set using a function of the form SET XXX REPRESENTATION, where XXX may be POLYLINE, POLYMARKER, TEXT, INTERIOR and EDGE. For example, the function for polyline is:

SET POLYLINE REPRESENTATION
parameters:

in	workstation identifier	integer
in	index	integer
in	linetype	integer
in	linewidth scale factor	real
in	polyline colour index	integer

This sets the workstation-dependent attributes of the primitive in entry *index* of the polyline bundle table on workstation *workstation identifier*.

It is good programming style to define all the representations required at the start of an application program, and then to subsequently select the appropriate one. The alternative is to scatter definitions of representations throughout the program, which is not a good idea. To see why, consider the changes involved in moving a program from one PHIGS installation to another. We want to make the best use of the workstations at our disposal, so it is likely that we will want to adjust each representation accordingly. Collecting all the definitions of representations into one place makes this much easier.

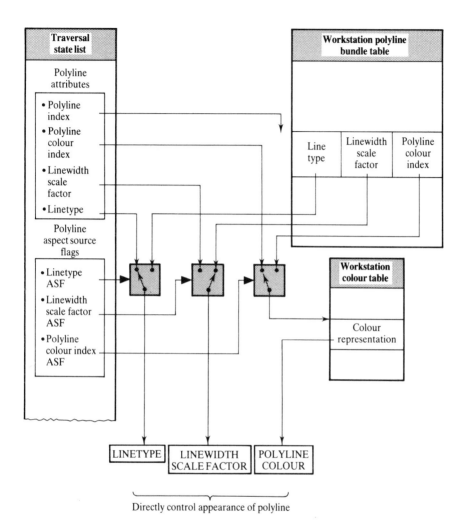

Figure 9.18 Aspects, attributes and ASFs.

9.10 Aspect source flags

For each of the primitive aspects, the application can specify whether the individual or bundled method is used to control it, by setting an **Aspect Source Flag** (**ASF**) for each aspect. Figure 9.18 illustrates how this works. It is normal practice to select either individual or bundled control as the default for an application, and which method is adopted is really a matter of programming style. For programs which are intended to be portable, the bundled method does offer some advantages, since it is easier to organize aspect specifications into calls to SET

XXX REPRESENTATION in a single place in the program, and then subsequently to use primitive indices to access the representations. The function to set an ASF is:

☐E☐   SET INDIVIDUAL ASF
parameters:
      in   aspect identifier   name of aspect
      in   aspect source   (BUNDLED, INDIVIDUAL)

It is possible to mix the use of individual and bundled control for different aspects, but this can be very confusing, and is best avoided.

Chapter 10
Archiving

So far we have described how to create and edit models, and how to produce pictures of them on workstations. In this chapter we cover the facilities for **saving** *models in* **archive files**, *and subsequently* **retrieving** *them into the CSS.*

Many programs which are used repeatedly contain code to create parts of the model which are essentially the same from run to run. PHIGS therefore provides a mechanism for saving parts of the CSS to a special kind of file called an **archive**, and retrieving structures from an archive into the CSS. This is illustrated in Figure 10.1.

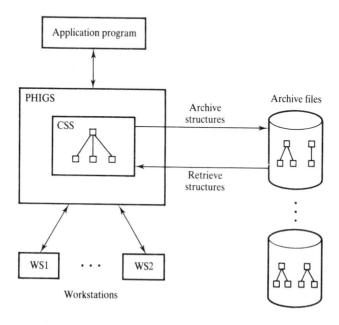

Figure 10.1   The archive file mechanism.

157

10.1   Creating an archive

An archive file is opened using:

▢   OPEN ARCHIVE FILE
parameters:
      in   archive identifier   integer
      in   file   file name

File is the name of the external file which will contain the archive. The application assigns each archive file an identifier using the *archive identifier* parameter, and it is this name (rather than the name of the external file) which is subsequently used to refer to the archive. If the archive file already exists, it will be opened. Otherwise, a new file will be created. An archive file cannot be opened for read-only access; it is always a readable and writeable file. More than one archive may be open at a time, up to an implementation-dependent maximum number, which may be inquired using INQUIRE PHIGS FACILITIES.

Once the application has finished with an archive, it should be closed, using:

▢   CLOSE ARCHIVE FILE
parameters:
      in   archive identifier   integer

10.2   Saving structures to archives

There are a number of functions for storing structures on an archive, and we shall look at each in turn. The following is the simplest, and copies all the structures in the CSS to the archive specified by *archive identifier*:

▢   ARCHIVE ALL STRUCTURES
parameters:
      in   archive identifier   integer

This is quite different from *posting* a structure to a workstation: if a posted structure is subsequently edited it may be updated automatically on the workstation. This does not happen with any of the archive functions, which effectively take snapshots of the CSS which are stored on archives. It is the responsibility of the application to keep the contents of archives synchronized with the CSS.

We can copy the whole CSS to an archive as follows:

    OPEN ARCHIVE (archive identifier, file name)
    ARCHIVE ALL STRUCTURES (archive identifier)
    CLOSE ARCHIVE (archive identifier)

Returning to the cube program, instead of posting the structure to the workstation

for display, we shall save it to an archive it for later use. To do this we open
an archive file, write the structure to the archive, and then close the archive, as
follows:

```
#include <phigs.h>

#define ARID 1

#include "makecube.c"

main()
{
    popenphigs(0,0);

    MakeCube();

    popenarchivefile(ARID,"cube.arc");

    parchiveallstruct(ARID);

    pclosearchivefile(ARID);

    pclosephigs()
}
```

Section 10.5 gives the 'other half' of the cube program, which restores the structure from the archive.

Sometimes, it may not be appropriate to archive all the structures in the CSS.
For example, in a molecular modelling system, the display might include menus
and prompt messages as well as molecules, and the application may wish to save
only molecules in an archive. In this case one of the following two functions may
be used:

☐ ARCHIVE STRUCTURE NETWORKS
parameters:

in	archive identifier	integer
in	list of root structure identifiers	list of integers

The supplied list of root structures together with all their descendants (children,
grandchildren and so on) are archived to the archive file specified by *archive
identifier*.

The next function is similar, but only those structures specified in *list of
structure identifiers* are archived:

☐ ARCHIVE STRUCTURES
parameters:

in	archive identifier	integer
in	list of structure identifiers	list of integers

10.3   Conflict resolution

The problem of conflict resolution arises in many aspects of computing, in various guises. For example, suppose you use a text editor to create a file called 'fred'. Then, sometime later, you attempt to create a file with the same name. You might expect the operating system to tell you that the file you are about to create already exists. Alternatively, you may know that 'fred' already exists and intend the new version to overwrite the older version.

This kind of conflict also arises with archives. Suppose we have already created an archive containing structure *A*. What should PHIGS do if we now open the same archive and attempt to write another structure also called *A* to it? In some circumstances, we may want an error to be reported (and no overwriting to occur); or, it may be desirable to let the new *A* overwrite the *A* already in the archive. We specify the required action by setting an *archive conflict flag*, using the function:

☐   SET CONFLICT RESOLUTION
parameters:

in	archive conflict flag	(UPDATE, ABANDON, MAINTAIN)
in	retrieve conflict flag	(UPDATE, ABANDON, MAINTAIN)

To illustrate, suppose an archive file already contains a structure, *A*, and we call ARCHIVE STRUCTURES specifying *A* and *B* to be copied from the CSS into the archive. This is illustrated in Figure 10.2. Structure *B* will be straightforwardly written to the archive, but structure *A* poses a problem. Because the archive already contains a structure called *A*, a conflict of names occurs. What happens next depends on the setting of *archive conflict flag*, which may take the following values:

- UPDATE   The structure *A* from the CSS overwrites the *A* which is already on the archive file.

- ABANDON   The entire archiving operation is abandoned, and an error is reported. The state of the archive is as if ARCHIVE STRUCTURES had never been called. That is, neither *A* nor *B* is written, and the archive contains only the original structure *A*.

- MAINTAIN   The new *A* is not written to the archive, and so the archive contains only *B* – the storage of which caused no conflict – and the original *A*.

The *archive conflict flag* applies to all archives; there is no separate flag associated with each archive. We shall discuss *retrieve conflict flag* in Section 10.5.

Before:

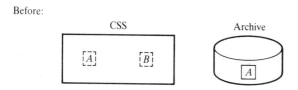

After calling ARCHIVE STRUCTURES (archive, [A, B]):

Conflict resolution flag	Final state of archive	Action
UPDATE		Original $\boxed{A}$ in archive is lost. $\boxed{A}$ and $\boxed{B}$ are written.
ABANDON		Neither $\boxed{A}$ nor $\boxed{B}$ are written.
MAINTAIN		Original $\boxed{A}$ remains in archive. $\boxed{B}$ is written.

Figure 10.2   Controlling conflict resolution.

10.4   Anticipating conflicts

To enable the application to pre-empt conflicts there are two functions which compare the contents of an archive file with the CSS. The first returns a list of structures that exist in both the CSS and the archive:

☐   INQUIRE ALL CONFLICTING STRUCTURES
    parameters:
        in   archive identifier   integer
        out error   integer
        out list of structure identifiers   list of integers

The second function determines any conflicts which may exist for all the structures in a particular structure network:

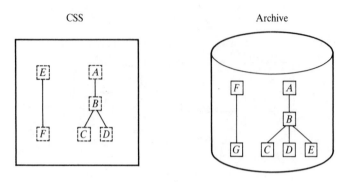

CSS   Archive

INQUIRE ALL CONFLICTING STRUCTURES (archive, error, list)
        list = A, B, C, D, E, F

INQUIRE CONFLICTING STRUCTURES IN NETWORK (archive, A, CSS, error, list)
        list = A, B, C, D

INQUIRE CONFLICTING STRUCTURES IN NETWORK (archive, A, ARCHIVE, error, list)
        list = A, B, C, D, E

Figure 10.3   Inquiring conflicting structures.

☐   INQUIRE CONFLICTING STRUCTURES IN NETWORK
     parameters:

in	archive identifier	integer
in	structure identifier	integer
in	structure network source	(CSS, ARCHIVE)
out	error	integer
out	list of structure identifiers	list of integers

If *structure network source* is CSS, the function obtains from the CSS a list of all the structures which are descendants of *structure identifier*. This list of structure identifiers is then compared with the contents of the archive file, and those structure identifiers which are common are returned in *list of structure identifiers*. If *structure network source* is ARCHIVE, the descendants of *structure identifier* are obtained from the archive, and are compared with the structures in the CSS. The use of these functions is illustrated in Figure 10.3.

10.5   Retrieving structures from archives

The following function copies all the structures in the specified archive file to the CSS:

☐ RETRIEVE ALL STRUCTURES
parameters:
    in   archive identifier   integer

This function is subject to a conflict resolution flag, *retrieve conflict flag*, which is set using SET CONFLICT RESOLUTION. Conflict resolution for retrieving from an archive operates in exactly the same way as storing to an archive, as described in Section 10.3. We specify the action using:

☐ SET CONFLICT RESOLUTION
parameters:
    in   archive conflict flag   (UPDATE, ABANDON,
                                         MAINTAIN)
    in   retrieve conflict flag   (UPDATE, ABANDON,
                                         MAINTAIN)

Retrieve conflict flag takes one of three values, which correspond to those of *archive conflict flag*:

- UPDATE   The structures retrieved from the archive overwrite those in the CSS.

- ABANDON   The entire retrieval operation is abandoned, and an error message is generated. The CSS is not disturbed.

- MAINTAIN   Structures which do not cause conflicts are retrieved. Structures which cause conflicts are not.

Structures copied into the CSS from an archive are not automatically posted to any workstations. In fact, to display the model, the application must have prior knowledge of which structures in the archive are the roots of structure networks. It can then retrieve a list of structures and their descendants from the archive, using:

☐ RETRIEVE STRUCTURE NETWORKS
parameters:
        in   archive identifier   integer
        in   list of root structure identifiers   list of integers

The following function is the analogue of ARCHIVE STRUCTURES, and retrieves the structures specified in *list of root structure identifiers*.

☐ RETRIEVE STRUCTURES
parameters:
        in   archive identifier   integer
        in   list of structure identifiers   list of integers

We shall now give the program to read the archive containing the cube structure, and retrieve the structure into the CSS. Then, we shall edit it to make it spin, exactly as in Chapter 2.

```c
#include <phigs.h>

#define CUBE 1
#define WS 1
#define ARID 1
#define WSTYPE 0
#define PRIORITY 1
#define PI 3.141592654

main()
{
    static Ppoint3 origin = {0.5,0.5,0.5};
    static Pvector3 shift = {0.0,0.0,0.0};
    static Pvector3 scale = {1,1,1};

    Pint err, i;
    Pmatrix3 transform;
    float angle;

    popenphigs(0, 0);                       /* Open PHIGS. */

    popenws(WS, 0, 0);                      /* Open a workstation. */

    popenarchivefile(ARID,"cube.arc");  /* Open the archive. */
    pretrieveallstruct(ARID);               /* Retrieve the cube. */
    pclosearchivefile(ARID);                /* Close the archive. */

    psetdisplayupdatest(WS, PASAP, PUQUM);

    ppoststruct(WS, CUBE, PRIORITY);    /* Post the structure. */

    popenstruct(CUBE);                      /* Open the structure. */

    pseteditmode(PEDIT_REPLACE);        /* Select REPLACE mode. */

    psetelemptr(1);

    for (i=0; i<361; i++){                  /* Edit the */
        angle = i*PI/180;                   /* transformation. */
        pbuildtran3(&origin, &shift, angle,angle,angle,
                    &scale, &err, transform);
        psetlocaltran3(transform, PREPLACE);
    }

    pclosews(WS);                           /* Close the workstation. */
    pclosephigs();                          /* Close PHIGS. */
}
```

10.6   Archive inquiry functions

Because an application program explicitly creates the CSS, it can keep track of which structure identifiers are used and which ones are roots of structure networks. During retrieval the application may not have this information: there can be no guarantee that the correct archive file has been opened, or that its contents are as expected. Therefore, PHIGS provides functions for an application to inquire about the contents of an archive file before attempting any retrieval operations. There are three functions for this purpose, as follows:

☐ RETRIEVE STRUCTURE IDENTIFIERS
  parameters:
in	archive identifier	integer
in	list of structure identifiers	list of integers

This returns a list of structures which are present in the specified archive.

☐ RETRIEVE PATHS TO ANCESTORS
  parameters:
in	archive identifier	integer
in	structure identifier	integer
in	path order	(TOPFIRST, BOTTOMFIRST)
in	path depth	integer
out	paths	list of paths

This is similar in operation to INQUIRE PATHS TO ANCESTORS (see Section 11.2.8), but it obtains the information from the specified archive file.

☐ RETRIEVE PATHS TO DESCENDANTS
  parameters:
in	archive identifier	integer
in	structure identifier	integer
in	path order	(TOPFIRST, BOTTOMFIRST)
in	path depth	integer
out	paths	list of paths

This is similar to INQUIRE PATHS TO DESCENDANTS (see Section 11.2.7). Figure 10.4 illustrates the use of these functions. An application may have several archive files open at a time, and the following function returns a list of the archive identifiers and corresponding file names of open archive files:

☐ INQUIRE ARCHIVE FILES
  parameters:
out	error	integer
out	list of archive identifiers	list of integers
out	list of archive file names	list of names

Archive

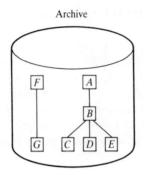

RETRIEVE STRUCTURE IDENTIFIERS (archive, list)
list = A, B, C, D, E, F, G

RETRIEVE PATHS TO ANCESTORS (archive, D, BOTTOMFIRST, error, paths)
paths = $<D, B, A>$

RETRIEVE PATHS TO DESCENDANTS (archive, A, TOPFIRST, error, paths)
paths = $<A, B, C>, <A, B, D>, <A, B, E>$

Figure 10.4   Inquiring the contents of an archive.

10.7   Deleting structures from archives

We can delete structures from an archive using the following functions:

☐   DELETE ALL STRUCTURES FROM ARCHIVE
parameters:
    in   archive identifier   integer

This function removes all structures from the specified archive file. The following function deletes the structures in *list of root structure identifiers*, and all their descendants:

☐   DELETE STRUCTURE NETWORKS FROM ARCHIVE
parameters:
    in   archive identifier   integer
    in   list of root structure identifiers   list of integers

This function has a peculiarity. Suppose that both structures A and B contain EXECUTE STRUCTURE elements which refer to structure C. If we call DELETE STRUCTURE NETWORKS FROM ARCHIVE specifying A, both A and C will be deleted, even though C is a descendant of B. Unlike the CSS, the corresponding EXECUTE STRUCTURE element will not be removed from B. It is valid for a structure in an archive to have EXECUTE STRUCTURE elements which refer to structures that are not in the archive.

The following function deletes the structures in *list of structure identifiers*:

☐ DELETE STRUCTURES FROM ARCHIVE
parameters:

in	archive identifier	integer
in	list of structure identifies	list of integers

In common with the previous function, this can also result in structures with descendants which are not in the archive.

Chapter 11
More about the CSS

---

*In this chapter we describe additional facilities for managing data in the CSS:
grouping using* **names** *and* **filters**, **inquiring** *about the CSS*, **searching** *for structure elements*, **generalized structure elements** *and* **application data**.

Sometimes it is convenient to group together items in the CSS independently
of the hierarchical relationships that exist between them. For example, for the
bicycle shown in Figure 11.1, we might wish to group together all those parts
made by a particular manufacturer, or those made from a certain material, and so
on. For this purpose PHIGS provides a mechanism to attach one or more **names**
to an output primitive structure element, such that all primitives with the same
names can be considered to belong to the same group. We shall look first at how
to construct groups using names, and then at how to manipulate the groups.

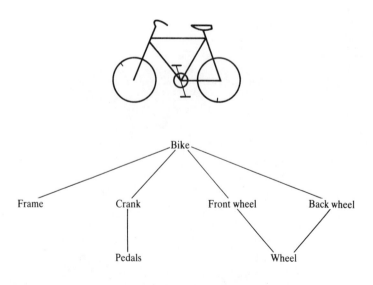

Figure 11.1   The bicycle.

The principle is simple: during the traversal of a structure a list of names called the **name set** is maintained, as part of the Traversal State List (TSL). Whenever an output primitive structure element is encountered in traversal, the names which are in the name set at that time become permanently attached to the primitive, just like other primitive attributes such as linetype or character height. When traversal begins, the name set is initially empty, but its contents are changed when either of two special structure elements is encountered during the traversal: one to add new names to the set and one to remove existing names from the set. The functions to create these elements are, respectively:

E | ADD NAMES TO SET
parameters:
    in   names to add   list of names

E | REMOVE NAMES FROM SET
parameters:
    in   names to remove   list of names

Imagine we want to group the crank and the frame together because they are made by the same manufacturer, Smith. We can use names to do this, by including an ADD NAMES TO SET element in the definition of each structure. We would do this for the crank structure as follows:

```
OPEN STRUCTURE (crank)
ADD NAMES TO SET (Smith)          % Element to attach the name.
POLYLINE 3 (crank points)         % Polyline to draw the crank.
REMOVE NAMES FROM SET (Smith)     % Element to remove the name.
EXECUTE STRUCTURE (pedals)
CLOSE STRUCTURE
```

Now, when the structure is traversed, the name Smith is attached to the polyline which draws the crank. The name set obeys exactly the same rules as other attributes: Smith will also be attached to all subsequent output primitives in the *crank* structure, unless the name set is changed again. In the same way, a child structure will inherit the current name set from its parent, and a posted structure will inherit its name set (which will be initially empty) from the PHIGS description table, and so on. This can be very useful: for the bicycle, we could give all the parts the name Smith by simply including the ADD NAMES TO SET element at a high enough position in the structure network, such as the *bike* structure.

In this example, however, the name Smith only applies to the polyline for the crank, because the next element in the structure removes the name from the name set. If this were not done, Smith would still be in the name set when the *pedals* structure is executed, and all its primitives would inherit the name. With complex networks, it is important to be careful with the assignation of names, and it is safer to localize modifications to the name set to avoid names becoming attached to the wrong primitives.

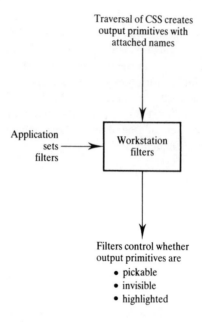

Traversal of CSS creates
output primitives with
attached names

Application
sets
filters

Workstation
filters

Filters control whether
output primitives are
- pickable
- invisible
- highlighted

Figure 11.2   Workstation filters.

11.1   Names and filters

Assigning names is only useful if there is a way to refer subsequently to the named groups. This is done by applying **workstation filters** to names to control three different properties of output primitives, **pickability**, **invisibility** and **highlighting**, as shown in Figure 11.2. We shall look at each property in turn:

- Pickability   The pickability of an output primitive determines whether or not it is sensitive to the operator pointing at it using a pick device. If a primitive is specified to be *not pickable*, the primitive can never be selected using pick input. This can be very useful; for example, an interactive diagram editing program might display a status line – distinct from the diagram – which gives information about the current state of the program and the drawing parameters that are in effect. If the operator can choose which part of the diagram to edit by picking, it would not be sensible to allow the operator to select the status line to be edited. One way to achieve this is to use names to make all the output primitives not pickable in the structures which draw the status line.

- **Invisibility**   Output primitives may be visible or invisible on a workstation. If part of a picture is to be displayed only in certain circumstances, rather than erasing and redrawing it when necessary, which may be slow if the picture is complex, it is often more efficient to draw it only once, and then subsequently control its visibility. The intention is that this mechanism will be implemented within the hardware of the workstation itself, and many devices do in fact provide this facility.

- **Highlighting**   It is often necessary to draw the operator's attention to part of the picture by temporarily making some primitives highlighted, so that they stand out from the rest of the display. This might be done by making them brighter, drawing them in a special colour reserved for highlighting, or by flashing them on and off.

We can illustrate the use of grouping, names and filters using the bicycle example. Here, each structure element is annotated to show how it will change the contents of the name set during traversal.

OPEN STRUCTURE (bike)	% Initially, name set = [ ].
ADD NAMES TO SET (Smith)	% Name set = [Smith].
EXECUTE STRUCTURE (frame)	
EXECUTE STRUCTURE (crank)	
ADD NAMES TO SET (Jones)	% Name set = [Smith, Jones].
EXECUTE STRUCTURE (front wheel)	
REMOVE NAMES FROM SET (Smith)	% Name set = [Jones].
EXECUTE STRUCTURE (back wheel)	
CLOSE STRUCTURE	

This has the effect of attaching names to output primitives in structures as follows:

Structure	Names
frame	Smith
crank	Smith
front wheel	Smith, Jones
back wheel	Jones

Now, before an output primitive is actually displayed on a workstation, each of its attached names (if it has any) is compared against a number of filters contained in the workstation, as shown in Figure 11.3. Each filter contains a list of names which determine the invisibility, pickability and highlighting attributes for the primitive. There is a pair of filters for invisibility, a pair for highlighting, and a pair for every pick input device on the workstation, as follows:

- the invisibility inclusion and exclusion filters

- the highlighting inclusion and exclusion filters

- the pick inclusion and exclusion filters (for each pick device)

Although this arrangement may seem complicated, the way the filters work is in fact quite straightforward. Consider the polyline which draws the frame of the bicycle, and which has the attached name Smith. Before the polyline is displayed

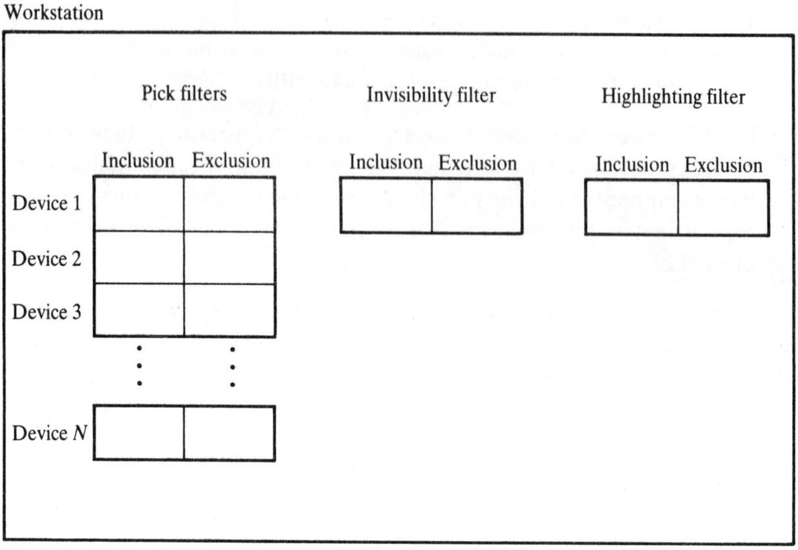

Workstation

Figure 11.3 Workstation filters.

on the workstation, any names it has (Smith) are compared against the two high-lighting filters on the workstation. If Smith appears in the list of names contained in the highlighting **inclusion** filter, the polyline will be displayed on the workstation, and it will be highlighted. If, however, Smith is in the highlighting **exclusion** filter, the polyline will still be displayed, but it will not be highlighted. The same tests are made for the invisibility inclusion and exclusion filters and (while a pick input operation is in progress) for the pickability inclusion and exclusion filters.

To illustrate this mechanism, imagine that the highlighting and invisibility filters of a particular workstation are set as shown below (an entry of '–' means that the filter does not contain any names):

Filter	*Inclusion part*	*Exclusion part*
invisibility	–	Smith
highlighting	Smith	Jones
pick (for device *n*)	Smith	–

If the bicycle structure is now posted to this workstation, the following attributes would be assigned for the output primitives in each structure (the *pickable* attribute refers only to the use of pick device number *n* on the workstation):

Structure	Names	Attributes
frame	Smith	visible, highlighted, pickable
crank	Smith	visible, highlighted, pickable
front wheel	Smith, Jones	visible, not highlighted, pickable
back wheel	Jones	visible, not highlighted, not pickable

If we now change the contents of the workstation's invisibility inclusion filter to be [Jones], then all those primitives with the name Jones will become invisible: this will cause the front and back wheels to disappear, and the displayed picture will be automatically updated.

The contents of each of the workstation filters are set using the following functions:

☐ SET HIGHLIGHTING FILTER

parameters:

in	workstation identifier	integer
in	inclusion set names	list of names
in	exclusion set names	list of names

☐ SET INVISIBILITY FILTER

parameters:

in	workstation identifier	integer
in	inclusion set names	list of names
in	exclusion set names	list of names

☐ SET PICK FILTER

parameters:

in	workstation identifier	integer
in	pick device number	integer
in	inclusion set names	list of names
in	exclusion set names	list of names

These functions do not create structure elements; they are analogous to setting workstation representations.

Names are actually integers, and that at least those in the range $0-63$ must be provided. A particular implementation may provide more, and you can find out about your own implementation using the INQUIRE PHIGS FACILITIES function, or consulting your *Local Guide*. As always, it is good practice use symbolic constants for names, instead of explicit integers which you can very quickly lose track of.

11.1.1 A common problem with picking

You may discover that you cannot pick anything at all! In fact, this is the default situation, where all output primitives are visible, not highlighted, and not pickable. It is necessary to attach names explicitly and set the pick filters accordingly for any output primitives which you require to be pickable. The following example illustrates how to create a structure containing a polyline which will be pickable using pick input device *dev* on workstation *ws*:

```
OPEN STRUCTURE (example)
ADD NAMES TO SET (poly)
POLYLINE 3 (...)
REMOVE NAMES FROM SET (poly)
CLOSE STRUCTURE

SET PICK FILTER (ws, dev, [ poly ], [ ])
```

Because the pick filter inclusion set contains the name *poly*, and the exclusion set is empty, any primitives which have the name *poly* will be pickable (primitives which do not have the name *poly* will remain not pickable). A simple way to make all primitives in a structure network pickable is to place an appropriate ADD NAMES TO SET element in the root structure, so that the name is inherited by all its descendants.

11.1.2 A more formal definition

What happens if a name appears in both the inclusion and exclusion parts of a filter, or if a name appears in neither? To be eligible for an attribute, such as highlighting, the primitive's name set must have at least one member in the appropriate inclusion set, and should not have any member in the exclusion set. We can summarize the various combinations as follows, for the name Smith and the highlighting filters:

Name	Inclusion set	Exclusion set	Effect
Smith	–	–	not highlighted
Smith	Smith	–	highlighted
Smith	–	Smith	not highlighted
Smith	Smith	Smith	not highlighted

We can express this formally. If we define:

N as the current name set (in the TSL)
S as a set of names
I as the highlighting/invisibility/pick inclusion set
E as the highlighting/invisibility/pick exclusion set
$\varnothing$ as the empty set

then the effect of ADD NAMES TO SET (*S*) is to modify *N* as follows (the symbol $\cup$ indicates the union of two sets):

$$N \leftarrow N \cup S$$

The effect of REMOVE NAMES FROM SET (*S*) is:

$$N \leftarrow N - S$$

A primitive will be eligible for highlighting, invisibility or picking if the following condition is true (the symbol $\cap$ signifies the intersection of two sets):

$$(N \cap I \neq \varnothing) \quad \text{AND} \quad (N \cap E = \varnothing)$$

If $N = \varnothing$ or $I = \varnothing$ then no primitive will ever be included, and if $E = \varnothing$ nothing that is included will be excluded.

11.2   Inquiring about the CSS

As well as functions for creating and editing structures and structure networks, there is a set of functions to enable the application to inquire about the contents of the CSS. This facility is vital for a variety of reasons:

- To write general-purpose portable code for processing structures and structure networks, it is necessary to know which structure is currently open, what the value of the element pointer is, what type of element it is pointing at, and so on.

- Structures and structure networks are very easy to create, modify and delete, and it is correspondingly very easy to lose track of the contents of the CSS. Keeping notes or manually examining the source code of your program to find out exactly what is in the CSS is of course possible, but it is time consuming and unreliable.

- Many graphics programs are highly interactive, with an operator using input devices to edit the picture. Because the CSS may be constantly changing, the only reliable way to determine its contents at any time is to inquire this information.

Each inquiry function returns an integer error number: if this is 0, it indicates that the inquiry was performed successfully, and that the information returned in the other parameters is valid; if it has any other value, something has gone wrong, and any information returned will not be reliable. Error codes are listed in Appendix E.

11.2.1   Inquiring which structures are in the CSS

One of the simplest inquiries to make about the CSS is to ask what structures it contains. The following function returns a list of the identifiers of all the structures in the CSS:

☐ INQUIRE STRUCTURE IDENTIFIERS
  parameters:
  > *out* error   integer
  > *out* structure identifiers   list of integers

11.2.2 Inquiring the status of a structure

This function gives the application general information about a single structure:

☐ INQUIRE STRUCTURE STATUS
  parameters:
  > *in*   structure identifier   integer
  > *out* error   integer
  > *out* structure status   (NON-EXISTENT, EMPTY,
  >   NON-EMPTY)

If the specified structure does not exist, the function returns NON-EXISTENT; otherwise, it returns EMPTY or NON-EMPTY, according to whether the structure contains elements.

11.2.3 Inquiring about the open structure

Because structure elements may only be manipulated when a structure is open, it is important that the application can inquire which, if any, structure is open for editing at a particular time. This is done using:

☐ INQUIRE OPEN STRUCTURE
  parameters:
  > *out* error   integer
  > *out* open structure status   (NONE, OPEN)
  > *out* structure identifier   integer

If there is a structure open when the function is called, OPEN and the identifier of the structure are returned. If there is no structure open, NONE is returned.

11.2.4 Inquiring the element pointer

During structure editing, it is vital to be sure of the position of the element pointer, since this is the position at which element deletion and insertion occur. The following function returns the current position of the element pointer.

☐ INQUIRE ELEMENT POINTER
  parameters:
  > *out* error   integer
  > *out* element position   integer

A structure must be open when this function is called, otherwise an error is reported.

11.2.5 Inquiring about structure elements

There are two functions for inquiring about a structure element: one for determining its type, and one for obtaining its contents:

☐ INQUIRE ELEMENT TYPE AND SIZE
   parameters:
in	structure identifier	integer
in	element position	integer
out	error	integer
out	element type	*see text*
out	element size	integer

This function returns the type of an element – whether it is a FILL AREA SET 3, TEXT 3, ADD NAMES TO SET, and so on – together with its size. The data type used to represent *element type* depends on the language binding, but there will be a different value for each type of structure element (Appendix E lists all element types). PHIGS does not specify what units are used to measure the size of an element, and you should refer to your *Local Guide* for details.

☐ INQUIRE ELEMENT CONTENT
   parameters:
in	structure identifier	integer
in	element position	integer
out	error	integer
out	element content	record

This returns a data record holding all the information contained in the structure element at *element position* in *structure identifier*; for a POLYLINE 3 element this would be a list of 3D MC points; for a SET LINETYPE element it would be a single integer, and so on. Because of the large variation in the types of the data, the format of the data record depends on the language binding.

For convenience, there are alternative versions of these functions, which return information about the element at the element pointer in the currently open structure:

☐ INQUIRE CURRENT ELEMENT TYPE AND SIZE
   parameters:
out	error	integer
out	element type	*see text*
out	element size	integer

and

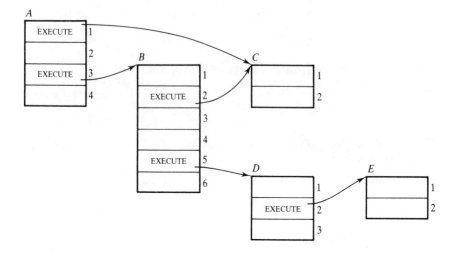

Figure 11.4   A structure network to illustrate inquiry.

INQUIRE CURRENT ELEMENT CONTENT
parameters:
      out error   integer
      out element content   record

11.2.6   Inquiring about structure networks

As well as the contents of individual structures, the application also needs to be able to inquire about their hierarchical relationships. For example, given a particular structure, we may wish to find all its immediate children – that is, all those structures referenced by EXECUTE STRUCTURE elements in the structure. Or, we may wish to find all the descendants of the structure, which comprise all the children of its children, and their children, and so on. Conversely, given a structure, we may wish to determine which other structures in the CSS reference the structure, either directly or via other structures.

    This information is treated consistently using the concept of a **path**. A path is a route in the CSS that leads, via EXECUTE STRUCTURE elements from a position in one structure, to a position in some other structure. Each member of the path comprises a structure identifier and an element number. For example, in Figure 11.4, the path from *A* to *C* would be < *A*.3, *B*.2, *C*.0 >. Because *C* has no children, its element number in the path is, by convention, set to 0.

    There are two functions to inquire about paths in the CSS: INQUIRE PATHS TO DESCENDANTS and INQUIRE PATHS TO ANCESTORS.

11.2.7   Inquire paths to descendants

This function returns a list of paths which are referenced by a specified structure:

☐   INQUIRE PATHS TO DESCENDANTS
    parameters:
in	structure identifier	integer
in	path order	(TOPFIRST, BOTTOMFIRST)
in	path depth	integer
out	error	integer
out	paths	list of paths

We can determine all the paths to the descendants of *A* by calling the function as follows:

INQUIRE PATHS TO DESCENDANTS (*A*, TOPFIRST, 0, error, paths)

This will set *paths* to be a list containing three paths:

< *A*.1, *C*.0 >
< *A*.3, *B*.2, *C*.0 >
< *A*.3, *B*.5, *D*.2, *E*.0 >

The *path order* and *path depth* parameters provide further control over exactly how the inquiry is performed. *Path order* determines whether the entries in each path are listed starting either with the topmost structure in the network, or the bottommost. If we had used BOTTOMFIRST instead of TOPFIRST, the result would have been:

< *C*.0, *A*.1 >
< *C*.0, *B*.2, *A*.3 >
< *E*.0, *D*.2, *B*.5, *A*.3 >

This example returns complete paths from the specified structure down to structures which have no more children, and thus tells us all the descendants of the structure. Often we may wish to restrict the scope of the inquiry, to obtain lists of immediate children, grandchildren or great-great-grandchildren, and so on, and we can do this using the *path depth* parameter. If *path depth* is 0, as it was in the examples above, the complete paths are returned. Using other values enables us to specify that only a portion of the complete paths is required. For example, if we set *path depth* to 2, and inquire the descendants of *A*, specifying TOPFIRST, the following paths will be obtained:

< *A*.1, *C*.0 >
< *A*.3, *B*.2 >
< *A*.3, *B*.5 >

Similarly, setting *path depth* to 2 and *path order* to BOTTOMFIRST will give:

< C.0, A.1 >
< C.0, B.2 >
< E.0, D.2 >

There are two points to note about the paths which are returned. First, there is no implied ordering of each of the paths within the list of paths. Thus, in the previous example, it would be equally valid for the paths to be returned as:

< C.0, B.2 >
< E.0, D.2 >
< C.0, A.1 >

Second, all the paths that are returned must be unique. When *path depth* is used to truncate a number of paths, some of the resulting paths might be the same. For example, if we specify *path order* as 1 and TOPFIRST, we would expect to obtain the following descendants of *A*:

< A.1 >
< A.3 >
< A.3 >

However, because two of these paths are identical, this path is returned only once:

< A.1 >
< A.3 >

11.2.8   Inquire paths to ancestors

This function returns a list of paths which reference a specified structure:

☐   INQUIRE PATHS TO ANCESTORS
parameters:

in	structure identifier	integer
in	path order	(TOPFIRST, BOTTOMFIRST)
in	path depth	integer
out	error	integer
out	paths	list of paths

We could determine all the ancestors of *C* using:

INQUIRE PATHS TO ANCESTORS (*C*, BOTTOMFIRST, 0, error, paths)

and the following paths will be returned:

< C.0, A.1 >
< C.0, B.2, A.3 >

We could determine which structures directly reference *C* using:

INQUIRE PATHS TO ANCESTORS (*C*, BOTTOMFIRST, 2, error, paths)

which would give:

> < *C*.0, *A*.1 >
> < *C*.0, *B*.2 >

11.2.9   Inquiring about posted structures

The following function returns a list of the topmost structures of structure networks which have been posted to a particular workstation:

☐ INQUIRE POSTED STRUCTURES
parameters:

in	workstation identifier	integer
out	error	integer
out	posted structure identifiers	list of integers

Once the list of posted roots of structure networks has been obtained, for each structure the INQUIRE PATHS TO DESCENDANTS function (Section 11.2.7) may be used to determine which other structures have been posted by virtue of being descendants of explicitly posted structures.

Conversely, we may wish to know to which workstations a particular structure has been posted. The following function returns this information:

☐ INQUIRE SET OF WORKSTATIONS TO WHICH POSTED
parameters:

in	structure identifier	integer
out	error	integer
out	workstation identifiers	list of integers

11.3   Element search

As we saw in Chapter 5, structures are edited using the element pointer, and we can set the element pointer at specific element numbers or labels. This is convenient when we already know what elements are in a structure, but there are times when we may want to search within structures for a particular type or types of element. It is easy enough for an application to do this: it can set the element pointer to a suitable starting position, and then repeatedly examine the element at the pointer to determine whether it is of the required type. If it is, the search is finished; otherwise the element pointer can be incremented, and the test repeated until the end of the structure is reached. This might be programmed as follows:

```
finished := false
position := starting position
```

repeat
  SET ELEMENT POINTER (position)
  INQUIRE CURRENT ELEMENT TYPE AND SIZE (error, type, size)
  found := (type = required type)
  finished := (position = number-of-elements-in-structure)
  if not finished **then**
      position := position + 1
until (found) **or** (finished)

This is a common operation, and PHIGS provides the ELEMENT SEARCH function:

☐ ELEMENT SEARCH
   parameters:

in	structure identifier	integer
in	start element number	integer
in	search direction	(BACKWARD, FORWARD)
in	element inclusion set	list of names
in	element exclusion set	list of names
out	error	integer
out	status	(FAILURE, SUCCESS)
out	found element number	integer

The search starts from a specified element in the structure, and searches either forwards or backwards according to *search direction*. An element will be found only if its type is included in *element inclusion set*, and is not excluded by *element exclusion set* (if an element type is in both sets, it will be excluded, according to the same rules as for the workstation filters described in Section 11.1). The search stops when either the start or the end of the structure is reached, or an element is found. If an element is found, *status* is set to SUCCESS, and the element number is returned in *found element number*; if no element of the appropriate type is found, *status* is set to FAILURE. For example, recall the cube structure from Chapter 5:

cube structure	0
LABEL *transformation*	1
SET LOCAL TRANSFORMATION 3	2
LABEL *front face*	3
POLYLINE 3 front face	4
LABEL *back face*	5
POLYLINE 3 back face	6
LABEL *links*	7
POLYLINE 3 link 1	8
POLYLINE 3 link 2	9
POLYLINE 3 link 3	10
POLYLINE 3 link 4	11
LABEL *text*	12
TEXT 3 "It's a"	13
TEXT 3 "square world!"	14

To search this structure for its first POLYLINE 3 element, we can use ELEMENT SEARCH as follows:

ELEMENT SEARCH (cube, 0, FORWARD, [POLYLINE 3], [ ],
                    error, status, foundpos)

Since the search starts at the first element, *foundpos* will be set to 4. Now, we can search for the next element which is not a label, using:

ELEMENT SEARCH (cube, foundpos+1, FORWARD, [ALL], [LABEL],
                    error, status, foundpos)

This will set *foundpos* to 6.

11.4   Incremental spatial search

The INCREMENTAL SPATIAL SEARCH (ISS) function searches a structure network for an output primitive which lies within a specified distance of a particular reference point in world coordinates. For example, if the operator uses a locator to input a point, the application can call ISS to determine which output primitives in which structures are near the point. The specification of ISS is:

☐ INCREMENTAL SPATIAL SEARCH 3

parameters:

in	reference point	3D WC point
in	search distance	real
in	start path	path
in	modelling clipping flag	(CLIP, NOCLIP)
in	search ceiling index	integer
in	normal filter list	list of filters
in	inverted filter list	list of filters
out	error	integer
out	found path	path

The search starts at a position in the structure network specified by *start path*. To perform the search, PHIGS effectively performs a traversal of the structure network (but does not send output to workstations) applying modelling transformations in the normal way. Whether or not modelling clipping is applied depends on the value of *modelling clipping flag*. If an output primitive element is located which is within *search distance* of *reference point*, the search is successful, and the result is a path from the root of the specified network to the element located.

The simplest way to use ISS is to begin with the *start path* as a complete path starting from the root structure of the network being searched. For example, in the structure network shown in Figure 11.5, let us assume that the polylines at elements 3 and 5 of structure *C*, and element 3 of structure *D*, are close to some

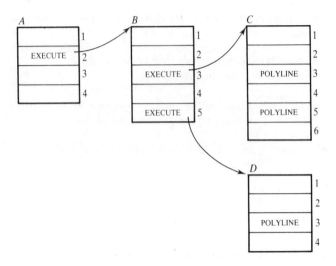

Figure 11.5   An example to illustrate incremental spatial search.

position *P* in WC. Given *P*, we can use ISS to locate these primitives as follows. To search the whole network (starting in structure *A*) we would specify *start path* as < *A*.0 >. ISS starts searching from the next element (*A*.1), and locates the first polyline near to *P* in structure *C*, returning *found path* as < *A*.2, *B*.3, *C*.3 >.

To find the next primitive near *P* we can call ISS again, this time setting *start path* as the path we have just obtained. The polyline at element 5 in *C* will be located, setting *found path* to < *A*.2, *B*.3, *C*.5 >. We can continue by using this path as the next *start path*, and then ISS will locate the polyline in *D*, returning < *A*.2, *B*.5, *D*.3 >.

Structure networks are often complex, and it may be convenient to restrict the parts of the network that are considered in the search. There are two ways to do this; the first is to use the *search ceiling index* parameter, which specifies that the search is to stop when the end of a particular structure is reached. In the example, if we specify *start path* as < *A*.2, *B*.3, *C*.5 >, and *search ceiling index* as 3, the search will stop when the end of the structure in position 3 of *start path* is reached (structure *C*). This means that the polyline at element 5 of *D* will not be located. To search without restriction, *search ceiling index* should be set to 1.

The second method is to use filters to control which elements in the structure network are actually considered in the search. These filters operate on the name set associated with an output primitive element, and each filter comprises an inclusion set and an exclusion set. To be accepted by a filter, the name set must contain at least one name which also occurs in the inclusion set, and which does not occur in the exclusion set – this is exactly the same mechanism we described in Section 11.1.2 for the workstation invisibility and highlighting filters. However, in ISS it is slightly more complicated, because there are two kinds of filter, normal and inverted, which operate in opposite senses. For an element to be considered during the search, it must be *accepted* by the normal filter list, and *rejected* by the inverted filter list.

An example of the use of the filters would be to restrict the search to elements which, for a particular workstation, are visible and pickable (using a particular pick device). This can be done very easily, by setting the normal filters to be a copy of the pick filter of the appropriate input device, and the inverted filters to be a copy of the workstation's invisibility filter. Here, structure elements whose name sets are accepted by the normal filters correspond to output primitives which are pickable, and elements whose name sets are rejected by the inverted filter correspond to primitives which are visible. To include all the elements in a structure network for searching, both the normal and inverted filter lists should be empty.

11.5   The generalized structure element

Manufacturers may wish to provide special features in their implementations which extend the functionality of the ISO definition of PHIGS. In the spirit of providing non-standard features in a standard manner, there is a special kind of structure element called the **Generalized Structure Element (GSE)**. GSEs are meant for enhancing the basic functionality, not for extending existing features. In particular GSEs are not permitted to create output primitives – this is the role of the generalized drawing primitive element (see Section 3.10). The function to create a GSE is:

| E | GENERALIZED STRUCTURE ELEMENT
     parameters:
          in   GSE identifier   implementation defined type
          in   GSE data   record

Each GSE has a *GSE identifier* which describes what it does, and when a GSE is inserted into a structure, no check is made of its validity. Similarly, if during traversal an unrecognized type of GSE is encountered, no error occurs, and the element is ignored. Since different implementations will probably offer different GSEs (and many will offer none at all), programs which make extensive use of GSEs are not likely to be portable.

To illustrate a possible use for a GSE, we will briefly mention a facility which PHIGS does not provide – conditional traversal. Traversal starts at the root of a posted structure network and visits every element in every structure in the network, in a strict order. As far as the application is concerned, traversal is an atomic action, which cannot be interrupted or controlled. An implementation could use GSEs to give the application more control over traversal, by providing special elements which, when encountered during traversal, actually affect the subsequent course of the traversal. This facility might be used, for example, to 'switch off' part of the structure network, so that it is effectively unposted. A GSE could also perform actions such as 'abandon the whole traversal at this element' or 'do not traverse the rest of this structure', and so on.

11.6   Application data

Often, applications will wish to store information about the model in addition to graphical data. For this purpose there is a special kind of structure element:

| E | APPLICATION DATA |
| *parameters:* |
| | *in* application data | record |

The way in which this element is used, and the format in which the data is en-coded, are entirely the responsibilities of the application. For example, for the bicycle, the application may wish to describe the materials used for each part, and their order numbers and cost. During traversal, application data elements have no effect, and PHIGS never interprets or modifies their contents.

11.7   Special interfaces

Implementations may provide special facilities designed to be used alongside PHIGS, and there is a special function for accessing them:

| ☐ | ESCAPE |
| *parameters:* |
	in escape function identifier	integer
	in input data record	record
	in output data record	record

Your *Local Guide* will list any functions of this kind. There are some restrictions on what an ESCAPE function is allowed to do: in particular, it must not generate graphical output or create a structure element.

Chapter 12
Dealing with errors

This chapter describes the facilities for handling error conditions which are detected by PHIGS during the execution of application programs.

The application must be notified when an error occurs, so that it can take appropriate corrective action. One approach would be to print out the error on the terminal from which the application program is being run, or to send a message to every open workstation, but PHIGS provides more flexible methods. There are two ways in which PHIGS communicates errors to the application:

- Some functions have an error parameter, and if an error occurs during the execution of the function, a number indicating the nature of the error is returned in the parameter. It is the responsibility of the application to check the value of this parameter to see if an error has occurred.

- If an error occurs in a function which does not have an error parameter, the ERROR HANDLING function is automatically called, and the error number is passed to this function.

In this chapter we describe the second of these methods. This applies only to functions which do not have an error parameter.

12.1   Error handling

When an error occurs, a function called ERROR HANDLING is automatically called. It is defined as follows:

☐ ERROR HANDLING
   parameters:
         in   error number   integer
         in   function name   name
         in   error file   file name

PHIGS passes as parameters to this function the number of the error, the name of the function called which caused the error, and the name of the error file specified when OPEN PHIGS was called. ERROR HANDLING differs from ordinary PHIGS functions in that it may be *redefined* by the application, so that the application's version is called instead of the standard version. The application can then respond to the error however it pleases, since it knows which error occurred, and the name of the PHIGS function which caused it.

We first consider the default situation, where the application does not redefine ERROR HANDLING. In this case, PHIGS performs a sensible action: ERROR HANDLING merely records the error by calling the ERROR LOGGING function:

☐ ERROR LOGGING
    parameters:
          in   error number   integer
          in   function name   name
          in   error file   file name

This writes an error message corresponding to *error number* and the name of the function responsible on *error file*. Error messages are listed in Appendix E.

This method of handling errors in two separate stages (ERROR HANDLING and ERROR LOGGING) gives the application the flexibility to treat errors in the most appropriate way. The application may itself call ERROR LOGGING to record the error, but it is not permitted to redefine the ERROR LOGGING function. For example, an application may define its own version of ERROR HANDLING to do something special if error 6 occurs, but just report the error otherwise, as follows:

```
ERROR HANDLING (error number, function name, error file)
% Application's definition of ERROR HANDLING function.
  begin
  if error number = 6 then
    % Do something special.
  else
    ERROR LOGGING (error number, function, error file)
  end
```

There are restrictions placed on what an application may do in its own ERROR HANDLING function: the only PHIGS functions it may call are any of the inquiry functions (which may not cause errors), ERROR LOGGING and EMERGENCY CLOSE PHIGS. The application can control whether or not ERROR HANDLING is called when an error occurs using:

☐ SET ERROR HANDLING MODE
    parameters:
             in   error handling mode   (OFF, ON)

If *error handling mode* is OFF, ERROR HANDLING will not be called when an error occurs. If the mode is ON (the default), it will be called. The current state of the

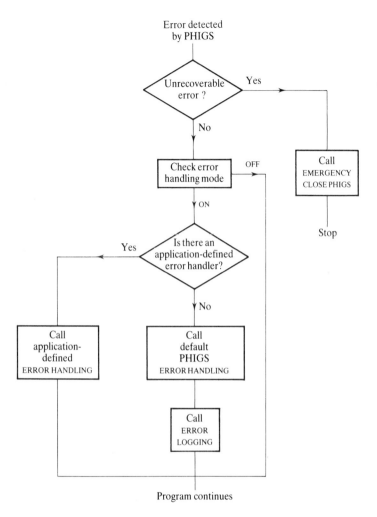

Figure 12.1 Error handling.

error handling mode can be inquired using:

☐ INQUIRE ERROR HANDLING MODE
  parameters:
  | *out* error | integer |
  | *out* error handling mode | (OFF, ON) |

In the case of functions that have output parameters in which error codes are returned (this includes all the inquiry functions, and other functions such as EL-EMENT SEARCH), ERROR HANDLING is never called, whether or not it has been redefined by the application. Figure 12.1 summarizes the error handling process.

12.2   Emergency close PHIGS

In some situations the application may decide that the nature of the error is such that the program should be terminated immediately. Because the state may be indeterminate in such cases, there is a function which attempts to save as much graphical information as possible, and closes PHIGS down gracefully:

☐   EMERGENCY CLOSE PHIGS
    parameters: none

The precise action of this function is implementation dependent, but as far as is possible, its effect is the same as calling the following functions, in this order:

1. CLOSE STRUCTURE (if open);

2. CLOSE ARCHIVE FILE (for each open archive file);

3. UPDATE WORKSTATION (for each open workstation);

4. CLOSE WORKSTATION (for each open workstation);

5. CLOSE PHIGS.

EMERGENCY CLOSE PHIGS may be called at any time by the application, not just from within the ERROR HANDLING function. It may also be called automatically in the case of unrecoverable internal errors.

12.3   Operating states

There are four **operating state variables**, which define the current status of PHIGS. The state variables, and their possible values are as follows:

- **system state**
  PHOP: PHIGS is open.
  PHCL: PHIGS is closed.

- **workstation state**
  WSOP: at least one workstation is open.
  WSCL: no workstations are open.

- **structure state**
  STOP: a structure is open.
  STCL: a structure is not open.

- **archive state**
  AROP: at least one archive file is open.
  ARCL: no archive files are open.

The initial values of these variables are PHCL, WSCL, STCL and ARCL. Functions may only be called in certain operating states, or an error will occur. For example, OPEN STRUCTURE may only be called when the system state is PHOP and the structure state is STCL. If either of these conditions is not met, the following error (number 6) occurs:

> *6: Ignoring function, function requires state* (PHOP, *, STCL, *).

An asterisk indicates that the value of the respective operating state is irrelevant to the function. Many functions cause an operating state to change: calling CLOSE STRUCTURE when a structure is open changes the structure state from STOP to STCL, and does not affect any other operating state. The current values of each of the operating states can be inquired, using the functions INQUIRE SYSTEM STATE VALUE, INQUIRE WORKSTATION STATE VALUE, INQUIRE STRUCTURE STATE VALUE, and INQUIRE ARCHIVE STATE VALUE.

Chapter 13
PHIGS PLUS graphical output

PHIGS PLUS is a set of extensions to PHIGS to support additional facilities for curves and surfaces, and lighting and shading. Most implementations of PHIGS now support PHIGS PLUS to some extent, although the extensions have not yet been agreed as a standard and are therefore still subject to change. In this chapter we cover the additional output primitives provided by PHIGS PLUS.

PHIGS does not include 'higher level' primitives such as curves and surfaces, and techniques for lighting and shading. Many of these are directly supported by modern high-performance displays, making it important for PHIGS programs to be able to address them.

Recognizing this, in late 1986 an ad hoc working group was formed by interested parties in the USA, with the intention of proposing a set of extensions to PHIGS to enable these capabilities to be addressed in a standard manner, compatible with the overall philosophy of PHIGS. The set of proposed extensions was submitted to ISO and has since been developed into PHIGS PLUS (*Plus Lumière Und Surfaces*). Although at the time of writing it is not an international standard, there is enough agreement for us to consider some of its capabilities, even though the details may change by the time the standard is finalized. In essence, PHIGS PLUS enhances PHIGS by providing:

- primitives for defining curves and surfaces

- lighting models

- shading of surfaces

- depth cueing

- colour mapping and direct colour specification

The output primitives are listed in Table 13.1 and described below. There are both 2D and 3D versions of these functions, but we shall describe only the 3D versions. The appearance of the term *with data* in a function name implies that additional information – application data, colours and vertex normal vectors – may be supplied as part of the definition.

Table 13.1 PHIGS PLUS output primitives.

Polyline set with data
Fill area set with data
Set of fill area set with data
Triangle strip with data
Quadrilateral mesh with data
Non-uniform B-spline curve
Non-uniform B-spline surface
Cell array plus

13.1 Polyline set with data

This primitive extends polyline in two ways. First, it allows us to define a set of unconnected polylines as a single primitive. This can be useful for displaying a variety of composite shapes constructed from individual polylines.

Second, we can supply an application-dependent value at each point in the polyline set. During display, these values may be linearly interpolated along the length of each polyline segment and then mapped to an appropriate colour. This has a variety of uses. For example, it could be used to display a graph, with the colour representing the variation of some parameter along the length of a polyline. Alternatively, we might use it to display a surface in the form of a mesh, where each vertex has an associated value – perhaps a temperature value – although, as we shall see shortly, there are other primitives specifically designed for surface display. The function for defining this primitive is:

E   POLYLINE SET 3 WITH DATA
     parameters:
          in   data per vertex flag   (COORDINATES,
                                                 COORDINATE COLOUR)
          in   colour type   integer
          in   vertex data   *see text*

The *vertex data* includes the coordinates of vertices and other optional values such as colour. Which of these is present is determined by the *data per vertex flag*, which specifies whether only the coordinates are supplied, or whether colour information is also present for each vertex. *Colour type* specifies whether colour is defined indirectly (as in PHIGS) or using one of the direct colour models supported by PHIGS PLUS, described in the next chapter.

Plate 12 shows a terrain map displayed using polylines with colour interpolation, in which colour is employed to encode height above (and below) sea level.

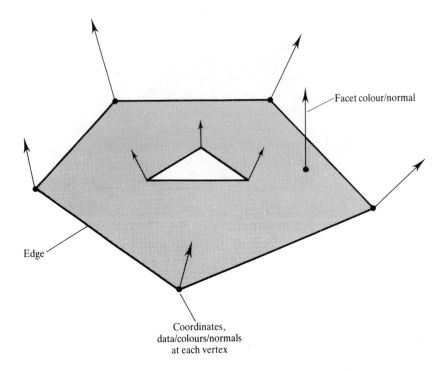

Facet colour/normal

Edge

Coordinates,
data/colours/normals
at each vertex

Figure 13.1 Fill area set with data.

13.2 Fill area set with data

This defines a set of filled areas, in a similar manner to its PHIGS counterpart,
FILL AREA SET 3. Here, however, we can specify additional information at each
vertex. The different parameters which can be added include **vertex colours**,
vertex normals, a **facet colour**, a **facet normal**, and application data, as shown
in Figure 13.1. These values, when supplied, may be used for surface shading.
The function for defining this primitive is:

E FILL AREA SET 3 WITH DATA
parameters:

in	data per facet flag		*see* Table 13.2
in	data per edge flag		(NONE,
			EDGE VISIBILITY FLAGS)
in	data per vertex flag		*see* Table 13.3
in	colour type		integer
in	facet data		*see text*
in	edge flags		*see text*
in	vertex data		*see text*

Table 13.2   Data per facet flag values.

no facet data
facet colours
facet normals
facet data
facet colour and normal
facet colour and data
facet normal and data
facet colour, normal and data

The possible values for *data per facet flag* are shown in Table 13.2. The values indicate which of the optional other values are present.

PHIGS PLUS allows precise control over the display of the edges belonging to filled areas. It is possible to determine which edges are displayed by supplying **edge visibility flags** for each edge. The *data per edge flag* indicates whether this visibility information is present or not, and can take the values NONE (not supplied), or EDGE VISIBILITY FLAGS (edge flags supplied). In the latter case, the *edge flags* parameter contains a list of visibility values for each edge.

13.3   Set of fill area set with data

This primitive defines a set of fill area sets. Each of the fill area sets must be planar, but the set of fill area sets does not have to fulfil this requirement. This gives a useful degree of flexibility in describing non-planar objects (see Plate 16). For example, we could use this single primitive to define a cube whose faces contain holes. Each face would constitute one fill area set, with the boundary as one area and the holes as other areas in the set.

Another feature of this primitive is that it employs a single list containing

Table 13.3   Data per vertex flag values.

coordinates only
coordinates and colours
coordinates and normals
coordinates and data
coordinates, colours and normals
coordinates, colours and data
coordinates, normals and data
coordinates, colours, normals and data

vertex data. Index values are used to access this list, allowing the vertex data to be shared. For example, in the case of the cube we can store the vertex data for each corner just once and then share it between its three adjacent faces. This saving in space is worthwhile because the amount of data stored for each vertex can be quite large. The function for specifying this primitive is:

E	SET OF FILL AREA SET 3 WITH DATA	
	parameters:	
in	data per facet flag	*see* Table 13.2
in	data per edge flag	(NONE,
		EDGE VISIBILITY FLAGS)
in	data per vertex flag	*see* Table 13.3
in	colour type	integer
in	facet data	*see text*
in	edge flags	*see text*
in	vertex data	*see text*
in	vertex indices	list of indices

The parameters are essentially similar to those for FILL AREA SET 3 WITH DATA, with the addition of the *vertex indices* parameter. However, because of its more complicated data representation, which permits vertex data to be shared, some of the other parameters become lists of values, or even lists of lists of values. For example, instead of a single list of values for the facet data, we now have to supply a list of lists of such values, with one list per facet. Similarly, where previously we had a list of edge flags we must supply a list of lists of edge flags, one for each fill area in the set of fill areas, and so on. We will not go into more detail here; suffice it to say that this degree of complexity is not something which the everyday application programmer wishes to grapple with. SET OF FILL AREA SET 3 WITH DATA would normally be used to write higher-level utility functions – one to display a cube, another to display a tetrahedron, and so on.

13.4   Triangle strip with data

The triangle strip primitive is illustrated in Figure 13.2. It comprises a series of triangles which are defined by a single list of vertices connected in a fixed order. A sequence of $n-2$ triangles is defined by n vertices. The kth triangle has vertices k, $k+1$ and $k+2$. The definition of the primitive can contain any combination of vertex colours, vertex normals, facet colours and facet normals. The main advantage of this primitive is that the vertex data is stored just once. Triangles are guaranteed to be planar, and some display systems have special hardware for drawing triangles very rapidly. The function definition is:

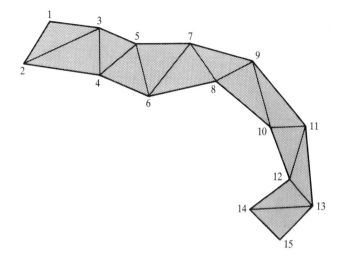

Figure 13.2   Triangle strip with data.

|E| TRIANGLE STRIP 3 WITH DATA

|E| TRIANGLE STRIP 3 WITH DATA
parameters:

in	data per facet flag	*see* Table 13.2
in	data per edge flag	(NONE,
		EDGE VISIBILITY FLAGS)
in	data per vertex flag	*see* Table 13.3
in	colour type	integer
in	facet data	*see text*
in	edge flags	*see text*
in	vertex data	*see text*

The meanings of the parameters are similar to those described for SET OF FILL AREA SET 3 WITH DATA. Note that the *edge flags* can be different for each edge. The *vertex data* includes the vertex coordinates.

13.5   Quadrilateral mesh with data

The quadrilateral mesh primitive comprises a 2D array of quadrilaterals, defined by a grid of vertices, as shown in Figure 13.3 and Plate 13. Two index values are used to reference each grid point. Like the triangle strip, vertex data is shared by adjacent facets, offering a useful saving in storage space, and the data can include any combination of application data, vertex colours, vertex normals, facet colours and facet normals. The function definition once again has a similar list of parameters to SET OF FILL AREA SET 3 WITH DATA, and is defined as:

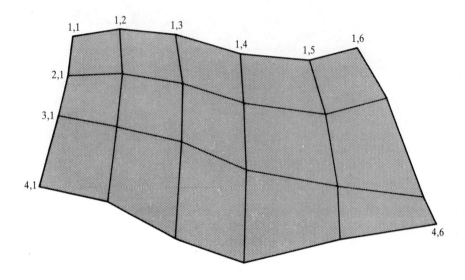

Figure 13.3   Quadrilateral mesh with data.

QUADRILATERAL MESH 3 WITH DATA
parameters:

in	data per facet flag	*see* Table 13.2
in	data per edge flag	(NONE,
		EDGE VISIBILITY FLAGS)
in	data per vertex flag	*see* Table 13.3
in	colour type	integer
in	facet data	*see text*
in	edge flags	*see text*
in	vertex data	*see text*

13.6   Non-uniform B-spline curve

A non-uniform B-spline is a curve (or surface) whose shape is controlled by a number of parameters which include its **control points**. Different shapes can be obtained by using the appropriate control points, and the mathematical formulation is such that there is an intuitive and well-behaved relationship between the control points and the shape of the curve. Non-uniform B-splines are often called **NURBs**, although this term strictly refers to **rational** B-splines only.

Non-uniform B-splines can be used to represent a variety of curved shapes, including all the conic sections, and also shapes which include straight edges and sharp corners. The most important property of a non-uniform rational B-spline from the point of view of PHIGS PLUS is that it is *closed under a perspective transformation*. This means that if the curve undergoes a transformation (for example by the viewing pipeline), the transformed shape of the curve can be obtained by transforming the original control points, and then using the transformed points to generate the curve. To see why this is an important property, consider a circle specified as centre and radius. We can transform the centre by the modelling and viewing transformations, but how should the radius be transformed? If perspective is involved, the circle could distort into an ellipse or a hyperbola. This is because the formulation is not closed: it cannot guarantee to produce the same data representation after transformation.

A non-uniform B-spline curve is defined as follows:

$$\mathbf{r}(t) = \sum_{i=1}^{n} \mathbf{p}_i N_i^k(t), \quad t_{min} \le t < t_{max}$$

Here, the curve is the set of points $\{\mathbf{r}(t)\}$ swept out as t takes all the values between t_{min} and t_{max}. $\{\mathbf{p}_i\}$ is a set of n **control points**, and $\{N_i^k(t)\}$ a set of **basis functions**, which are defined by the following recurrence relation:

$$N_i^0(t) = \begin{cases} 1 & \text{if } t_i \le t < t_{i+1} \\ 0 & \text{otherwise} \end{cases}$$

$$N_i^k(t) = \frac{(t - t_{i-k}) * N_{i-1}^{k-1}(t)}{(t_i - t_{i-k})} + \frac{(t_{i+1} - t) * N_i^{k-1}(t)}{(t_{i+1} - t_{i-k+1})}$$

k is called the **order** of the curve. For instance, if $k = 4$, the basis function $\{N_i^4(t)\}$ will include terms in t^3, t^2 and t. The set of real numbers

$$\{t_1, \dots, t_{n+k}\}$$

is called the **knot vector**. For example, a cubic knot vector ($k = 4$) for $n = 6$ control points might be:

$$\{0, 0, 0, 0, 0.25, 0.75, 1, 1, 1, 1\}$$

A knot vector must satisfy a number of conditions. The t_i must be a monotonically increasing sequence, and the first and last knots must be repeated k times. Knots are usually normalized to the range [0,1], although this is not necessary. If $t_i - t_{i-1}$ is the same for all i, the B-spline is termed **uniform**; otherwise it is **non-uniform**. The non-uniform formulation provides the greatest flexibility, and is the type used in PHIGS PLUS.

13.6.1   Rational B-splines

There are two types of B-spline: **rational** and **non-rational**. Only rational B-splines have the property of being closed under a perspective transformation, which is why they are used in PHIGS PLUS.

Given a 3D control point $\mathbf{p}_i$, we can create the corresponding homogeneous point $\mathbf{p}_i^h$ by adding a fourth coordinate, w_i, as follows:

$$\mathbf{p}_i^h = \begin{bmatrix} \mathbf{p}_i \\ w_i \end{bmatrix}$$

PHIGS PLUS requires that $w_i > 0$, and usually we shall have $w_i = 1$. The corresponding 4D B-spline curve is the set of points $\{\mathbf{r}^h(t)\}$, such that:

$$\mathbf{r}^h(t) = \sum_{i=1}^{n} \mathbf{p}_i^h N_i^k(t), \quad t_{\min} \le t < t_{\max}$$

As with homogeneous points the 3D point is obtained by dividing the first three coordinates by the fourth (see Appendix C). The 3D curve $\{\mathbf{r}^h(t)\}$ is therefore:

$$\mathbf{r}(t) = \frac{\sum_{i=1}^{n} \mathbf{p}_i^h N_i^k(t)}{\sum_{i=1}^{n} w_i N_i^k(t)}$$

This is the formulation used in PHIGS PLUS.

13.6.2   Examples of non-uniform B-spline curves

Figure 13.4 shows a cubic ($k = 4$) non-uniform B-spline curve and its 7 control points, using the following knot vector of 11 elements:

$$\{0, 0, 0, 0, 0.25, 0.5, 0.75, 1, 1, 1, 1\}$$

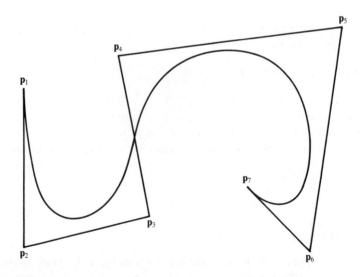

Figure 13.4   A cubic non-uniform B-spline curve.

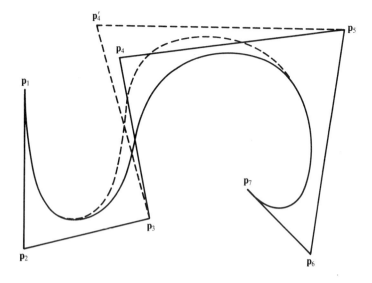

Figure 13.5 The effect of moving $\mathbf{p}_4$ to $\mathbf{p}_4'$.

This is an example of a non-rational B-spline, since $w_i = 1$. This example illustrates some general properties. The curve passes through the first and last control points ($\mathbf{p}_1$ and $\mathbf{p}_7$), and the tangent at $\mathbf{p}_1$ is proportional to $\mathbf{p}_2 - \mathbf{p}_1$. Similarly, the tangent at $\mathbf{p}_7$ is proportional to ($\mathbf{p}_7 - \mathbf{p}_6$). Figure 13.5 shows the effect of moving control point $\mathbf{p}_4$ to $\mathbf{p}_4'$, and the resulting curve is shown dotted. Note that we have not changed the knot vector, and that the curve moves in an intuitive way (some other methods of drawing curves do not have this property).

We can create sharp corners by moving adjacent control points close together, as shown in Figure 13.6, which shows the crest of the University of

Figure 13.6 A picture comprising 106 B-splines.

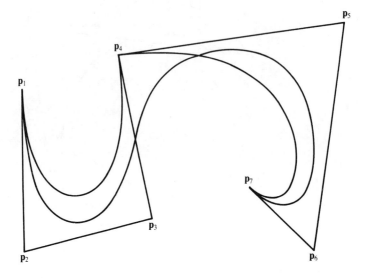

Figure 13.7   Using repeated knots to create sharp corners.

Manchester, constructed from 106 different B-spline curves. Exact corners may be created by adjusting the knot vector, and repeating the *knots* rather than control points. Figure 13.7 shows a corner at $\mathbf{p}_4$, created by changing the knot vector to:

$$\{0, 0, 0, 0, 0.25, 0.25, 0.25, 1, 1, 1, 1\}$$

Here, the control points are the same as for Figure 13.4. Figure 13.8 shows some more examples of non-uniform B-spline curves.

13.6.3   The non-uniform B-spline curve primitive

The following function defines a non-uniform B-spline curve:

E	NON-UNIFORM B-SPLINE CURVE

parameters:

in	order (k)	integer
in	knot vector $(\{t_i\})$	list of $(n+k)$ reals
in	rationality	(RATIONAL, NON-RATIONAL)
in	control points $(\{\mathbf{p}_i\}$ or $\{\mathbf{p}_i^h\})$	list of n 3D or 4D MC points
in	t_{min}, t_{max}	2 reals

If the RATIONAL form is used then the control points are 4D MC points, while for the NON-RATIONAL form, they are 3D points. The attributes of B-spline curves are described in the next section.

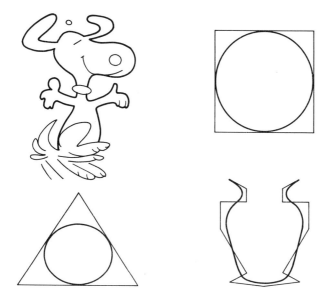

Figure 13.8   Examples of non-uniform B-spline curves.

13.6.4   The attributes of non-uniform B-spline curve

Because curves are usually drawn using straight-line approximations, non-uniform B-spline curve shares the attributes of polyline. An additional attribute, curve approximation criteria, controls the method used to generate the straight-line approximation:

E̲ SET CURVE APPROXIMATION CRITERIA
   parameters:
   in   approximation type   integer
   in   approximation data   data record

There are a number of standard methods provided:

- **Workstation-dependent**   A workstation-dependent technique is used.

- **Constant parametric subdivision between knots**   The curve is evaluated at n points between each pair of knots.

- **Chordal size in WC (or NPC or DC)**   Each line segment is shorter than a specified size.

- **Chordal deviation in WC (or NPC or DC)**   The maximum deviation ε (shown exaggerated in Figure 13.9) is less than a specified tolerance.

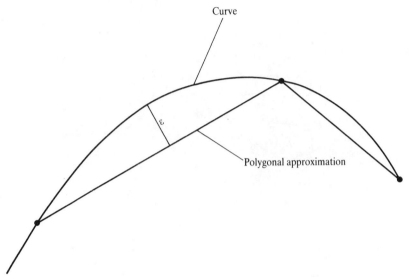

Figure 13.9   Controlling the chordal deviation.

13.7   Non-uniform B-spline surface

Non-uniform B-splines can also be used to draw surfaces. A non-uniform B-spline surface is a set of points defined over two independent variables u and v, and the formulation is analogous to the B-spline curve:

$$\mathbf{r}^h(u, v) = \sum_{i=1}^{n} \sum_{j=1}^{m} N_i^k(u) N_j^l(v) \mathbf{p}_{ij}^h$$

There are now *two* knot vectors:

$$\{u_1, \ldots, u_{n+k}\} \quad \text{and} \quad \{v_1, \ldots, v_{m+l}\}$$

and u and v must obey the same conditions as the knots for a B-spline curve. The following function creates a non-uniform B-spline surface:

[E]   NON-UNIFORM B-SPLINE SURFACE
parameters:

in	u order (k)	integer
in	v order (l)	integer
in	u knot vector	list of $n + k$ reals
in	v knot vector	list of $m + l$ reals
in	rationality	(RATIONAL, NON-RATIONAL)
in	control points ($\{\mathbf{p}_{ij}\}$ or $\{\mathbf{p}_{ij}^h\}$)	list of $n * m$ 3D or 4D MC points
in	trimming definition	list of list of trim curves

An example is shown in Figure 13.10. As with B-spline curves, there is an intu-

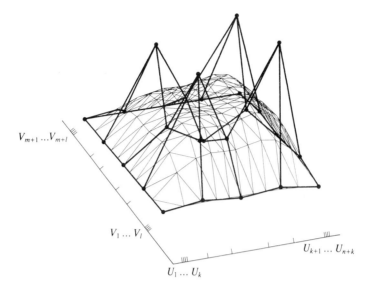

$V_{m+1}...V_{m+l}$

$V_1 ... V_l$

$U_{k+1} ... U_{n+k}$

$U_1 ... U_k$

Figure 13.10 A non-uniform B-spline surface, and its *u* and *v* knot vectors.

itive relationship between the positions of the control points and the shape of the resulting surface. For example, taking a quadratic in *u* produces a circle, and in conjunction with a linear function in *v* produces a section of a cone, as shown in Plate 17. The surface may be closed (such as a sphere), and using repeated knots and control points enables a wide range of shapes to be represented. Figure 13.11 shows some other examples of non-uniform B-spline surfaces.

13.7.1   The attributes of non-uniform B-spline surface

A non-uniform B-spline surface has all the attributes of fill area set and quadrilateral mesh, plus two others: surface approximation criteria and parametric surface characteristics.

Whereas chords are used to approximate curves, planar elements (such as quadrilaterals) are used to approximate a surface. Exactly how this is done is controlled by the surface approximation criteria attribute. The parametric surface characteristics control the methods used to render the surface, such as isoparametric curves or contour curves. Plates 18 and 19 show a B-spline surface created by revolving a B-spline curve around an axis. Plates 22 and 23 illustrate that placing the control points of a rational B-spline on the corners, mid-points of edges and faces of a cube generates a sphere. Similarly, we can arrange the control points in a rectangular manner to produce a torus, as shown in Plates 20 and 21.

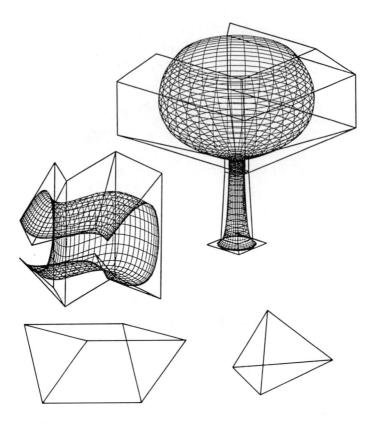

Figure 13.11   Some examples of non-uniform B-spline surfaces.

13.7.2   Trimming surfaces

Instead of drawing the whole surface, a number of trimming curves may be specified, which cause only portions of the surface to be drawn. A trimming curve
defines a region of valid u and v values, and the surface is the set of points obtained
by evaluating the B-spline for each (u, v) value in the range. An example is shown
in Figure 13.12. Each trimming curve is converted to a loop by joining the last
part to the first, but the loops must not intersect themselves or each other. The
region of the surface which is displayed is defined by the 'inside' of the loops.
By joining together a number of B-spline surfaces we can represent shapes of
considerable complexity, such as the car shown in Plate 7.

13.7.3   Further reading

The non-uniform B-spline formulation is very powerful, and space does not permit a more detailed treatment. For thorough coverage of B-spline curves and
surfaces the reader is referred to [Bartels *et al.*, 1987] and [Farin, 1990].

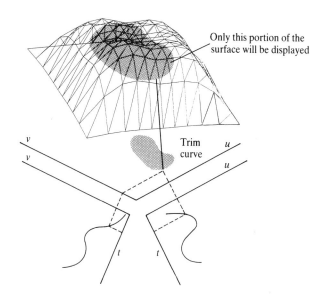

Figure 13.12   An example of trimming a non-uniform B-spline surface.

13.8   Cell array plus

The CELL ARRAY PLUS primitive is identical to its PHIGS counterpart, CELL ARRAY 3, except that a general colour (see Section 14.1) may be assigned to each cell. Its specification is:

E   CELL ARRAY 3 PLUS
   parameters:
        in   parallelogram   three 3D MC points
        in   colour type   integer
        in   colour   array of colours

The *colour type* parameter identifies how the colours are defined: either indirectly, or using one of the direct colour models. The array of colour values contains one entry per cell defining its colour.

Chapter 14

The PHIGS PLUS rendering pipeline

This chapter describes the facilities which PHIGS PLUS provides for rendering images using its **rendering pipeline**, *which includes* **colour specification, lighting, shading, depth cueing** *and* **colour mapping**.

Conceptually, the **rendering pipeline** fits into the PHIGS output pipeline after the application of modelling and viewing transformations. It implements a number of steps, summarized in Figure 14.1:

- **Data mapping** is concerned with mapping application-dependent data values, optionally supplied as part of the *with data* primitives, onto colours.

- **Lighting** has to do with different types of light source, and with the way in which light reflected from primitives is calculated.

- **Shading** controls the way in which application data, colours and vertex normals are interpolated across the surfaces of primitives.

- **Depth cueing** is a technique for modifying the intensity of an image according to the distance of the primitives from the viewpoint.

- **Colour mapping** determines how the computed colours are actually displayed.

Figure 14.1   Stages in the rendering pipeline.

A number of these steps are interdependent. The effects they produce can only be explained when we understand the whole process. For this reason, we will examine these topics in a slightly different order and, in particular, we will defer discussion of data mapping until after we have described the reflectance equations for different types of light source. Plates 26 to 31 show the same scene rendered using a number of the techniques which we shall describe in this chapter.

14.1 Colour specification

In PHIGS, colours are referred to indirectly via an index, which accesses a workstation colour table where each entry contains the components of the colour. This method of specifying colours is not appropriate for shaded coloured pictures, because many different colour combinations may be needed and it is not generally possible to predict in advance what these will be. PHIGS PLUS extends the basic colour model of PHIGS by allowing us to specify colours directly, using different **colour models**. This is referred to as **general colour** specification. Instead of using an index, a general colour comprises a type and a tuple of numbers. There are two possible cases:

- A type followed by a colour index. The index is used to obtain the colour components from a colour table in the same way defined by PHIGS.

- A type followed by several colour component values. Usually there will be three values, such as the red, green and blue components. In this case the colour components are used directly.

Whichever method is used, the resulting colour component values are substituted into the equations used for shading the primitives during subsequent stages of the rendering pipeline, as will be described in Section 14.3. The derivation of the colour is summarized in Figure 14.2, which also illustrates how PHIGS indirect colour fits in, while Table 14.1 shows the possible values for the *type* parameter in a general colour specification. Colour types are described in Appendix F.

Table 14.1   Colour type values.

0	INDIRECT
1	RGB
2	CIE LUV
3	HSV
4	HLS

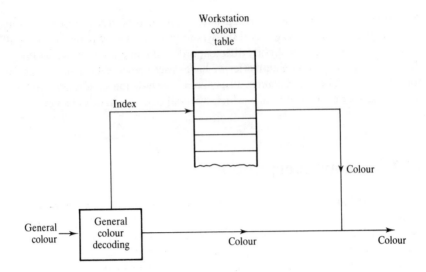

Figure 14.2   Derivation of general colour.

14.2   Lighting and reflectance

During scan conversion, a reflectance equation is applied to find the colour and intensity for each pixel. The equations used are implementation dependent, although the Phong reflectance model is commonly employed. Here we examine this model briefly; greater detail can be found in standard computer graphics texts.

The reflectance equation is used to calculate the colour and intensity of light reflected from the surface of an object in the direction of the viewer. The Phong reflectance equation has three main terms: **ambient light**, **diffusely reflected directional light**, and **specularly reflected directional light**. These terms are usually summed for all active light sources, yielding an equation of the form:

$$C = \sum_{i=1}^{n}(C_{a_i} + C_{d_i} + C_{s_i})$$

where C is the total light reflected from a point on the surface, n is the number of light sources, and C_{a_i}, C_{d_i} and C_{s_i} are the ambient, diffuse and specular components respectively for light source i. These terms depend on a number of parameters:

- The **positions** and **strengths** of the different light sources, which determine how much light strikes each object in a scene. The light may be attenuated according to the distance of the light source from the object. The different types of light source are described in the next section.

- The **surface characteristics** of the objects, which determine how much of the incident light is reflected towards the viewer. These characteristics include the surface's colour, a **diffuse reflection coefficient** and a **specular reflection coefficient**. The ambient and diffuse components are reflected equally in all directions, but the specular component is highly directional. It is a maximum in the direction of a ray whose reflection angle is equal to the incident angle of the incoming light. The 'spread' of the specular component is controlled by the **specular exponent**.

- The **geometry** of the surfaces. The energy of the light incident upon a surface depends on the angle between the arriving light rays and the surface. In the case of diffusely reflected light, the energy can be calculated from the cosine of the angle between a vector towards the light source and a vector normal to the surface. Multiplying this incident energy by the diffuse reflection coefficient gives the amount of light reflected diffusely. For specularly reflected light a vector in the direction of the viewer is required in order to calculate the specular light reflected in that direction.

14.3 Light sources and reflectance equations

PHIGS PLUS supports four kinds of light source. The reflectance equations for each of these are given below, using the parameters defined in Table 14.2 and illustrated in Figure 14.3.

- **Ambient**   Ambient lights are provided to model overall background illumination, such as daylight scattered by the earth's atmosphere. The lights are non-directional – that is, they are assumed to illuminate all objects equally, independently of surface orientations or positions. For an ambient light source:

$$C_a = K_a L_c O_d$$
$$C_d = 0$$
$$C_s = 0$$

- **Directional**   A directional light source has **colour** and **direction**, but is conceptually located at infinity, so that all light rays arriving in the scene will be parallel:

$$C_a = 0$$
$$C_d = K_d L_c O_d \hat{V}_n . \hat{V}_l$$
$$C_s = K_s O_s L_c (\hat{V}_e . \hat{V}_r)^{O_c}$$

The reflection vector is easily calculated from the direction of the incoming light ray, $\hat{V}_l$, and the surface normal vector $\hat{V}_n$:

$$\hat{V}_r = 2(\hat{V}_n . \hat{V}_l)\hat{V}_n - \hat{V}_l$$

Table 14.2   Parameters for reflectance equations.

L_d	light source direction unit vector
L_c	light source colour
L_p	light source position vector
L_e	light source concentration exponent
C_1, C_2	attenuation coefficients
A_s	spread angle
L_a	light attenuation
O_p	object position vector
O_d	object diffuse colour
O_s	object specular colour
O_e	object specular exponent
K_a	ambient reflection coefficient
K_d	diffuse reflection coefficient
K_s	specular reflection coefficient
$\hat{V}_e$	unit vector from object to view point
$\hat{V}_r$	unit reflection vector from object
$\hat{V}_l$	unit vector from object to light source
$\hat{V}_n$	unit surface normal vector of object
C_a	ambient contribution from light source
C_d	diffuse contribution from light source
C_s	specular contribution from light source

- **Positional**   A positional light is located at a finite **position**, and has a colour, and an **attenuation parameter**, L_a, which determines how the intensity of light falling on primitives changes with distance:

$$
\begin{aligned}
C_a &= 0 \\
C_d &= K_d L_c O_d (\hat{V}_n . \hat{V}_l) L_a \\
C_s &= K_s O_s L_c (\hat{V}_e . \hat{V}_r)^{O_c} L_a
\end{aligned}
$$

The attenuation parameter depends on the attenuation coefficients C_1 and C_2, and the distance from the object to the light source:

$$
L_a = \frac{1}{C_1 + (C_2 \| O_p - L_p \|)}
$$

- **Spot**   A spot light is a positional light with a **concentration exponent** and **spread angle**, which together define a cone of light:

$$
\begin{aligned}
C_a &= 0 \\
C_d &= K_d L_c O_d (\hat{V}_n . \hat{V}_l)(\hat{L}_d . - \hat{V}_l)^{L_c} L_a \\
C_s &= K_s O_s L_c (\hat{V}_e . \hat{V}_r)^{O_c} (\hat{L}_d . - \hat{V}_l)^{L_c} L_a
\end{aligned}
$$

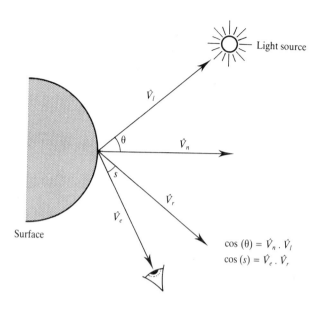

Figure 14.3   Parameters for reflectance equations.

C_d and C_s will be zero if the vector O_p is outside the cone defined by the spread angle A_s.

14.4   Defining and controlling light sources

The parameters associated with a particular light source are stored in a workstation table accessed by an index. They can be set with the function:

☐   SET LIGHT SOURCE REPRESENTATION
parameters:

in	workstation identifier	integer
in	light source index	integer
in	light source type	integer
in	data record	record

The *light source type* parameter identifies whether the light is an ambient, directional, positional, or spot source, and the *data record* contains the parameters appropriate to a light of that type. During traversal, different light sources are activated or deactivated by SET LIGHT SOURCE STATE structure elements, created by the function:

Table 14.3 Reflectance characteristics.

1	no reflectance calculation performed
2	ambient effects only
3	ambient and diffuse effects
4	ambient, diffuse and specular effects

E   SET LIGHT SOURCE STATE
parameters:

in	activation list	list of light source indices
in	deactivation list	list of light source indices

As their names imply, the two lists supplied as parameters determine which lights are turned on or off by this element.

14.5   Defining reflectance properties

The reflectance properties of surfaces can be set with the function:

E   SET REFLECTANCE PROPERTIES
parameters:

in	ambient reflection coefficient	real
in	diffuse reflection coefficient	real
in	specular reflection coefficient	real
in	specular colour	general colour
in	specular exponent	real

This function sets the attributes individually. If bundled attributes are used instead, these properties are accessed by an index, which can be defined with the function SET REFLECTANCE INDEX, while the representation is set with SET REFLECTANCE REPRESENTATION. It is also possible to decide on a selective basis which of the specific effects – ambient, diffuse and specular – are to be applied. These can be selected with the function:

E   SET REFLECTANCE CHARACTERISTICS
parameters:

in	reflectance characteristics	integer

where the parameter values are as shown in Table 14.3. Plates 25, 32 and 33 illustrate the use of reflectance properties.

14.6   Shading

The equations presented in Section 14.3 show how a colour and intensity can be derived for the light reflected from the surface of a primitive in the direction of the viewpoint. These equations depend on the orientation of the surface, as defined by its surface normal vector $\hat{V}_n$. A common technique in computer graphics is to use polygon meshes – such as fill areas, triangle strips or quadrilateral meshes – to approximate curved surfaces. In the simplest form of shading, we compute a single surface normal vector for each facet and then shade it accordingly. However, the facets are then clearly visible, and the resulting discontinuities across the edges between adjacent facets destroy any illusion that we are viewing a curved surface. This can be seen in several of the colour plates, such as Plates 19 and 21.

One way to improve upon this is to interpolate the surface normal vectors supplied at each vertex. Ideally, the normal at a vertex is calculated to correspond to the direction of the true curved surface at that position.

With **Gouraud interpolation**, the graphics system calculates the colour and intensity at each vertex using the vertex normals, and then interpolates these colour values across the facet. At internal edges this creates a smoothly changing intensity which more closely resembles a curved surface – see, for example, Plate 32. However, unless one of the vertices happens to coincide with the position of a specular reflection we will not obtain any specular highlights with this approach.

Further improvements can be obtained with **Phong interpolation**, which interpolates the vertex normals, and then applies the reflectance equation at every interior pixel. Clearly this involves more computation, but it produces specular highlights, as seen in Plates 33 and 34.

Caution is needed with both of these methods, because – with the exception of triangular facets – the resulting colour and intensity values are sensitive to changes in transformations. In other words, if we change our 3D viewing transformation there may be small, but nonetheless discernible, changes in the shading which make it appear that the surface is actually changing shape.

14.6.1   Interior shading methods

PHIGS PLUS does not use conventional terms such as Gouraud or Phong shading, but instead introduces its own terminology. For example, the following five interior shading methods are defined:

- **None**   A colour is calculated for each facet, based on its surface normal. If the facet normal is supplied by the application then this is used; otherwise, the normal is calculated internally. Plate 29 shows an example.

- **Colour**   The colour and surface normal at each vertex are substituted into the reflectance equation. The colours derived from this are interpolated to obtain individual pixel values (Gouraud interpolation). Plates 30 and 32 illustrate colour shading.

- **Data**   The application data values supplied at each vertex are interpolated to obtain corresponding values at each pixel. These values are then mapped to colours, as will be described in Section 14.7, and the colours are used to evaluate the reflectance equations.

- **Normal**   The vertex normals and colours (if supplied) are interpolated to obtain values at each pixel, and these are substituted into the reflectance equation (Phong interpolation). See Plates 31 and 34.

- **Dot**   The vector dot products used in the reflectance equations are evaluated at each vertex, using the local vertex normals. These quantities are $(\hat{V}_n.\hat{V}_l)$, $(\hat{V}_e.\hat{V}_r)$, and $(\hat{L}_d. - \hat{V}_l)$ in the equations presented in Section 14.3. These dot product values are then interpolated across the surface of the primitive. This method is sometimes referred to as cheap Phong interpolation. It yields a result close to full Phong interpolation, but avoids the need to compute unit vectors from interpolated normals at every interior point.

The function to select the desired method is:

[E]   SET INTERIOR SHADING METHOD
    parameters:
        in   shading method   integer

Shading methods are illustrated in Plates 24 and 25. Note that they *only* apply if the interior style for the area primitive in question is set to SOLID.

14.6.2   Computing surface normal vectors

The facet normal is calculated by PHIGS PLUS, unless it is supplied explicitly by the application program as part of the *with data* options of the various primitives. In the case of the fill area primitives, PHIGS PLUS calculates the normal by taking the cross product of two vectors, derived from the first three non-collinear points in the list of fill area vertices. The direction of the resulting vector depends on the relative positions of the three points, and may be the opposite of what was intended if the fill area happens to be concave at the second point. It is always safest to supply the normal vector explicitly.

In the case of the triangle strip, PHIGS PLUS computes the facet normal from successive triples of points. It automatically reverses the normals of alternate facets to obtain a consistent direction. This is needed because the direction of the numbering of the points on alternate triangles reverses, being clockwise for one and then anticlockwise for the next. In the case of quadrilateral mesh, each facet normal is computed from the cross product of the two diagonals of the facet.

If an application wishes to supply explicit facet normals then it can compute these in any convenient manner. Two common methods are to calculate the true surface normal at this point, or to compute the normal from the facet vertices, using local knowledge to avoid the previously mentioned problem of concave shapes. The function COMPUTE FILL AREA SET GEOMETRIC NORMAL is provided to assist with this.

Vertex normals can be calculated directly from surface equations, or can be taken as the average of the surrounding facet normals.

14.7   Data mapping and colour interpolation

So far, we have described how PHIGS PLUS applies primitive attributes, such as colour and reflectance coefficients. However, things are actually slightly more complicated than this, because the *with data* primitives allow us optionally to specify application-dependent data values, as well as colours and normals, at each vertex.

The *with data* primitives allow application data to be associated with primitive vertices. These values are mapped to colours before the reflectance calculations are performed. There are five defined values for the **data mapping method**:

1. **None**   No data mapping is performed.

2. **Single value, uniform**   This maps a single value to a colour selected from a list of n colours, numbered from C_1 to C_n. Values less than some lower limit, d_l, are mapped to C_1. Values greater than or equal to some upper limit, d_u, are mapped to C_n. Between these limits, the data values are mapped linearly onto entries in the list between C_2 and C_{n-1}. We can define this more formally as:

$$\delta = \frac{d_u - d_l}{n - 2}, \quad n > 2$$

$$C = C_1, \quad d < d_l$$

$$C = C_{i+2}, \quad (d_l + i\delta) \le d < d_l + (i+1)\delta, \quad 0 \le i \le n - 3$$

$$C = C_n, \quad d \ge d_u$$

3. **Single value, non-uniform**   Here, we again have a table of n colours, but in addition we have a list of transition data values, d_1 to d_{n-1}, corresponding to the transitions between successive colours. Colour C_1 will be selected if $d < d_1$, C_i when $d_{i-1} \le d < d_i$, and C_n when $d \ge d_{n-1}$.

4. **Bi-value, uniform**   This is similar to the single value, uniform method, except that two data values are used to select a colour from a set of colour lists. Linear interpolation is used with the first data value to select which list of colours to use. Then, a linear interpolation is employed with the second value, to select the specific colour from the chosen list as described previously for single value, uniform mapping.

5. **Bi-value, non-uniform**   Here again, we have two data values. Corresponding to these there are two lists of transition values. The two values are compared with their respective lists to select a colour. We can visualize this as a 2D array of values, whose array indices are selected by comparing the supplied data values with the transition values associated with each index.

The function SET DATA MAPPING METHOD is provided to select the required method and to specify the necessary parameters. The equivalent functions for bundled attributes are SET DATA MAPPING INDEX and SET DATA MAPPING REPRESENTATION.

If a data mapping technique is selected, and the appropriate data values are specified at each vertex, then PHIGS PLUS will derive the corresponding vertex colours. These vertex colours will override any explicitly specified vertex colours, unless the *data mapping method* NONE is selected.

During surface shading, the vertex colours, if available, are interpolated across the surface of the primitive, using bi-linear interpolation. Suppose that no vertex colours are supplied. In this case PHIGS PLUS will check to see whether individual facet colours have been supplied. If they are present, then they are used; otherwise, the interior colour attribute associated with the particular type of primitive in question will be used instead.

The colour derived in this way is referred to as the **intrinsic colour** of the primitive. Note that colour computations are performed with the user-selected rendering colour model. While this has a clear interpretation for RGB, unusual effects are likely to result if the other models are used. The rendering colour model is selected with SET RENDERING COLOUR MODEL.

There is one further feature concerned with deriving colours. This is the notion of *front* and *back faces*. Those primitives which are used to display areas are defined so that they are considered to have two sides, either of which may be visible. It is sometimes useful to be able to distinguish which side of the primitive can actually be seen. For example, suppose we wish to display a surface representing a function of two variables. By colouring its two sides differently we are able to discriminate between the top and bottom of the surface, which can be useful if the surface is very bumpy and we are viewing it from the side.

We can define different colour and reflectance values for the front and back faces. During processing, the (implicit or explicit) facet normal is used to determine the orientation of a facet with respect to the viewer, and thus to determine which of the two sets of values to use during shading. There are functions for setting the back face properties, corresponding to their front face counterparts, such as SET BACK DATA MAPPING METHOD, and SET BACK REFLECTANCE PROPERTIES. It is also possible to control whether front and back faces are distinguished, by setting the **face distinguishing mode** to ON or OFF, using the function SET FACE DISTINGUISHING MODE.

There is one other use for front and back faces. During hidden surface removal we can request PHIGS PLUS to ignore either front or back faces. This is known as **face culling**, and is controlled by the function SET FACE CULLING MODE, which can accept as a parameter the values (NONE, BACKFACE, FRONT-

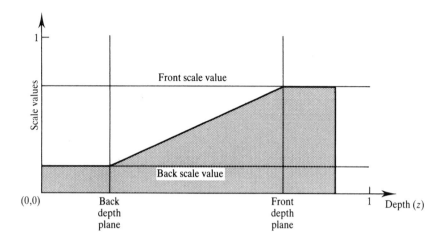

Figure 14.4   Depth cueing.

FACE). Culling of back faces is often worthwhile, because it eliminates around 50% of faces from further processing, which can result in significant speed gains during rendering.

14.8   Depth cueing

Depth cueing is a technique which adjusts the colour of a primitive according to its distance from the viewer. This corresponds to its z coordinate in NPC space. The technique is commonly employed to reduce the intensity of primitives which are further from the viewer, thereby creating an illusion of depth. It also helps to reduce clutter in an image by making the frontmost details brighter and clearer than those at the back of the scene (see Plates 27 and 28).

A general formulation is adopted in which the z coordinate controls the mixing of the primitive's colour and a depth cue colour. The parameters which affect this are the *front depth cue* and *back depth cue reference planes* which determine the range of z values over which a linear interpolation is performed, and the *front* and *back scale factors* which determine the ratio in which the primitive's colour and depth cue colour are mixed for points in front of and behind, respectively, the front and back planes. This is illustrated in Figure 14.4. One application of this general approach is to allow colours to desaturate with depth (distance) – as happens in the real world.

Depth cueing is controlled via a bundle. The particular set of values to apply is selected by using SET DEPTH CUE INDEX, and the representation is set with:

☐ SET DEPTH CUE REPRESENTATION
   parameters:

in	workstation identifier	integer
in	depth cue index	integer
in	depth cue mode	(SUPPRESSED, ALLOWED)
in	depth cue reference planes	2 reals
in	depth cue scale factors	2 reals
in	depth cue colour	general colour

The depth cue reference planes are defined by their NPC z coordinates, as shown in Figure 14.4, in which the front and back scale values, each in the range $0-1$, can also be seen.

14.9   Colour mapping

The last stage of the rendering pipeline is to display the colours which have been calculated with the reflectance equations. The first step in this process is to convert the colours from the model used to calculate them into the colour model which is to be used for their display. In practice, the set of colours contained in an image can be very large. Unless we are fortunate enough to have a workstation which can display true colours then we will have to use some method for mapping the desired colours onto those actually available. To make this as flexible as possible, there is a **colour mapping** stage which supports true colour mapping, and two kinds of pseudo-colour mapping.

With **true colour mapping** the desired colours are passed to the workstation and must be reproduced as faithfully as possible using an implementation-dependent method. Possible solutions include use of full colour devices (with perhaps 24 bits per pixel), and use of dithering.

With **pseudo-colour** a weighting function is used to combine the given colours to form an index. This index is then employed to access a **pseudo-colour table** from which the final colours are found. These must then be represented as faithfully as possible by the workstation. In effect, pseudo-colour offers a mechanism for controlling the final mapping of colours. As an example, consider a picture specified with HSV parameters. The weighting function parameters could be defined such that only the V values are of any consequence, providing a simple way to map a colour picture to a greyscale display.

A variation of pseudo-colour is **pseudo-N colour**. Here, N look-up tables are employed, one for each colour component, and separate indices are computed for each, which gives greater flexibility.

The colour mapping method is accessed via a bundle, using SET COLOUR MAPPING INDEX, and the representation is set with:

Table 14.4   Colour mapping methods.

1	true colour mapping
2	pseudo-colour mapping
3	pseudo-N colour mapping

☐ SET COLOUR MAPPING REPRESENTATION

parameters:

in	workstation identifier	integer
in	colour mapping index	integer
in	colour mapping method	integer
in	data record	record

The colour mapping methods are shown in Table 14.4. The data record contains colour values appropriate to the selected method.

14.10   An example

Appendix B contains a complete example PHIGS PLUS program written in C and implemented using SunPHIGS 1.1. The program illustrates a number of PHIGS and PHIGS PLUS features including structure definition, use of the polyline and quadrilateral mesh primitives, defining light sources, and controlling the rotation of the displayed image via a view definition. The program also uses a menu (a choice device) and the keyboard (a string device) for entering input values using event mode. Plates 14 and 15 show examples of the program in action on a Sun workstation.

Appendix A
Viewing example program

This appendix presents the C program described in Chapter 6 which uses viewing to simulate flying around a scene in a helicopter.

The scene is modelled using two main structures: one for the ground and one for the hotel. The hotel itself is made from several other structures which define its basic shape, its sign and the helicopter landing-pad on the roof. The scene is posted using view representation 1, which is subsequently modified by updating the view up vector according to latitude and longitude values entered using two valuators in sample mode. A choice device is used in sample mode for posting the scene to a workstation which produces hard copy, and for terminating the program.

A.1   A note about viewing parameters

In this example we have kept things simple by centring the middle of the hotel at the WC point $(0, 0, 0)$. This is done using a modelling transformation. The view orientation parameters used are as follows:

View reference point	$(0, 0, 0)$
View plane normal	set according to latitude and longitude
View up vector	$(0, 0, 1)$

The view mapping parameters used are:

Window limits	-1.25 to 1.25 for x and y
Projection viewport	0 to 1 in x, y and z
Projection type	PARALLEL
Projection reference point	$(0, 0, 0)$
View plane distance	0.9
Back plane distance	-2.0
Front plane distance	2.0
View clipping limits	0 to 1 in x, y and z
xy clipping indicator	NOCLIP
Back clipping indicator	NOCLIP
Front clipping indicator	NOCLIP

A.2   The program

```c
#include <phigs.h>
#include <stdio.h>
#include <math.h>

/* Some constants. */

#define WS1      1
#define WS2      2
#define DEVICE1 1
#define DEVICE2 2
#define PI       3.14159

/* Structure identifiers. */

#define SCENE       1
#define BASE        2
#define HOTEL       3
#define PAD         4
#define SIGN        5

#define BASESIZE     0.9
#define HOTELWIDTH   0.3
#define HOTELDEPTH   0.1
#define HOTELHEIGHT  0.5
#define DOORWIDTH    0.03
#define DOORHEIGHT   0.15

Pviewrep3 view;        /* View representation used for scene. */

/**************************************************************
makebase: Creates the structure for the base of the scene. */
void makebase()
{
   Ppoint3 basepts[] = {{0,0,0}, {BASESIZE,0,0},
                        {BASESIZE,BASESIZE,0},
                        {0, BASESIZE,0,}};
   popenstruct(BASE);
   psetintstyle(PHOLLOW);
   pfillarea3(4, basepts);
   pclosestruct();
}

/* makepad: Creates the structure for the helicopter landing-pad
   on the roof of the hotel. */
void makepad()
{
   Ppoint3 landpad[5] = {{-HOTELDEPTH/3 , HOTELDEPTH/3, 0},
                         {HOTELDEPTH/3, HOTELDEPTH/3, 0},
```

```
                          {HOTELDEPTH/3 ,-HOTELDEPTH/3, 0},
                          {-HOTELDEPTH/3, -HOTELDEPTH/3, 0}};
   popenstruct(PAD);
   psetintstyle(PSOLID);
   pfillarea3(4, landpad);
   pclosestruct();
}

/*******************************************************
makesign: Creates the structure for the hotel sign. */
void makesign()
{
   Pchar *hsign = "HOTEL";
   Pvector3 d[2] = {{1.0, 0.0, 0.0}, {0.0, 1.0, 0.0}};
   Ppoint3 tll = {HOTELWIDTH/2, 3*HOTELHEIGHT/4, 0};
   Ptxalign txa = {PTH_CENTRE, PAV_HALF};

   popenstruct(SIGN);
   psetcharheight(0.06);
   psettextpath(PTP_RIGHT);
   psettextalign(&txa);
   ptext3(&tll, d, hsign);
   pclosestruct();
};

/*****************************************************
makehotel: Creates the structure for the hotel. */
void makehotel()
{
   Ppoint3 hotelbase[] = {{0, 0, 0}, {0, HOTELDEPTH, 0},
                          {HOTELWIDTH, HOTELDEPTH, 0},
                          {HOTELWIDTH, 0, 0}, {0, 0, 0}};
   Ppoint3 hoteltop[] = {{0, 0, HOTELHEIGHT},
                          {0, HOTELDEPTH, HOTELHEIGHT},
                          {HOTELWIDTH, HOTELDEPTH, HOTELHEIGHT},
                          {HOTELWIDTH, 0, HOTELHEIGHT},
                          {0, 0, HOTELHEIGHT}};
   Ppoint3 hoteldoor[] = {{HOTELWIDTH/2-DOORWIDTH, 0, 0},
                          {HOTELWIDTH/2+DOORWIDTH,0,0},
                          {HOTELWIDTH/2+DOORWIDTH, 0, DOORHEIGHT},
                          {HOTELWIDTH/2-DOORWIDTH, 0, DOORHEIGHT},
                          {HOTELWIDTH/2-DOORWIDTH,0,0}};
   Pint err;
   Pmatrix3 padmat,textmat;
   Ppoint3 link1[] = {{0, 0, 0}, {0, 0, HOTELHEIGHT}};
   Ppoint3 link2[] = {{0, HOTELDEPTH, 0},
                       {0, HOTELDEPTH, HOTELHEIGHT}};
   Ppoint3 link3[] = {{HOTELWIDTH, HOTELDEPTH, 0},
                       {HOTELWIDTH, HOTELDEPTH, HOTELHEIGHT}};
   Ppoint3 link4[] = {{HOTELWIDTH, 0, 0},
```

```
                              {HOTELWIDTH, 0, HOTELHEIGHT}};
Pchar *hotelsign = "HOTEL";
Pvector3 axtxtdir[2] = { {1.0, 0.0, 0.0}, {0.0, 1.0, 0.0}};
Pvector3 textdir[2] = { {0.0, 1.0, 0.0}, {0.0, 0.0, 1.0}};
Pvector3 textdir2[2] = { {1.0, 0.0, 0.0}, {0.0, 0.0, 1.0}};
Ppoint3 textloc2 = {HOTELWIDTH/6 ,HOTELDEPTH/2.0, HOTELHEIGHT};
Ppoint3 textloc1 = {HOTELWIDTH, HOTELDEPTH/2, HOTELHEIGHT*5/6};
Ptxalign txalign = {PTH_NORMAL, PAV_HALF};
Pvector3 padpos = {5*HOTELWIDTH/6, HOTELDEPTH/2, HOTELHEIGHT};
Ppoint3 xaxis[2] = { {0,0,0}, {0.5,0,0} };
Ppoint3 yaxis[2] = { {0,0,0}, {0,0.5,0} };
Ppoint3 zaxis[2] = { {0,0,0}, {0,0,0.75} };
Ppoint3 x_txt = {0.52,0,0};
Ppoint3 y_txt = {0.0,0.52,0};
Ppoint3 z_txt = {0,0,0.77};

popenstruct(HOTEL);
psetlinewidth(3.0);                    /* Hotel's X, Y and Z axes. */
psetlinetype(PLN_SOLID);
ppolyline3(2, xaxis);
psetlinetype(PLN_DASH);
ppolyline3(2, yaxis);
psetlinetype(PLN_DOT);
ppolyline3(2, zaxis);
psetcharheight(0.07);
ptext3(&x_txt, axtxtdir, "X");
ptext3(&y_txt, axtxtdir, "Y");
ptext3(&z_txt, axtxtdir, "Z");

psetlinetype(PLN_SOLID);          /* Base, top and sides. */
ppolyline3(5, hotelbase);
ppolyline3(5, hoteltop);
psetlinewidth(5.0);
ppolyline3(2, link2);
ppolyline3(2, link3);
psetlinewidth(1.0);
ppolyline3(2, link1);
ppolyline3(2, link4);

ppolyline3(5, hoteldoor);         /* Draw the door. */
psettextprec(PPSTROKE);           /* The downward sign. */
psetcharheight(0.04);
psettextpath(PTP_DOWN);
ptext3(&textloc1, textdir, hotelsign);

protatex(PI/2, &err, textmat); /* The front sign. */
psetlocaltran3(textmat, PREPLACE);
pexecutestruct(SIGN);

ptranslate3(&padpos, &err, padmat); /* The landing pad. */
```

```
   psetlocaltran3(padmat, PREPLACE);
   pexecutestruct(PAD);
   pclosestruct();
}

/**********************************
build_model: Assembles the model. */
void build_model()
{
   Pmatrix3 hotelshift, baseshift,textmat;
   Pvector3 hotelposition = {-HOTELWIDTH/2, -HOTELDEPTH/2,
                             -HOTELHEIGHT/2};
   Pvector3 baseposition = {-BASESIZE/2, -3*BASESIZE/4,
                             -HOTELHEIGHT/2};
   Pint err;

   makebase();             /* Create BASE structure. */
   makesign();             /* Create SIGN structure. */
   makepad();              /* Create PAD structure. */
   makehotel();            /* Define HOTEL structure. */

   popenstruct(SCENE);  /* Define the SCENE structure. */
   psetviewind(1);      /* Use view index 1. */

   ptranslate3(&baseposition, &err, baseshift);
   psetlocaltran3(baseshift, PREPLACE);
   pexecutestruct(BASE);

   ptranslate3(&hotelposition, &err, hotelshift);
   psetlocaltran3(hotelshift, PREPLACE);
   pexecutestruct(HOTEL);

   pclosestruct();
}

/*********************************************************
setview: Defines the initial view, returned in vrep. */
void setview(Pint ws, Pviewrep3 *vrep)
{
   Ppoint3  vrp;
   Pvector3 vpn, vup;
   Pint  err;
   Pviewmapping3 vmap;
   Plimit3 lims = {0.0, 1.0, 0.0, 1.0, 0.0, 1.0};
   vrp.x = 0.0; vrp.y = 0.0; vrp.z = 0.0;
   vpn.x = 0.0; vpn.y = -1.0; vpn.z = 0.0;
   vup.x = 0.0; vup.y = 0.0; vup.z = 1.0;

   pevalvieworientationmatrix3(&vrp, &vpn, &vup, &err,
                               vrep->orientation_matrix);
```

```
      if (err != 0) {printf("Error in view orientation = %d", err);}

      vrep->clip_limit = lims;
      vrep->clip_xy = vrep->clip_back = vrep->clip_front = PNOCLIP;
      vmap.window.xmin = -1.25; vmap.window.xmax = 1.25;
      vmap.window.ymin = -1.25; vmap.window.ymax = 1.25;
      vmap.viewport = lims;
      vmap.proj = PPARALLEL;
      vmap.prp.x = (vmap.window.xmin + vmap.window.xmax) / 2.0;
      vmap.prp.y = (vmap.window.ymin + vmap.window.ymax) / 2.0;
      vmap.prp.z = 1.0;
      vmap.view_plane = 0.9;
      vmap.front_plane = 2.0;
      vmap.back_plane = -2.0;
      pevalviewmappingmatrix3( &vmap, &err, vrep->mapping_matrix);
      if (err != 0) {printf("Error in view mapping = %d", err);}

      psetviewrep3(WS1, 1, vrep);
}


/******************************************************************
changeview: Accepts a view rep which has a valid view
mapping matrix, and changes the view orientation, and sets
a view rep. */
void changeview(Pint ws, Pviewrep3 *vrep)
{
   Pfloat latitude, longitude;
   Ppoint3  vrp;
   Pvector3 vpn, vup;
   Pint  err;
   Plimit3 lims = {0.0, 1.0, 0.0, 1.0, 0.0, 1.0};
   vrp.x = 0.0; vrp.y = 0.0; vrp.z = 0.0;
   vpn.x = 0.0; vpn.y = -1.0; vpn.z = 0.0;
   vup.x = 0.0; vup.y = 0.0; vup.z = 1.0;

   psampleval(WS1, DEVICE1, &longitude);
   psampleval(WS1, DEVICE2, &latitude);
   vpn.x = cos(latitude*PI/180) * cos(longitude*PI/180);
   vpn.y = cos(latitude*PI/180) * sin(longitude*PI/180);
   vpn.z = sin(latitude*PI/180);

   pevalvieworientationmatrix3(&vrp, &vpn, &vup, &err,
                               vrep->orientation_matrix);
   if (err != 0) {printf("Error in view orientation = %d", err);}

   vrep->clip_limit = lims;
   vrep->clip_xy = vrep->clip_back = vrep->clip_front = PNOCLIP;
   psetviewrep3(ws, 1, vrep);
}
```

```
/********************************************************************
init_input: Initializes two valuators in sample mode, and a
choice device in event mode. */
init_input()
{
   Pchoicestatus initstatus = PCH_OK;
   Pint initvalue = 1;
   Pvalrec vrec;
   Plimit ea;
   Pint err;
   Pdspsize dispsize;
   Pchoicerec crec;
   static Pchar *strs[] = {"Hardcopy", "Exit"};

   pinqdisplayspacesize(211, &err, &dispsize);
   ea.xmin = dispsize.device.x*0.7;
   ea.xmax = dispsize.device.x*0.85;
   ea.ymin = dispsize.device.y*0.7;
   ea.ymax = dispsize.device.y*0.85;
   vrec.valpet1_datarec.low = 0.0;
   vrec.valpet1_datarec.high = 360.0;
   vrec.valpet1_datarec.title_string = "Longitude";
   pinitval( WS1, DEVICE1, 0.0, 1, &ea, &vrec);
   psetvalmode( WS1, DEVICE1, PSAMPLE, PES_ECHO);

   ea.xmin = dispsize.device.x*0.7;
   ea.xmax = dispsize.device.x*0.85;
   ea.ymin = dispsize.device.y*0.55;
   ea.ymax = dispsize.device.y*0.7;
   vrec.valpet1_datarec.low = -90.0;
   vrec.valpet1_datarec.high = 90.0;
   vrec.valpet1_datarec.title_string = "Latitude";
   pinitval( WS1, DEVICE2, 0.0, 1, &ea, &vrec);
   psetvalmode( WS1, DEVICE2, PSAMPLE, PES_ECHO);

   ea.xmin = dispsize.device.x*0.7;
   ea.xmax = dispsize.device.x*0.85;
   ea.ymin = dispsize.device.y*0.4;
   ea.ymax = dispsize.device.y*0.55;

   crec.choicepet1_datarec.number = 2;
   crec.choicepet1_datarec.strings = strs;
   crec.choicepet1_datarec.title_string = "Choice device";

   pinitchoice(WS1, DEVICE1, initstatus,
               initvalue, 1, &ea, &crec);
   psetchoicemode(WS1, DEVICE1, PEVENT, PES_ECHO);
}
```

```
/*********************************************************************
hardcopy: Opens a hardcopy workstation, and posts SCENE to it. */
hardcopy()
{
    popenws(WS2, "scene.ps", 61); /* Implementation dependent. */
    psetviewrep3(WS2, 1, &view);  /* Set up the current view. */
    ppoststruct(WS2, SCENE, 0.0); /* Post SCENE. */
    pclosews(WS2);
}

/* main ***********************************************************/
main()
{
    Pevent event;                 /* Event input data. */
    Pchoice choice;

    popenphigs(0, 0);             /* Open PHIGS. */
    popenws(WS1, 0, 0);           /* Open a workstation. */

    setview(WS1, &view);          /* Define the initial view. */

    build_model();                /* Create the model. */

    psetdisplayupdatest(WS1, PASAP, PUQUM); /* Set fast update. */

    ppoststruct(WS1, SCENE, 0.0); /* Post the root structure. */

    init_input();                 /* Initialize input devices. */
    while (1)
      {
      changeview(WS1, &view);     /* Change the view. */
      pawaitevent(0.0, &event);   /* See if choice picked. */

      if (event.class == PI_CHOICE)
        { pgetchoice(&choice);
          if (choice.choice == 1) {hardcopy(); break;}
          if (choice.choice == 2) {break;}
        }
      }

    pclosews(WS1);                /* Close workstation. */
    pclosephigs();                /* Close PHIGS. */
}
```

Appendix B
PHIGS PLUS example program

This appendix contains a complete PHIGS PLUS example program, written in C and using the SunPHIGS 1.1 implementation of PHIGS. The program has been tested by the authors, but may differ slightly from what is needed on other systems because PHIGS PLUS is not yet finalized as a standard.

B.1 Introduction

The program is designed to display a surface which represents a function of two variables. The surface may be computed, or the data describing it may be obtained experimentally. In either case, input to the program is from a file, whose format is given in the next section. The surface is assumed to comprise a 2D array of 'spot heights', and the PHIGS PLUS quadrilateral mesh primitive is employed to display it, using shading. The surface is subject to a viewing transformation, which can be altered by pressing the arrow keys on an alphanumeric keyboard.

The program is controlled by a menu which contains the following commands:

- **Shade** This generates a shaded view of the surface, using the quadrilateral mesh primitive, with two light sources, one ambient and one directional. A z-buffer is used for Hidden Surface Removal (HSR).

- **Move** This allows the viewpoint to be altered by pressing the arrow keys on the alphanumeric keyboard. Pressing the 'left' arrow simulates moving the eye to the left, with the 'right' arrow key as its counterpart. The 'up' and 'down' arrow keys simulate moving up and down. In fact, these keys control angles of rotation, which we can think of as longitude and latitude. The functions which update these angles contain checks to make sure the angles do not go out of range. When the program is in this mode, the surface is displayed as a wireframe mesh using polylines. This is for reasons of speed – polylines are displayed much more quickly than quadrilateral meshes on the Sun workstation, so the wireframe method permits quicker feedback.

- **Light** This operates in a similar manner to altering the viewpoint, but in this case it is the light source direction which is altered. An arrow is displayed to show the current direction, and this can be altered using the 'left', 'right', 'up' and 'down' arrow keys. Wireframe mode is used here as well.

- **File**   This is selected when a new data file is to be read. The keyboard is switched to request mode and the operator is prompted for a name. The prompt is displayed as the initial string. This works, but is probably bad practice, because if the operator erases characters then the edit position changes. This causes the name to be positioned differently in the input buffer from what the program expects, so that an incorrect name results.

B.2   The data file format

Here is a fragment of a data file describing a surface. Only the first and last few lines are given because the complete file is too large.

The first two values give the number of grid points in each direction, in this case we have a 41×41 grid of points. The next two points give the x and z step sizes. In this example, the grid point spacing in each direction is one unit. The remainder of the data file contains the y (height) values for each grid point. In this case there will be 41×41 values.

```
    41    41    1.000000  1.000000
  -88.23036      -90.06970      -91.85558      -93.26171
  -93.99392      -93.94831      -93.20770      -91.96466
      .
      .
      .
 -111.0175      -112.0482      -113.0876      -114.2531
 -115.5245      -116.8404      -118.1761      -119.5470
 -120.9626
```

B.3   The program

```c
#include <phigs/phigs.h>        /* SunPHIGS declarations file */
#include <math.h>
#include <stdio.h>

#define PICTURE 1               /* structure numbers */
#define SHADED 2
#define WIREFRAME 3
#define WIREMESH 4
#define ARROW 5
#define WS 1                    /* workstation identifier */
#define PRIORITY 1              /* structure priority */
#define PI 3.141592654
```

```
#define SCALE 0.8
#define VIEWINDEX 1
#define LIGHT1INDEX 1
#define LIGHT2INDEX 2
#define BUFFERSIZE 40                    /* size of text input buffer */
#define EDITPOS 16        /* initial edit position for text input */

/****************************************************************
 Message function
 ****************************************************************/

static void
message(index)           /* display messages in the text subwindow */
  int index;
{
Pchar buf[40];                               /* characters go here */

  switch(index) {                     /* switch on message number */
    case 1:sprintf(buf, "Reading coordinates..\n");
      break;
    case 2:sprintf(buf, "Calculating facet normal vectors..\n");
      break;
    case 3:sprintf(buf,"Building wireframe and shaded model..\n");
      break;
    case 4:sprintf(buf, "Can't open file..\n");
      break;
    case 5:sprintf(buf, "Change view..\n");
      break;
    case 6:sprintf(buf, "Change light direction..\n");
      break;
    case 7:sprintf(buf, "Shading picture..\n");
      break;
    case 8:sprintf(buf, "Scaling points..\n");
      break;
    case 9:sprintf(buf, "This may take a while..\n");
      break;
  }
  pmessage(WS, buf);
}

/****************************************************************
 Light source functions
 ****************************************************************/

Pint index[] = {LIGHT1INDEX, LIGHT2INDEX};

static void
activate_light_source()                    /* activate light source */
{
Pintlst activation, deactivation;
```

```
    activation.number = 2;
    activation.integers = index;
    deactivation.number = 0;
    deactivation.integers = NULL;
    psetlightsrcstate(&activation, &deactivation);
}


/*****************************************************************/

static void
set_light_source(direction)                     /* set up light source */
  Pvector3 direction;
{
Plightsrcbundl rep;

  rep.type = 2;                                         /* directional */
  rep.rec.directional.colour.type = 1;          /* general colour */
  rep.rec.directional.colour.val.general.x = 1;  /* white light */
  rep.rec.directional.colour.val.general.y = 1;
  rep.rec.directional.colour.val.general.z = 1;
  rep.rec.directional.dir = direction;
  psetlightsrcrep(WS, LIGHT1INDEX, &rep);      /* this is light 1 */
}


/*****************************************************************/

static void
echo(x_angle, y_angle)         /* rotate arrow for light direction */
  float x_angle, y_angle;
{
static Pvector3 origin = {0.0, 0.0, 0.0};
static Pvector3 scale = {1.0, 1.0, 1.0};
static Pvector3 shift = {0.5, 0.5, SCALE/2.0};
Pint err;
Pmatrix3 matrix;
float angle = 0;

  popenstruct(ARROW);
    psetelemptr(2);
    pseteditmode(PEDIT_REPLACE);/* replace arrow transformation */
    pbuildtran3(&origin, &shift, x_angle, y_angle, angle,
                &scale, &err, matrix);
    psetlocaltran3(matrix, PREPLACE);
    pseteditmode(PEDIT_INSERT);            /* go back to insert mode */
  pclosestruct();
}


/*****************************************************************/
```

```
static void
calculate_direction(i, j)/* calculate direction of light source */
  int i, j;                            /* from angles i & j */
{
Pvector3 lightdir;
float anglei, anglej, R;

  anglei = i*PI/180;
  anglej = j*PI/180;
  echo(anglei, anglej);        /* display arrow in new position */
  lightdir.y = -cos(anglei);
  R = sqrt(1 - lightdir.y * lightdir.y);
  lightdir.x = -R*sin(anglej);
  lightdir.z = -R*cos(anglej);
  set_light_source(lightdir);  /* update light source direction */
}

/****************************************************************/

static void
change_light(direction)        /* change direction of light source */
  Pint direction;
{
static int i, j;
int stopflag = 0;      /* stopflag used to limit "up/down" motion */
  switch(direction) {
    case PCURSOR_KEY_UP:              /* move light direction "up" */
      if (i == 0) {
        stopflag = 1;
        break;}
      i = i-5;
      break;
    case PCURSOR_KEY_DOWN:       /* move light direction "down" */
      if (i == 180) {
        stopflag = 1;
        break;}
      i = i+5;
      break;
    case PCURSOR_KEY_LEFT:       /* move light direction "left" */
      if (j == 0)
        j = 360;
      j = j-5;
      break;
    case PCURSOR_KEY_RIGHT:      /* move light direction "right" */
      if (j == 360)
        j = 0;
      j = j+5;
      break;
    case 0:                       /* reset to default position */
      i = 0;
```

```
        j = 0;
        break;
    }
    if (stopflag == 0)
      calculate_direction(i, j);
}


/******************************************************************
  Viewing functions
 ******************************************************************/

static void
init_rep(rep)                               /* initialize view rep */
  Pviewrep3 *rep;
{
static Plimit window = {-0.8, 0.8, -0.8, 0.8};      /* NPC window */
static Plimit3 viewport = {0, 1, 0, 1, 0, 1}; /* whole viewport */
static Ppoint3 prp = {0, 0, 10};        /* projection reference pt */
static Plimit3 clip_limit = {0, 1, 0, 1, 0, 1}; /* clipp limits */
Pint err2, view_plane = 0, front_plane = 5, back_plane = -5;
Pviewmapping3 mapping;
Pprojtype proj = PPERSPECTIVE;                  /* perspective view */
Pclip clip_xy = PNOCLIP,clip_front = PNOCLIP,clip_back = PNOCLIP;
                          /* clipping is disabled because it is
                                    scaled to be entirely visible */
  mapping.window = window;
  mapping.viewport = viewport;
  mapping.proj = proj;
  mapping.prp = prp;
  mapping.view_plane = view_plane;
  mapping.back_plane = back_plane;
  mapping.front_plane = front_plane;
  pevalviewmappingmatrix3(&mapping, &err2, rep->mapping_matrix);
  rep->clip_limit = clip_limit;
  rep->clip_xy = clip_xy;
  rep->clip_back = clip_back;
  rep->clip_front = clip_front;
}


/******************************************************************/

static void
set_view_rep(vpn)                            /* set view rep with vpn */
  Pvector3 vpn;
{
static Pviewrep3 rep;
static Ppoint3 vrp = {0.5, 0.5, SCALE/2.0};
static Pvector3 vup = {0, 1, 0};            /* y-axis is vertical */
static initflag;
Pint err1;
```

```
  pevalvieworientationmatrix3(&vrp, &vpn, &vup, &err1,
                              rep.orientation_matrix );
  if (initflag == 0) {
    init_rep(&rep);
    initflag = 1;}
  psetviewrep3(WS, VIEWINDEX, &rep);
}

/****************************************************************/

static void
calculate_vpn(i, j)        /* calculate new vpn from angles i & j */
  int i, j;
{
Pvector3 vpn;
float anglei, anglej, R;

    anglei = i*PI/180;
    anglej = j*PI/180;
    vpn.y = sin(anglei);
    R = sqrt(1 - vpn.y*vpn.y);
    vpn.x = R*sin(anglej);
    vpn.z = R*cos(anglej);
    set_view_rep(vpn);
}

/****************************************************************/

static void
change_view(direction)                 /* change view plane normal */
  Pint direction;
{
static int i, j;
int stopflag = 0;

  switch(direction) {                  /* depends on key pressed */
    case PCURSOR_KEY_UP:
      if (i == 85) {
        stopflag = 1;
        break;}
      i++;
      break;
    case PCURSOR_KEY_DOWN:
      if (i == -85) {
        stopflag = 1;
        break;}
      i--;
      break;
    case PCURSOR_KEY_LEFT:
```

```
      if (j == 0) j = 360;
      j--;
      break;
    case PCURSOR_KEY_RIGHT:
      if (j == 360) j = 0;
      j++;
      break;
    case 0:
      i = 0;
      j = 0;
      break;
  }
  if (stopflag == 0)
    calculate_vpn(i, j);
}

/*****************************************************************
 Compute area properties
 *****************************************************************/

static void
area_properties()                              /* set area properties */
{
Pareaprops properties;
Pgcolr colour;

  properties.ambient_coef = 0.2;
  properties.diffuse_coef = 0.9;
  properties.specular_coef = 0.2;
  properties.specular_colour.type = 1;          /* general colour */
  properties.specular_colour.val.general.x = 1;      /* specular */
  properties.specular_colour.val.general.y = 1;       /* colour */
  properties.specular_colour.val.general.z = 1;
  properties.specular_exp = 10;
  properties.transpar_coef = 0;
  psetareaprop(&properties);/* front and back faces are similar */
  psetbackareaprop(&properties);
  colour.type = 0;
  colour.val.index = 6;
  psetbackintcolour(&colour);
}

/*****************************************************************
 Structure creation
 *****************************************************************/

static void
picture()                                /* post the shaded picture */
{
  punpostallstruct(WS);                        /* unpost all structures */
```

```
  psethlhsrmode(WS, 1);                                /* z-buffer HSR */
  ppoststruct(WS, PICTURE, PRIORITY);      /* post shaded picture */
}

/****************************************************************/

static void
wireframe()                                  /* post the wireframe */
{
  punpostallstruct(WS);                    /* unpost all structures */
  ppoststruct(WS, WIREFRAME, PRIORITY);   /* post wireframe pict */
  psethlhsrmode(WS, 0);                    /* no HSR for this method */
}

/****************************************************************/

static void
structures()              /* create wireframe and shaded picture */
{
  popenstruct(WIREFRAME);                  /* create new structure */
    psetviewind(VIEWINDEX);  /* affected by view transformation */
    pexecutestruct(WIREMESH);   /* call un-transformed structure */
  pclosestruct();
  popenstruct(PICTURE);                    /* ditto for shaded picture */
    psethlhsrid(1);                        /* enable HSR for this one */
    activate_light_source();               /* and shine lights on it */
    psetedgecolourind(1);                  /* edge colour for facets */
    psetfacedistgmode(PDISTG_YES);     /* distinguish front/back */
    psetbackintstyle(PSOLID);                    /* solid fill */
    psetbackintshadmethod(1);                   /* flat shading */
    psetbackintreflecteq(3);      /* reflectance characteristics */
    psetintstyle(PSOLID);              /* ditto for front faces */
    psetintshadmethod(1);
    psetintreflecteq(4);
    area_properties();
    psetviewind(VIEWINDEX);
    pexecutestruct(SHADED);                  /* call the structure */
    psethlhsrid(0);              /* disable HSR for anything else */
  pclosestruct();

}

/****************************************************************/

Ppoint3 shaft[] = {{0.0, 0.6, 0.0}, {0.0, 0.2, 0.0}};
Ppoint3 head1[] = {{0.05, 0.25, 0.0}, {0.0, 0.2, 0.0},
                   {-0.05, 0.25, 0.0}};
Ppoint3 head2[] = {{0.0, 0.25, 0.05}, {0.0, 0.2, 0.0},
                   {0.0, 0.25, -0.05}};
static void
```

```
arrow()                                   /* create arrow structure */
{
static Pvector3 origin = {0.0, 0.0, 0.0};
static Pvector3 scale = {1.0, 1.0, 1.0};
static Pvector3 shift = {0.5, 0.5, SCALE/2.0};
Pint err;
Pmatrix3 matrix;
float angle = 0;

  popenstruct(ARROW);
    psetviewind(VIEWINDEX);                       /* arrow is affected by
                                                     view transformation */
    pbuildtran3(&origin, &shift, angle, angle, angle, &scale,
                &err, matrix);        /* compute transformation */
    psetlocaltran3(matrix, PREPLACE);
    psetlinecolourind(4);
    psetlinewidth(4);
    ppolyline3(2, shaft);                         /* draw arrow parts */
    ppolyline3(3, head1);
    psetlinecolourind(2);
    ppolyline3(3, head2);
  pclosestruct();
}

/******************************************************************
 Initialize light source direction and view direction
 ******************************************************************/

static void
initialize_vectors()               /* set initial light direction and
                                                view plane normal */
{
int reset = 0;

  change_view(reset);
  change_light(reset);
}

/******************************************************************
 Create wireframe using polylines
 ******************************************************************/

static void
y_lines(point, dim, size)          /*create polylines in y_direction*/
  Ppoint3 *point;
  Pdim dim;
  int size;
{
Ppoint3 *points, *temp;
int x_count, y_count;
```

```
  temp = (Ppoint3*)malloc(size * dim.y_dim);
  for (x_count = 0; x_count < dim.x_dim; x_count++) {
    points = temp;
    for (y_count = 0; y_count < (dim.y_dim * dim.x_dim);
    y_count = y_count + dim.y_dim) {
      *points = *(point + y_count + x_count);
      points++;}
      popenstruct(WIREMESH);
        ppolyline3(dim.y_dim, temp);
      pclosestruct();
  }
  free(temp);
}

/****************************************************************/

static void
x_lines(point, dim, size)      /* create polylines in x_direction */
  Ppoint3 *point;
  Pdim dim;
  int size;
{
Ppoint3 *points, *temp;
int x_count, y_count;

  temp = (Ppoint3*)malloc(size * dim.x_dim);
  for (y_count = 0; y_count < (dim.y_dim * dim.x_dim);
  y_count = y_count + dim.y_dim) {
    points = temp;
   for (x_count = 0; x_count < dim.x_dim; x_count++) {
      *points = *(point + x_count + y_count);
      points++;}
  .   popenstruct(WIREMESH);
        ppolyline3(dim.x_dim, temp);
      pclosestruct();
  }
  free(temp);
}

/****************************************************************/

static void
make_wiremesh(point, dim)        /* create a wireframe structure */
  Ppoint3 *point;
  Pdim dim;
{
int size;

  message(3);
```

```
    pseteditmode(PEDIT_INSERT);
    popenstruct(WIREMESH);
      psetlinecolourind(5);
    pclosestruct();
    size = sizeof(Ppoint3);
    x_lines(point, dim, size);
    y_lines(point, dim, size);
}


/*****************************************************************
 Calculate facet normals
 *****************************************************************/

static void          /* calculate facet normals from vertex coords */
calcnorm(points, cnm)
  Ppoint3  points[4];
  Pconorm3 *cnm;
{
static Pcobundl facetcolour = {1, 1, 0};
float sum, nx, ny, nz;
int i, j;

  nx = ny = nz = 0;
  for (i = 0; i < 4; i++) {
    j = i + 1;
    if (i == 3)
      j = 0;
    nx = nx + (points[i].y - points[j].y)*(points[i].z +
        points[j].z);
    ny = ny + (points[i].z - points[j].z)*(points[i].x +
        points[j].x);
    nz = nz + (points[i].x - points[j].x)*(points[i].y +
        points[j].y);
  }
  sum = sqrt(nx*nx + ny*ny + nz*nz);
  if (sum > 0.0) {
    nx = nx/sum;
    ny = ny/sum;
    nz = nz/sum;}
  cnm->normal.x = nx;
  cnm->normal.y = ny;
  cnm->normal.z = nz;
  cnm->colour.direct = facetcolour;
}


/*****************************************************************/

/* assign normal vectors to facets */
static void
normalvectors(point, conorm, dim)
```

```
  Ppoint3 *point;
  Pconorm3 *conorm;
  Pdim dim;
{
Ppoint3 pointarray[4];
int i, j, step;

  message(2);
  for (j = 0; j < ((dim.y_dim - 1) * (dim.x_dim - 1));
  j = j + dim.x_dim)
    for (i = 0; i < (dim.x_dim - 1); i++) {
      step = i + j;
      pointarray[0] = *(point + step);
      pointarray[1] = *(point + step + 1);
      pointarray[2] = *(point + step + dim.x_dim + 1);
      pointarray[3] = *(point + step + dim.x_dim);
      calcnorm(pointarray, conorm);
      conorm++;}
}

/******************************************************************
  Scale picture to fit display space
 ******************************************************************/

static void
scale(point, dim, max, min)          /* scale y coords of vertices */
  Ppoint3 *point;
  Pdim dim;
  float max, min;
{
int count;

  for (count = 0; count < (dim.x_dim * dim.y_dim); count++) {
    point->y = (point->y - min) / (max - min) * SCALE;
    point++;}
}

/******************************************************************
  Functions for reading data file
 ******************************************************************/

static void
read_pts(fp, point, dim, max, min)          /* read y coordinates */
  FILE *fp;
  Ppoint3 *point;
  Pdim dim;
  float *max, *min;
{
float x_step, z_step, x, z;
int i, j;
```

```
    message(1);
    *max = -1000000.0;
    *min = 1000000.0;
    fscanf(fp, "%f %f", &x_step, &z_step);
    z = 0;
    for (j = 0; j < dim.y_dim; j++) {
      x = 0;
      for (i = 0; i < dim.x_dim; i++) {
        point->x = x / ((dim.x_dim - 1) * x_step);
        point->z = z / ((dim.y_dim - 1) * z_step);
        fscanf(fp, "%f", &point->y);
        if (point->y > *max) *max = point->y;
        if (point->y < *min) *min = point->y;
        point++;
        x = x + x_step;
      }
      z = z + z_step;
    }
}


/******************************************************************/

static void                   /* read data for quadmesh and create */
read_data(fp)                            /*quadmesh structure */
  FILE *fp;
{
Pint fflag = 3, vflag = 0, colour_model = 1;
Pdim dim;
Pfacetdataarr3 fdata;
Pfacetvdataarr3 vdata;
float max, min;
int size;

    fscanf(fp, "%d %d", &dim.x_dim, &dim.y_dim);
    size = sizeof(Pconorm3);
    fdata.conorms = (Pconorm3*)malloc(size * (dim.x_dim-1)*
                                   (dim.y_dim-1));
    size = sizeof(Ppoint3);
    vdata.points = (Ppoint3*)malloc(size * dim.x_dim * dim.y_dim);
    read_pts(fp, vdata.points, dim, &max, &min);
    if (max != 0)
      scale(vdata.points, dim, max, min);
    normalvectors(vdata.points, fdata.conorms, dim);
    popenstruct(SHADED);
      pquad3data(fflag, vflag, colour_model, &dim, &fdata, &vdata);
    pclosestruct();
    make_wiremesh(vdata.points, dim);
    free(vdata.points);
    free(fdata.conorms);
```

```
}

/***************************************************************/

static void
read_file(dataflag, string)              /* open file to read data */
  int *dataflag;
  Pchar string[];
{
FILE *fopen(), *fp;

  fp = fopen(string, "r");
  if (fp == NULL)
    message(4);
  else {
    pdelstruct(SHADED);
    pdelstruct(PICTURE);
    pdelstruct(WIREFRAME);
    pdelstruct(WIREMESH);
    read_data(fp);
    *dataflag = 1;}
  fclose(fp);
}

/****************************************************************
 Functions for processing device input
 ****************************************************************/

static void
process_device1(dev1, dev2, dev3, dataflag, keyflag)
                          /* process input from device 1 (menu) */
  Pint dev1, dev2, dev3;
  int *dataflag, *keyflag;
{
static int pictureflag;
Pchoice choice;

  psetchoicemode(WS, dev2, PREQUEST, PES_ECHO);
  pgetchoice(&choice);
  switch (choice.choice) {
    case 1:
      if (*dataflag != 0) {
        message(7);
        picture();
        pictureflag = 1;}
      break;
    case 2:
      if (*dataflag != 0) {
        psetchoicemode(WS, dev2, PEVENT, PES_ECHO);
        message(5);
```

```
        *keyflag = 1;
        if (pictureflag == 1) {
          wireframe();
          pictureflag = 0;}}
      break;
    case 3:
      if (*dataflag != 0) {
        psetchoicemode(WS, dev2, PEVENT, PES_ECHO);
        message(6);
        *keyflag = 2;
        if (pictureflag == 1) {
          wireframe();
          pictureflag = 0;}
          ppoststruct(WS, ARROW, PRIORITY);}
      break;
    case 4:
      psetchoicemode(WS, dev1, PREQUEST, PES_ECHO);
      psetchoicemode(WS, dev2, PREQUEST, PES_ECHO);
      psetstringmode(WS, dev3, PEVENT, PES_ECHO);
      break;
    case 5:
      exit(0);
      break;
  }
}


/****************************************************************/

static void
process_device2(keyflag) /* process input from dev 2 (keyboard) */
  int keyflag;
{
Pchoice choice;

  pgetchoice(&choice);
  switch (keyflag) {
    case 1:
      change_view(choice.choice);
      break;
    case 2:
      change_light(choice.choice);
      break;
  }
}


/****************************************************************/

static void
process_device3(dev1, dev3, dataflag)          /* process input from
                                               device 3 (keyboard) */
```

```
   Pint dev1, dev3;
   int *dataflag;
{
Pchar string[BUFFERSIZE];

   pgetstring(string);
   psetchoicemode(WS, dev1, PEVENT, PES_ECHO);
   psetstringmode(WS, dev3, PREQUEST, PES_ECHO);
   punpostallstruct(WS);
   read_file(dataflag, string + EDITPOS - 1);
   if (*dataflag == 1) {
     initialize_vectors();
     structures();
     wireframe();}
}
```

/***/

```
static void                            /* process current event */
process_event(event, dev1, dev2, dev3)
   Pevent *event;
   Pint dev1, dev2, dev3;
{
static int dataflag, keyflag;

   switch(event->dev) {
   case 3:                                  /* device 1 (menu) */
     process_device1(dev1, dev2, dev3, &dataflag, &keyflag);
     break;
   case 11:                              /* device 2 (arrow key) */
     process_device2(keyflag);
     break;
   case 1:                    /* device 3 (string from keyboard) */
     process_device3(dev1, dev3, &dataflag);
     break;
   }
}
```

/***/

```
Pchar shade[] = "Shade";                   /* define menu items */
Pchar move[] =  "Move";
Pchar light[] = "Light";
Pchar file[] =  "File";
Pchar quit[] =  "Quit";
Pchar *menu[] = {shade, move, light, file, quit};
Pchar initstring[] = "Enter filename:";

static void                         /* initialize input devices */
initialize_input_devices(dev1, dev2, dev3)
```

```
   Pint dev1, dev2, dev3;
{
static Plimit echo_area = {0, 1, 0, 1};
static Pchoicepet0003 cdata = {5, menu};
static Pstringpet0001 sdata = {BUFFERSIZE, EDITPOS};
Pint pet1 = 3, pet2 = 1, pet3 = 1, init = 1;
Pchoicestatus status = PCH_NOCHOICE;
Pchoicerec choicedata;
Pstringrec stringdata;

  choicedata.choicepet3_datarec = cdata;
  stringdata.stringpet1_datarec = sdata;
  pinitchoice(WS, dev1, status, init, pet1,
            &echo_area, &choicedata);
  psetchoicemode(WS, dev1, PEVENT, PES_ECHO);
  pinitchoice(WS, dev2, status, init, pet2, &echo_area, NULL);
  pinitstring(WS, dev3, initstring, pet3, &echo_area, &stringdata);
}

/*****************************************************************/

static void
choices()                                        /* main event loop */
{
Pevent event;
Pint dev1 = 3, dev2 = 11, dev3 = 1;

  initialize_input_devices(dev1, dev2, dev3);
  pawaitevent(60.0, &event);
  while(event.class != PI_NONE) {
    process_event(&event, dev1, dev2, dev3);
    pawaitevent(600.0, &event);}
}

/*****************************************************************
  Initialize light sources, colours, create arrow
 *****************************************************************/

static void
initialize()              /* set colour reps, ambient light source
                                          and arrow structure */
{
static Pcobundl colour0 = {0.7, 0.7, 0.7};
static Pcobundl colour1 = {0.0, 0.0, 0.0};
Plightsrcbundl rep;

  psetcolourrep(WS, 0, &colour0);
  psetcolourrep(WS, 1, &colour1);
  rep.type = 1;
  rep.rec.ambient.colour.type = 1;
```

```
    rep.rec.ambient.colour.val.general.x = 1;
    rep.rec.ambient.colour.val.general.y = 1;
    rep.rec.ambient.colour.val.general.z = 1;
    psetlightsrcrep(WS, LIGHT2INDEX, &rep);
    arrow();
}

/*****************************************************************
  Main program
 *****************************************************************/

main()
{
Pwstype wst;

    popenphigs((Pchar*)0, PDEFAULT_MEM_SIZE);
    wst = phigs_ws_type_create( phigs_ws_type_sun_tool,
            PHIGS_TOOL_LABEL, "SunPHIGS Tool Workstation",
            PHIGS_COLOUR_MODE, 1,
            PHIGS_DOUBLE_BUFFER, PHIGS_DBL_HW, 0);
    popenws(WS, (Pconnid)NULL, wst);
    initialize();
    choices();
    pclosews(WS);
    pclosephigs();
}
/*****************************************************************/
```

Appendix C

Coordinate transformations

PHIGS employs a number of coordinate systems to simplify the specification and viewing of pictures. For example, a programmer may use several different local modelling coordinate systems for convenience, which must then be converted into a unified world coordinate system. We also encounter **view reference coordinates, normalized projection coordinates** and **device coordinates**.

We must therefore have some means for transforming, or mapping, between these different coordinate systems. PHIGS is designed for high performance, and the process of transforming between coordinates must be efficient. One way to achieve this is to use **homogeneous coordinates** to represent points and **matrices** to perform the mapping.

C.1   Homogeneous coordinates

Homogeneous coordinates are quite familiar to mathematicians. Once grasped, they are straightforward to use, although they can seem confusing at first. The source of confusion is that with homogeneous coordinates we represent an n-dimensional space with a coordinate system of $n + 1$ dimensions; thus, a point in three dimensions is represented by four homogeneous coordinates. The use of such a 4D coordinate system for 3D computer graphics has some very useful properties.

Consider a point in three dimensions. In homogeneous coordinates the position of the point is specified by four values, (x, y, z, w). However, these four values are not independent, which is to be expected because three values are sufficient to define a position uniquely in 3D space. In fact, points in the 3D 'real world' lie on the plane $w = 1$ in the 4D homogeneous space. To obtain the 3D coordinates of a point whose homogeneous coordinates are known, we must map the point to the plane $w = 1$, by dividing the w coordinate *into* the x, y and z terms.

It is, perhaps, easiest to visualize this with the aid of a diagram such as Figure C.1. Here, for simplicity, we show just the x, y and w axes. An arbitrary point p_1 (x_1, y_1, z_1, w_1) projects to the point p_2 $(x_2, y_2, z_2, 1)$, which is where a line from the origin to p_1 passes through the plane $w = 1$. From similar triangles we can obtain the relationships $x_2 = x_1/w_1$ and $y_2 = y_1/w_1$. Similarly, although not shown in the diagram, $z_2 = z_1/w_1$. This process is known as **normalization**, and is sometimes called **homogeneous division** because it entails dividing

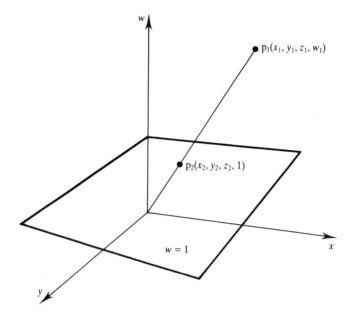

Figure C.1 Mapping points in homogeneous space to the $w = 1$ plane.

the x, y and z values by the w term. Let us consider an example: if p_1 had coordinates $(2, 3, 5, 4)$, its 'real world' coordinates, after normalization, would be $(0.5, 0.75, 1.25, 1)$. From the diagram we can see that an infinite number of points along the line $p_1 p_2$ map to the same normalized point. The point $(4, 6, 10, 8)$ has different homogeneous coordinates but represents the same real 3D point as p_1 in the example just given.

To summarize, if we know the four homogeneous coordinates of a point, we can obtain the 3D coordinates of the corresponding 'real world' point by dividing the x, y and z homogeneous coordinates by the value of the w coordinate. Conversely, if we know the 3D coordinates of a point, we can express it in homogeneous coordinates by setting $w = 1$.

We have conveniently ignored what happens if we try to divide by w when its value is zero, but will return to this in due course.

C.2   The matrix method for transformations

Using **column vector notation** we express a point (x, y, z, w) as:

$$
\begin{bmatrix}
x \\
y \\
z \\
w
\end{bmatrix}
$$

This notation is commonly used by mathematicians and is employed by PHIGS. Many text books on computer graphics use **row** vectors; the reason for this has never been entirely clear, except perhaps that these are easier to typeset!

In order to apply a transformation to our point we multiply it by a 4×4 matrix to yield the transformed coordinates (x', y', z', w') :

$$
\begin{bmatrix} x' \\ y' \\ z' \\ w' \end{bmatrix} = \begin{bmatrix} a & b & c & d \\ e & f & g & h \\ i & j & k & l \\ m & n & o & p \end{bmatrix} \cdot \begin{bmatrix} x \\ y \\ z \\ w \end{bmatrix}
$$

Expanding this, we obtain expressions for the individual transformed coordinates:

$$
\begin{aligned}
x' &= ax + by + cz + dw \\
y' &= ex + fy + gz + hw \\
z' &= ix + jy + kz + lw \\
w' &= mx + ny + oz + pw
\end{aligned}
$$

By setting the terms of the matrix to appropriate values we can achieve a wide range of effects, including translation, scaling, rotation and perspective projection. To illustrate this we look first at some simple examples in the next section.

C.3   Translation

First, we examine translation of a point, whose 3D coordinates are (x, y, z), by amounts (T_x, T_y, T_z) parallel to the coordinate axes. This can be done with a matrix of the form:

$$
\begin{bmatrix} 1 & 0 & 0 & T_x \\ 0 & 1 & 0 & T_y \\ 0 & 0 & 1 & T_z \\ 0 & 0 & 0 & 1 \end{bmatrix}
$$

Multiplying the vector for a point by this matrix we obtain:

$$
\begin{bmatrix} x' \\ y' \\ z' \\ w' \end{bmatrix} = \begin{bmatrix} 1 & 0 & 0 & T_x \\ 0 & 1 & 0 & T_y \\ 0 & 0 & 1 & T_z \\ 0 & 0 & 0 & 1 \end{bmatrix} \cdot \begin{bmatrix} x \\ y \\ z \\ 1 \end{bmatrix}
$$

yielding:

$$
\begin{aligned}
x' &= x + T_x \\
y' &= y + T_y \\
z' &= z + T_z
\end{aligned}
$$

Note that in this case $w' = 1$. This will always be the case when $w = 1$ and the first three terms in the bottom row of the matrix are all zero *and* the bottom, right-hand term in the matrix is 1. We shall examine later the case where these terms have other values.

C.4   Scaling about the coordinate origin

To scale by (S_x, S_y, S_z) parallel to the coordinate axes we must multiply each co-ordinate by its corresponding scale factor:

$$\begin{bmatrix} x' \\ y' \\ z' \\ w' \end{bmatrix} = \begin{bmatrix} S_x & 0 & 0 & 0 \\ 0 & S_y & 0 & 0 \\ 0 & 0 & S_z & 0 \\ 0 & 0 & 0 & 1 \end{bmatrix} \cdot \begin{bmatrix} x \\ y \\ z \\ 1 \end{bmatrix}$$

resulting in:

$$\begin{aligned} x' &= S_x x \\ y' &= S_y y \\ z' &= S_z z \end{aligned}$$

C.5   Rotation about the coordinate axes

For rotating by θ about the z axis we use:

$$\begin{bmatrix} x' \\ y' \\ z' \\ w' \end{bmatrix} = \begin{bmatrix} \cos\theta & -\sin\theta & 0 & 0 \\ \sin\theta & \cos\theta & 0 & 0 \\ 0 & 0 & 1 & 0 \\ 0 & 0 & 0 & 1 \end{bmatrix} \cdot \begin{bmatrix} x \\ y \\ z \\ 1 \end{bmatrix}$$

which produces:

$$\begin{aligned} x' &= \cos\theta x - \sin\theta y \\ y' &= \sin\theta x + \cos\theta y \\ z' &= z \end{aligned}$$

Note that we are using a right-handed coordinate system with the convention that a positive angle has an anticlockwise sense when looking in the negative direction along the axis. To obtain equivalent matrices for rotation about the x and y axes we can permute the rows and columns of the matrix. Rotation about x by an angle ϕ is obtained with:

$$\begin{bmatrix} 1 & 0 & 0 & 0 \\ 0 & \cos\phi & -\sin\phi & 0 \\ 0 & \sin\phi & \cos\phi & 0 \\ 0 & 0 & 0 & 1 \end{bmatrix}$$

while rotation about y by an angle η requires:

$$\begin{bmatrix} \cos\eta & 0 & \sin\eta & 0 \\ 0 & 1 & 0 & 0 \\ -\sin\eta & 0 & \cos\eta & 0 \\ 0 & 0 & 0 & 1 \end{bmatrix}$$

C.6   Perspective projection

A particularly interesting feature of homogeneous coordinates is their use for perspective projection. Perspective helps to convey a sense of depth in a 3D scene, and is characterized by the foreshortening of lengths and by parallel lines converging to one or more vanishing points. This effect can be modelled by a coordinate transformation which distorts 3D space.

To illustrate this we shall examine a matrix which results in a perspective distortion, whereby lines which are initially parallel to the z axis pass through a vanishing point on the z axis after transformation, as shown in Figure C.2. The matrix for this is:

$$\begin{bmatrix} 1 & 0 & 0 & 0 \\ 0 & 1 & 0 & 0 \\ 0 & 0 & 1 & 0 \\ 0 & 0 & p_z & 1 \end{bmatrix}$$

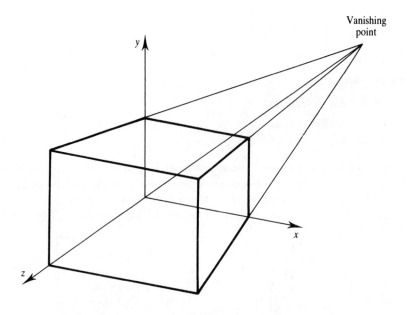

Figure C.2   Perspective vanishing point.

If we multiply the coordinates of the point $(x, y, z, 1)$ by this matrix, we obtain

$$
\begin{aligned}
x' &= x \\
y' &= y \\
z' &= z \\
w' &= p_z z + 1
\end{aligned}
$$

Because w' is no longer unity we must normalize the x, y and z values by dividing by w':

$$
\begin{aligned}
x'' &= \frac{x'}{w'} = \frac{x}{1 + p_z z} \\
y'' &= \frac{y'}{w'} = \frac{y}{1 + p_z z} \\
z'' &= \frac{z'}{w'} = \frac{z}{1 + p_z z} \\
&= \frac{1}{\frac{1}{z} + p_z}
\end{aligned}
$$

We can see from this that the normalized coordinates x'' and y'' diminish as the original z value increases, becoming zero when z reaches infinity. Furthermore, as $z \to \infty$ then $z'' \to 1/p_z$, and this is the desired vanishing point.

All that remains is to choose a suitable value for p_z. If we set $p_z = -1/z_{eye}$ then we obtain a result which is equivalent to viewing the picture from a point $z = z_{eye}$ on the z axis with the picture projected onto the plane $z = 0$. This particular transformation produces a one-point perspective projection with a single vanishing point located on the z axis. Two-point and three-point perspective projections can be obtained by setting the p_x and p_y terms in the matrix:

$$
\begin{bmatrix}
1 & 0 & 0 & 0 \\
0 & 1 & 0 & 0 \\
0 & 0 & 1 & 0 \\
p_x & p_y & p_z & 1
\end{bmatrix}
$$

With this method the effects of perspective foreshortening and the vanishing point derive from the division by w' during normalization. This result is one of the features of using homogeneous coordinates. A major benefit of this approach is that such a transformation can be combined with other transformations, as described in the next section. Clearly if $w' = 0$ we have a problem – we will attempt to divide by zero! In fact, we will also have a problem if there are any extremely small values of w', since division by these these may cause floating-point overflow. Points with negative values of w' correspond to points located *behind* the viewpoint. These occur in applications such as viewing architectural models, where we may wish to 'move inside' a model of a building to see what its interior looks like. PHIGS avoids this problem by performing homogeneous coordinate clipping to remove those parts of primitives which are behind, or very close to, the centre of projection. This clipping is applied *before* the division by w'.

C.7   Concatenating transformations

So far, we have only considered single transformations whose effects are relative to the coordinate origin. For example, the scale transformation described previously will cause pictures to grow or shrink about the origin.

More complex effects can be obtained by **concatenating** a number of simple transformations. Concatenation is performed by multiplying together the individual transformation matrices to yield a single **composite transformation matrix**. To illustrate this, consider scaling about an arbitrary point. We can break this down into three simple steps:

1. Translate the object so that the point about which the scaling is to be performed becomes coincident with the origin.

2. Scale the object to its desired size about the origin.

3. Translate the object so that the centre of scaling moves back to its original position.

Here, when we refer to transforming the object we mean transforming the points used to draw the picture. Thus, we must apply the transformation to *all* of the points which define the object. We have already seen how each of these steps can be performed. Suppose the point about which the scaling is to happen is (x_p, y_p, z_p), and the scale factor is to be S along each axis. First we translate the object by $(-x_p, -y_p, -z_p)$:

$$
\begin{bmatrix} x' \\ y' \\ z' \\ w' \end{bmatrix} = \begin{bmatrix} 1 & 0 & 0 & -x_p \\ 0 & 1 & 0 & -y_p \\ 0 & 0 & 1 & -z_p \\ 0 & 0 & 0 & 1 \end{bmatrix} \cdot \begin{bmatrix} x \\ y \\ z \\ 1 \end{bmatrix} = [T_1] \cdot \begin{bmatrix} x \\ y \\ z \\ 1 \end{bmatrix}
$$

Next, we scale these new coordinates by S:

$$
\begin{bmatrix} x'' \\ y'' \\ z'' \\ w'' \end{bmatrix} = \begin{bmatrix} S & 0 & 0 & 0 \\ 0 & S & 0 & 0 \\ 0 & 0 & S & 0 \\ 0 & 0 & 0 & 1 \end{bmatrix} \cdot \begin{bmatrix} x' \\ y' \\ z' \\ w' \end{bmatrix} = [T_2] \cdot \begin{bmatrix} x' \\ y' \\ z' \\ w' \end{bmatrix}
$$

Finally, we translate back:

$$
\begin{bmatrix} x''' \\ y''' \\ z''' \\ w''' \end{bmatrix} = \begin{bmatrix} 1 & 0 & 0 & x_p \\ 0 & 1 & 0 & y_p \\ 0 & 0 & 1 & z_p \\ 0 & 0 & 0 & 1 \end{bmatrix} \cdot \begin{bmatrix} x'' \\ y'' \\ z'' \\ w'' \end{bmatrix} = [T_3] \cdot \begin{bmatrix} x'' \\ y'' \\ z'' \\ w'' \end{bmatrix}
$$

Because the matrices T_1, T_2 and T_3 are square, and matrix multiplication is associative, we can combine these individual steps into a single transformation:

$$
\begin{bmatrix} x''' \\ y''' \\ z''' \\ w''' \end{bmatrix} = T_c \cdot \begin{bmatrix} x \\ y \\ z \\ 1 \end{bmatrix}
$$

where T_c is the composite transformation matrix:

$$T_c = T_3 \cdot T_2 \cdot T_1$$

The value of using homogeneous coordinates now becomes clear. A wide variety of effects can be achieved within a consistent, uniform framework in which each transformation is represented by a 4×4 matrix. Simple transformations can be combined, in some appropriate sequence, by multiplying the individual matrices to yield a single composite transformation matrix. Multiplying a point specified in the original coordinate system by this matrix applies the whole sequence of transformations in a single step.

The application of this technique within graphics systems makes performing transformations between different coordinate systems very efficient, because a single composite matrix can be found which transforms a point from the application's modelling coordinates directly into device coordinates in a single step.

C.7.1   Pre- and post-concatenation

The order in which matrices are combined is particularly important. If the order is wrong then the result will also be wrong. In a few cases the order is unimportant – when the matrix product is commutative – such as symmetrical scaling combined with rotation. In the example given previously, for scaling about an arbitrary point, the order in which the steps are applied to the object is termed the **logical order**. The corresponding order for combining the matrices is found by writing them down in a right to left order. In our example, the logical order for the transformations was T_1, T_2, T_3 but the order in which the matrices must be multiplied together was the *reverse* of this: $T_c = T_3 \cdot T_2 \cdot T_1$.

An alternative way to think of this is to regard the left-most matrix as defining a transformation which affects globally anything to the right of it. Thus, in the example $T_c = T_3 \cdot T_2 \cdot T_1$, the matrix T_3 will change the coordinate system which is used to specify T_2, which in turn will affect T_1.

The importance of the ordering is best illustrated by a simple 2D example, such as that shown in Figure C.3. In the left-hand part of the diagram a square is first uniformly scaled by a factor of 3.0, and then translated by $(10, 30)$ – note that this is the logical order in which the transformations are applied. The composite transformation matrix is $T_c = T_{\text{translate}} \cdot T_{\text{scale}}$. Note that the final position of the bottom, left-hand corner is $(10, 30)$ – the translation terms are *not* affected by the scale factor.

In the right-hand part of the diagram the transformations are applied in the opposite order. The composite matrix is $T_c = T_{\text{scale}} \cdot T_{\text{translate}}$. Now, it is the translated square which is scaled with respect to the origin, and as a result the bottom, left-hand corner ends up at $(30, 90)$ – the translation terms have been multiplied by the scale factor.

In PHIGS, the process of combining transformations to produce a composite transformation is referred to as concatenation, of which there are two varieties:

- With **pre-concatenation** a new composite matrix is obtained by placing

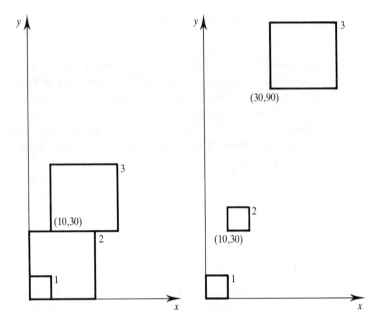

Figure C.3   Effect of matrix ordering.

the current composite matrix, T_c, *before* – that is, to the left of – the new matrix T_{new}, when multiplying them together:

$$T_c \leftarrow T_c \cdot T_{new}$$

This achieves the effect of defining a new local coordinate system *relative to* the old coordinate system.

- With **post-concatenation** the current matrix, T_c, is placed *after* – that is, to the right of – the new matrix:

$$T_c \leftarrow T_{new} \cdot T_c$$

This has the effect of changing the current transformation by making its effects *relative to* the new transformation.

The usual way to compute a composite matrix is to calculate each component transformation in turn, combining it with the composite matrix at each step. The sequence of matrices $T_3 \cdot T_2 \cdot T_1$ can be derived either by computing T_3 first, then T_2 and finally T_1 and using pre-concatenation, or in the reverse order using post-concatenation. In PHIGS, during structure traversal, modelling transformations are concatenated in this way. It is usual for matrices encountered at the top of the hierarchy to affect those at lower levels, so that in the example we have just used T_3 would be encountered first, then T_2 and finally T_1. In this case, they would be combined using pre-concatenation.

Appendix D
Using PHIGS with Fortran

Because Fortran names are limited to six characters, the names used in the Fortran binding are rather cryptic, to say the least. However, they are derived according to a system of abbreviations. For example, CHARACTER becomes CH, STRUCTURE becomes ST, and so on. For example, OPEN PHIGS becomes POPPH, and SET CHARACTER HEIGHT becomes PSCHH. The complete list of subroutine names in given in Appendix E.

D.1   Data records

Some functions, such as those which initialize input devices have *data record* parameters. Typically, this data is a collection of integers, reals and strings. In some languages (such as C and Ada) the binding can accommodate data records by defining structured data types, but in Fortran this is not possible. The Fortran solution is to represent a data record using a character array into which integers, reals and strings are packed. To enable reals, integers and strings to be converted to and from character arrays, the Fortran binding provides two utility routines: PACK DATA RECORD (PPREC) and UNPACK DATA RECORD (PUREC). PACK DATA RECORD takes a number of integers, reals and strings, and packs them into a character array:

```
SUBROUTINE PPREC(IL,IA,RL,RA,SL,LSTR,STR,
                 MLDR,ERRIND,LDR,DATREC)
```
Input parameters:
INTEGER IL	number of integer entries
INTEGER IA(*)	array containing integer entries
REAL RL	number of real entries
REAL RA(*)	array containing real entries
INTEGER SL	number of string entries
INTEGER LSTR(*)	length of each string entry
CHARACTER*(*)STR(*)	string entries
INTEGER MLDR	dimension of data record array

Output parameters:
INTEGER ERRIND	error indicator
INTEGER LDR	number of array elements used in DATREC
CHARACTER*80 DATREC(MLDR)	data record

To see how this function is used, consider the example of initializing a locator input device, to use prompt and echo type 4. This displays a rubber-band line connecting the initial locator position with the current measure of the locator. Because the line is effectively a polyline, it has the usual polyline attributes, and a data record is used to specify these. The format of the data record is as follows:

Entry	Meaning	Type	Example
1	linetype ASF	INTEGER	PINDIV
2	linewidth scale factor ASF	INTEGER	PINDIV
3	polyline colour index ASF	INTEGER	PINDIV
4	polyline index	INTEGER	0 (not relevant)
5	linetype	INTEGER	2
6	linewidth scale factor	REAL	1.4
7	polyline colour index	INTEGER	2

There are seven entries, which specify the polyline attributes using either the individual or bundled method. In this example we will use individual attributes; the polyline index entry is not relevant. We can use PPREC to build the data record, as follows:

```
C Declare and initialize the integer, real and string arrays.
      INTEGER IA(6)
      DATA IA /0, PINDIV, PINDIV, PINDIV, 0, 2, 2/
      REAL RA (1)
      DATA RA /1.4/
      CHARACTER*1 STR

C Declare and define the lengths of each array.
      INTEGER IL, RL, SL, LSTR
      DATA IL, RL, SL /7, 1, 0, 0/

C Declare variables to receive the data record.
      INTEGER MLDR, ERRIND, LDR
      CHARACTER*(80) DAREC(MLDR)

C Call pack data record
      CALL PPREC(IL,IA,RL,RA,SL,LSTR,STR,MLDR,ERRIND,LDR,DATREC)
```

Now we can initialize the locator device, passing in the data record DATREC, and its length LDR:

```
      CALL PINLC3(WKID, LOCDEV, IVIEW, IPX, IPY, IPZ,
     +            4, EVOL, LDR, DATREC)
```

D.2   The Fortran subset binding

The binding for the Fortran subset is different from that for full Fortran, as follows:

- Those subroutines in the full Fortran binding that have arguments of type CHARACTER*(*) have alternative subroutine definitions for the subset that use CHARACTER*80 character strings.

- For some subroutines, an additional INTEGER argument is used in the subset version which gives the number of characters in a string. In this case the subset subroutine has the same name as the subroutine for full Fortran, but with the addition of a final S. For other subroutines, this INTEGER argument is already present, and the subset version takes the same name as the full Fortran subroutine.

For example, here is the full Fortran binding for the TEXT 3 function:

```
SUBROUTINE PTX3(PX,PY,PZ,TDX,TDY,TDZ,CHARS)
Input parameters:
      REAL PX, PY, PZ                text position
      REAL TDX(2), TDY(2), TDZ(2)    text direction vectors
      CHARACTER*(*) CHARS            string
```

In the subset version, there is an extra INTEGER argument to give the length of the string, and the type of the string argument is CHARACTER*(80):

```
SUBROUTINE PTX3S(PX,PY,PZ,TDX,TDY,TDZ,LSTR,CHARS)
Input parameters:
      REAL PX, PY, PZ                text position
      REAL TDX(2), TDY(2), TDZ(2)    text direction vectors
      INTEGER LSTR                   length of string
      CHARACTER*(80) CHARS           string of characters
```

D.3   The square

```
C Access the PHIGS FORTRAN binding.
C The next line is implementation dependent.
      INCLUDE '/usr/common/include/phigs/phigs77.h'

C Define the data for the box.
      REAL XPTS(5), YPTS(5), ZPTS(5)
      DATA XPTS /.2, .4, .4, .2, .2/
      DATA YPTS /.3, .3, .5, .5, .3/
      DATA ZPTS /.0, .0, .0, .0, .0/

      INTEGER WSID, BOX, WST
      REAL PRI
```

```
      WSID = 1
      BOX = 1
      PRI = 1.0


C Open PHIGS. The parameters are implementation dependent.
      CALL POPPH(0, 0)
C Open a workstation. The parameters are implementation dependent.
      CALL POPWK(WSID, 0, 0)
C Open a structure.
      CALL POPST(BOX)
C Insert a polyline 3 element.
      CALL PPL3(5, XPTS, YPTS, ZPTS)
C Close the structure.
      CALL PCLST
C Set display update state for immediate updating.
      CALL PSDUS(WSID, PASAP, PNIVE)
C Post the structure.
      CALL PPOST(WSID, BOX, PRI)
C Close the workstation.
      CALL PCLWK(WSID)
C Close PHIGS.
      CALL PCLPH
      STOP
      END
```

D.4   The rotating cube

```
      PROGRAM CUBE

C Include the Fortran binding definitions.
      INCLUDE '/usr/common/include/phigs/phigs77.h'

      INTEGER WSID, CUBEID, I, ERR
      REAL PRI, PI, ANGLE, CMIN, CMAX

      REAL MATRIX(4,4)
      REAL TXVX(2), TXVY(2), TXVZ(2)
      DATA TXVX, TXVY, TXVZ/1.0, 0., 0.0, 1.0, 0., 0./
      DATA WSID, CUBEID, PRI, PI /1,1,1.0,3.14159/

C Initialize PHIGS.
      CALL POPPH(6, 0)

C Initialise a workstation.
      CALL POPWK(WSID, 0, PHIGSWSTTOOL)

C Set display update state for dynamic updating.
      CALL PSDUS(WSID, PASAP, PNIVE)
```

```
c Create a cube.
      CALL MAKCUB(CUBEID)

C Display the structure.
      CALL PPOST(WSID, CUBEID, PRI)

C Open the structure for 'replace mode' editing.
      CALL POPST(CUBEID)
      CALL PSEDM(PREPLC)
      CALL PSEP(1)

C Rotate the picture through 360 degrees about each axis.

      DO 10 I = 1,360
      ANGLE = I*PI/180
      CALL PBLTM3(0.5,0.5,0.5,   0.,0.,0.,
     +                  ANGLE, ANGLE, ANGLE,
     +                    1.0,1.0, 1.0,
     +                  ERR,
     +                  MATRIX)
      CALL PSLMT3(MATRIX, PCREPL)
 10      CONTINUE

      CALL PCLST

C Close down.
      CALL PCLWK(WSID)

      CALL PCLPH
        STOP
      END

      SUBROUTINE MAKCUB(ID)
C Include the Fortran binding definitions.
      INCLUDE '/usr/common/include/phigs/phigs77.h'

      INTEGER ID, ERR
      REAL ANGLE
      REAL CMIN,CMAX
      PARAMETER(CMIN=0.3, CMAX=0.7)

C Data for the front face.
        REAL FFACEX(5), FFACEY(5), FFACEZ(5)
        DATA FFACEX /CMIN,CMIN,CMAX,CMAX,CMIN/
        DATA FFACEY /CMIN,CMAX,CMAX,CMIN,CMIN/
        DATA FFACEZ /CMAX,CMAX,CMAX,CMAX,CMAX/

C Data for the back face.
        REAL BFACEX(5), BFACEY(5), BFACEZ(5)
```

```
          DATA BFACEX  /CMIN,CMIN,CMAX,CMAX,CMIN/
          DATA BFACEY  /CMIN,CMAX,CMAX,CMIN,CMIN/
          DATA BFACEZ  /CMIN,CMIN,CMIN,CMIN,CMIN/

C Data for the links.
          REAL LK1X(2),  LK2X(2),  LK3X(2),  LK4X(2)
          REAL LK1Y(2),  LK2Y(2),  LK3Y(2),  LK4Y(2)
          REAL LK1Z(2),  LK2Z(2),  LK3Z(2),  LK4Z(2)
          DATA LK1X,LK1Y,LK1Z  /CMIN,CMIN,CMIN,CMIN,CMIN,CMAX/
          DATA LK2X,LK2Y,LK2Z  /CMIN,CMIN,CMAX,CMAX,CMIN,CMAX/
          DATA LK3X,LK3Y,LK3Z  /CMAX,CMAX,CMAX,CMAX,CMIN,CMAX/
          DATA LK4X,LK4Y,LK4Z  /CMAX,CMAX,CMIN,CMIN,CMIN,CMAX/

          REAL MATRIX(4,4)
          REAL TXVX(2),  TXVY(2),  TXVZ(2)
          DATA TXVX, TXVY, TXVZ/1.0, 0., 0.0, 1.0, 0., 0./

C Open a structure for the cube.
          CALL POPST(ID)

C Compute initial transformation, with no rotation yet.
          CALL PBLTM3(0.5,0.5,0.5,  0.,0.,0.,
         +              0.0, 0.0, 0.0,
         +                1.0,1.0, 1.0,
         +              ERR,
         +              MATRIX)

C Insert a local transformation matrix.
          CALL PSLMT3(MATRIX, PCREPL)

C Draw the cube.
          CALL PPL3(5, FFACEX, FFACEY, FFACEZ)
          CALL PPL3(5, BFACEX, BFACEY, BFACEZ)
          CALL PPL3(2, LK1X, LK1Y, LK1Z)
          CALL PPL3(2, LK2X, LK2Y, LK2Z)
          CALL PPL3(2, LK3X, LK3Y, LK3Z)
          CALL PPL3(2, LK4X, LK4Y, LK4Z)

C Draw the text, with horizontal centre alignment.
          CALL PSTXAL(PACENT, PAVNOR)
          CALL PSCHH(0.02)
          CALL PTX3(0.5,0.6,0.7, TXVX,TXVY,TXVZ, 'It''s a')
          CALL PTX3(0.5,0.5,0.7, TXVX,TXVY,TXVZ, 'square world!')

C Close the structure.
          CALL PCLST

          RETURN
          END
```

Appendix E
Summary of functions, elements and errors

E.1 C and Fortran binding names

This section gives the C and Fortran binding names of all PHIGS functions listed alphabetically. The following notation is used:

- A **3** at the end of a function name indicates that a function has two forms, one for 2D graphics, and one for 3D. For example, the following:

PHIGS function	C	Fortran
POLYLINE 3	ppolyline3	PPL3

is shorthand for:

PHIGS function	C	Fortran
POLYLINE	ppolyline	PPL
POLYLINE 3	ppolyline3	PPL3

- **(S)** after a Fortran binding name indicates that there is a version of the function for the Fortran subset.

- = following a Fortran name indicates that there is a version of the function for the full binding and for the subset, but that the function has the same name in both.

PHIGS function	C	Fortran
ADD NAMES TO SET	paddnameset	PADS
ANNOTATION TEXT RELATIVE 3	pannotationtextrelative3	PATR3 (S)
APPLICATION DATA	papplicationdata	PAP
ARCHIVE ALL STRUCTURES	parallstruct	PARAST
ARCHIVE STRUCTURE NETWORKS	parstructnet	PARSN
ARCHIVE STRUCTURES	parstruct	PARST
AWAIT EVENT	pawaitevent	PWAIT

PHIGS function	C	Fortran
BUILD TRANSFORMATION MATRIX 3	pbuildtran3	PBLTM3
CELL ARRAY 3	pcellarray3	PCA3
CHANGE STRUCTURE IDENTIFIER	pchangestructid	PCSTID
CHANGE STRUCTURE IDENTIFIER AND REFERENCES	pchangestructidref	PCSTIR
CHANGE STRUCTURE REFERENCES	pchangestructref	PCSTRF
CLOSE ARCHIVE FILE	pclosearfile	PCARF
CLOSE PHIGS	pclosephigs	PCLPH
CLOSE STRUCTURE	pclosestruct	PCLST
CLOSE WORKSTATION	pclosews	PCLWK
COMPOSE MATRIX 3	pcomposematrix3	PCOM3
COMPOSE TRANSFORMATION MATRIX 3	pcomposetran3	PCOTM3
COPY ALL ELEMENTS FROM STRUCTURE	pcopyallelemsstruct	PCELST
DELETE ALL STRUCTURES	pdelallstruct	PDAS
DELETE ALL STRUCTURES FROM ARCHIVE	pdelallstructar	PDASAR
DELETE ELEMENT	pdelelem	PDEL
DELETE ELEMENT RANGE	pdelelemrange	PDELRA
DELETE ELEMENTS BETWEEN LABELS	pdelelemslabels	PDELLB
DELETE STRUCTURE	pdelstruct	PDST
DELETE STRUCTURE NETWORK	pdelstructnet	PDSN
DELETE STRUCTURE NETWORKS FROM ARCHIVE	pdelstructnetar	PDSNAR
DELETE STRUCTURES FROM ARCHIVE	pdelstructar	PDSTAR
ELEMENT SEARCH	pelemsrch	PELS
EMERGENCY CLOSE PHIGS	pemergencyclosephigs	PECLPH
EMPTY STRUCTURE	pemptystruct	PEMST
ERROR HANDLING	perrorhand	PERHND
ERROR LOGGING	perrorlog	PERLOG
ESCAPE	pescape	PESC
EVALUATE VIEW MAPPING MATRIX 3	pevalviewmappingmatrix3	PEVMM3
EVALUATE VIEW ORIENTATION MATRIX 3	pevalvieworientationmatrix3	PEVOM3
EXECUTE STRUCTURE	pexecutestruct	PEXST
FILL AREA 3	pfillarea3	PFA3
FILL AREA SET 3	pfillareaset3	PFAS3
FLUSH DEVICE EVENTS	pflushevents	PFLUSH
GENERALIZED DRAWING PRIMITIVE 3	pgdp3	PGDP3

PHIGS function	C	Fortran
GENERALIZED STRUCTURE ELEMENT	pgse	PGSE
GET CHOICE	pgetchoice	PGTCH
GET ITEM TYPE FROM METAFILE	pgettypemf	PGTITM
GET LOCATOR 3	pgetloc3	PGTLC3
GET PICK	pgetpick	PGTPK
GET STRING	pgetstring	PGTST (=)
GET STROKE 3	pgetstroke3	PGTSK3
GET VALUATOR	pgetval	PGTVL
INCREMENTAL SPATIAL SEARCH 3	pincrspasrch3	PISS3
INITIALIZE CHOICE 3	pinitchoice3	PINCH3
INITIALIZE LOCATOR 3	pinitloc3	PINLC3
INITIALIZE PICK 3	pinitpick3	PINPK3
INITIALIZE STRING 3	pinitstring3	PINST3 (=)
INITIALIZE STROKE 3	pinitstroke3	PINSK3
INITIALIZE VALUATOR 3	pinitval3	PINVL3
INQUIRE ALL CONFLICTING STRUCTURES	pinqallconfstruct	PQCST
INQUIRE ANNOTATION FACILITIES	pinqannotationfacil	PQANF
INQUIRE ARCHIVE FILES	pinqarfiles	PQARF
INQUIRE ARCHIVE STATE VALUE	pinqarst	PQARS
INQUIRE CHOICE DEVICE STATE 3	pinqchoicest3	PQCHS3
INQUIRE COLOUR FACILITIES	pinqcolourfacil	PQCF
INQUIRE COLOUR MODEL	pinqcolourmodel	PQCMD
INQUIRE COLOUR MODEL FACILITIES	pinqcolourmodelfacil	PQCMDF
INQUIRE COLOUR REPRESENTATION	pinqcolourrep	PQCR
INQUIRE CONFLICT RESOLUTION	pinqconfres	PQCNRS
INQUIRE CONFLICTING STRUCTURES IN NETWORK	pinqconfstructinnet	PQCSTN
INQUIRE CURRENT ELEMENT CONTENT	pinqcurelemcontent	PQCECO (=)
INQUIRE CURRENT ELEMENT TYPE AND SIZE	pinqcurelemtypesize	PQCETS
INQUIRE DEFAULT CHOICE DEVICE DATA 3	pinqdefchoicedata3	PQDCH3
INQUIRE DEFAULT DISPLAY UPDATE STATE	pinqdefdisplayupdatest	PQDDUS
INQUIRE DEFAULT LOCATOR DEVICE DATA 3	pinqdeflocdata3	PQDLC3
INQUIRE DEFAULT PICK DEVICE DATA 3	pinqdefpickdata3	PQDPK3

PHIGS function	C	Fortran
INQUIRE DEFAULT STRING DEVICE DATA 3	`pinqdefstringdata3`	PQDST3
INQUIRE DEFAULT STROKE DEVICE DATA 3	`pinqdefstrokedata3`	PQDSK3
INQUIRE DEFAULT VALUATOR DEVICE DATA 3	`pinqdefvaldata3`	PQDVL3
INQUIRE DISPLAY SPACE SIZE 3	`pinqdisplayspacesize3`	PQDSP3
INQUIRE DISPLAY UPDATE STATE	`pinqdisplayupdatest`	PQDUS
INQUIRE DYNAMICS OF STRUCTURES	`pinqdynstruct`	PQDSTR
INQUIRE DYNAMICS OF WORKSTATION ATTRIBUTES	`pinqdynwsattr`	PQDSWA
INQUIRE EDGE FACILITIES	`pinqedgefacil`	PQEDF
INQUIRE EDGE REPRESENTATION	`pinqedgerep`	PQEDR
INQUIRE EDIT MODE	`pinqeditmode`	PQEDM
INQUIRE ELEMENT CONTENT	`pinqelemcontent`	PQECO
INQUIRE ELEMENT POINTER	`pinqelemptr`	PQEP
INQUIRE ELEMENT TYPE AND SIZE	`pinqelemtypesize`	PQETS
INQUIRE ERROR HANDLING MODE	`pinqerrorhandmode`	PQERHM
INQUIRE GENERALIZED DRAWING PRIMITIVE 3	`pinqgdp3`	PQGDP3
INQUIRE GENERALIZED STRUCTURE ELEMENT FACILITIES	`pinqgsefacil`	PQGSEF
INQUIRE HIGHLIGHTING FILTER	`pinqhilightfilter`	PQHLFT
INQUIRE HLHSR FACILITIES	`pinqhlhsrfacil`	PQHRF
INQUIRE HLHSR MODE	`pinqhlhsrmode`	PQHRM
INQUIRE INPUT QUEUE OVERFLOW	`pinqinputoverflow`	PQIQOV
INQUIRE INTERIOR FACILITIES	`pinqintfacil`	PQIF
INQUIRE INTERIOR REPRESENTATION	`pinqintrep`	PQIR
INQUIRE INVISIBILITY FILTER	`pinqinvisfilter`	PQIVFT
INQUIRE LIST OF AVAILABLE GENERALIZED DRAWING PRIMITIVES 3	`pinqavailgdp3`	PQEGD3
INQUIRE LIST OF GENERALIZED STRUCTURE ELEMENTS	`pinqgse`	PQEGSE
INQUIRE LIST OF AVAILABLE WORKSTATION TYPES	`pinqwstypes`	PQEWK

PHIGS function	C	Fortran
INQUIRE LIST OF COLOUR INDICES	pinqcolourind	PQECI
INQUIRE LIST OF EDGE INDICES	pinqedgeind	PQEEDI
INQUIRE LIST OF INTERIOR INDICES	pinqintind	PQEII
INQUIRE LIST OF PATTERN INDICES	pinqpatind	PQEPAI
INQUIRE LIST OF POLYLINE INDICES	pinqlineind	PQEPLI
INQUIRE LIST OF POLYMARKER INDICES	pinqmarkerind	PQEPMI
INQUIRE LIST OF TEXT INDICES	pinqtextind	PQETXI
INQUIRE LIST OF VIEW INDICES	pinqviewind	PQEVWI
INQUIRE LOCATOR DEVICE STATE 3	pinqlocst3	PQLCS3
INQUIRE MODELLING CLIPPING FACILITIES	pinqmodelclipfacil	PQMCLF
INQUIRE MORE SIMULTANEOUS EVENTS	pinqmoreevents	PQSIM
INQUIRE NUMBER OF AVAILABLE LOGICAL INPUT DEVICES	pinqnuminput	PQLI
INQUIRE NUMBER OF DISPLAY PRIORITIES SUPPORTED	pinqnumdisplaypri	PQDP
INQUIRE OPEN STRUCTURE	pinqopenstruct	PQOPST
INQUIRE PATHS TO ANCESTORS	pinqpathances	PQPAN
INQUIRE PATHS TO DESCENDANTS	pinqpathdesc	PQPDE
INQUIRE PATTERN FACILITIES	pinqpatfacil	PQPAF
INQUIRE PATTERN REPRESENTATION	pinqpatrep	PQPAR
INQUIRE PHIGS FACILITIES	pinqphigsfacil	PQPHF
INQUIRE PICK DEVICE STATE 3	pinqpickst3	PQPKS3
INQUIRE POLYLINE FACILITIES	pinqlinefacil	PQPLF
INQUIRE POLYLINE REPRESENTATION	pinqlinerep	PQPLR
INQUIRE POLYMARKER FACILITIES	pinqmarkerfacil	PQPMF
INQUIRE POLYMARKER REPRESENTATION	pinqmarkerrep	PQPMR
INQUIRE POSTED STRUCTURES	pinqpostedstruct	PQPOST
INQUIRE PREDEFINED COLOUR REPRESENTATION	pinqpredcolourrep	PQPCR
INQUIRE PREDEFINED EDGE REPRESENTATION	pinqprededgerep	PQPEDR
INQUIRE PREDEFINED INTERIOR REPRESENTATION	pinqpredintrep	PQPIR

PHIGS function	C	Fortran
INQUIRE PREDEFINED PATTERN REPRESENTATION	pinqpredpatrep	PQPPAR
INQUIRE PREDEFINED POLYLINE REPRESENTATION	pinqpredlinerep	PQPPLR
INQUIRE PREDEFINED POLYMARKER REPRESENTATION	pinqpredmarkerrep	PQPPMR
INQUIRE PREDEFINED TEXT REPRESENTATION	pinqpredtextrep	PQPTXR
INQUIRE PREDEFINED VIEW REPRESENTATION	pinqpredviewrep	PQPVWR
INQUIRE SET OF OPEN WORKSTATIONS	pinqsetopenws	PQOPWK
INQUIRE SET OF WORKSTATIONS TO WHICH POSTED	pinqsetwsposted	PQWKPO
INQUIRE STRING DEVICE STATE 3	pinqstringst3	PQSTS3 (=)
INQUIRE STROKE DEVICE STATE 3	pinqstrokest3	PQSKS3
INQUIRE STRUCTURE IDENTIFIERS	pinqstructids	PQSID
INQUIRE STRUCTURE STATE VALUE	pinqstructst	PQSTRS
INQUIRE STRUCTURE STATUS	pinqstructstatus	PQSTST
INQUIRE SYSTEM STATE VALUE	pinqsystemst	PQSYS
INQUIRE TEXT EXTENT	pinqtextextent	PQTXX (S)
INQUIRE TEXT FACILITIES	pinqtextfacil	PQTXF
INQUIRE TEXT REPRESENTATION	pinqtextrep	PQTXR
INQUIRE VALUATOR DEVICE STATE 3	pinqvalst3	PQVLS3
INQUIRE VIEW FACILITIES	pinqviewfacil	PQVWF
INQUIRE VIEW REPRESENTATION	pinqviewrep	PQVWR
INQUIRE WORKSTATION CATEGORY	pinqwscategory	PQWKCA
INQUIRE WORKSTATION CLASSIFICATION	pinqwsclass	PQWKCL
INQUIRE WORKSTATION CONNECTION AND TYPE	pinqwsconntype	PQWKC
INQUIRE WORKSTATION STATE TABLE LENGTHS	pinqwssttable	PQWKSL
INQUIRE WORKSTATION STATE VALUE	pinqwsst	PQWKST
INQUIRE WORKSTATION TRANSFORMATION 3	pinqwstran3	PQWKT3
INTERPRET ITEM	pinterpret	PIITM
LABEL	plabel	PLB
MESSAGE	pmessage	PMSG (S)

PHIGS function	*C*	*Fortran*
OFFSET ELEMENT POINTER	poffsetelemptr	POSEP
OPEN ARCHIVE FILE	popenarfile	POPARF
OPEN PHIGS	popenphigs	POPPH
OPEN STRUCTURE	popenstruct	POPST
OPEN WORKSTATION	popenws	POPWK
POLYLINE 3	ppolyline3	PPL3
POLYMARKER 3	ppolymarker3	PPM3
POST STRUCTURE	ppoststruct	PPOST
READ ITEM FROM METAFILE	preadmf	PRDITM
REDRAW ALL STRUCTURES	predrawallstruct	PRST
REMOVE NAMES FROM SET	premovenameset	PRES
REQUEST CHOICE	preqchoice	PRQCH
REQUEST LOCATOR 3	preqloc3	PRQLC3
REQUEST PICK	preqpick	PRQPK
REQUEST STRING	preqstring	PRQST
REQUEST STROKE 3	preqstroke3	PRQSK3
REQUEST VALUATOR	preqval	PQQVL
RESTORE MODELLING CLIPPING VOLUME	prestoremodelclipvol	PRMCV
RETRIEVE ALL STRUCTURES	pretrieveallstruct	PRAST
RETRIEVE PATHS TO ANCESTORS	pretrievepathanc	PRPA
RETRIEVE PATHS TO DESCENDANTS	pretrievepathdec	PRPD
RETRIEVE STRUCTURE IDENTIFIERS	pretrievestructids	PRSID
RETRIEVE STRUCTURE NETWORKS	pretrivestructnet	PRESN
RETRIEVE STRUCTURES	pretrievestructs	PREST
ROTATE	protate	PRO
ROTATE X	protatex	PROX
ROTATE Y	protatey	PROY
ROTATE Z	protatez	PROZ
SAMPLE CHOICE	psamplechoice	PSMCH
SAMPLE LOCATOR 3	psampleloc3	PSMLC3
SAMPLE PICK	psamplepick	PSMPK
SAMPLE STRING	psamplestring	PSMST
SAMPLE STROKE 3	psamplestroke3	PSMSK3
SAMPLE VALUATOR	psampleval	PSMVL
SCALE 3	pscale3	PSC3
SET ANNOTATION STYLE	psetannotationstyle	PSANS
SET ANNOTATION TEXT ALIGNMENT	psetannotationalign	PSATAL
SET ANNOTATION TEXT CHARACTER HEIGHT	psetannotationcharheight	PSATCH
SET ANNOTATION TEXT CHARACTER UP VECTOR	psetannotationcharup	PSATCU
SET ANNOTATION TEXT PATH	psetannotationpath	PSATP

PHIGS function	*C*	*Fortran*
SET CHARACTER EXPANSION FACTOR	psetcharexpan	PSCHXP
SET CHARACTER HEIGHT	psetcharheight	PSCHH
SET CHARACTER SPACING	psetcharspace	PSCHSP
SET CHARACTER UP VECTOR	psetcharup	PSCHUP
SET CHOICE MODE	psetchoicemode	PSCHM
SET COLOUR MODEL	psetcolourmodel	PSCMD
SET COLOUR REPRESENTATION	psetcolourrep	PSCR
SET CONFLICT RESOLUTION	psetconfres	PSCNRS
SET DISPLAY UPDATE STATE	psetdisplayupdatest	PSDUS
SET EDGE COLOUR INDEX	psetedgecolourind	PSEDCI
SET EDGE FLAG	psetedgeflag	PSEDFG
SET EDGE INDEX	psetedgeind	PSEDI
SET EDGE REPRESENTATION	psetedgerep	PSEDR
SET EDGETYPE	psetedgetype	PSEDT
SET EDGEWIDTH SCALE FACTOR	psetedgewidth	PSEWSC
SET EDIT MODE	pseteditmode	PSEDM
SET ELEMENT POINTER	psetelemptr	PSEP
SET ELEMENT POINTER AT LABEL	psetelemptrlabel	PSEPLB
SET ERROR HANDLING MODE	pseterrorhandmode	PSERHM
SET GLOBAL TRANSFORMATION 3	psetglobaltran3	PSGMT3
SET HIGHLIGHTING FILTER	psethilightfilter	PSHLFT
SET HLHSR IDENTIFIER	psethlhsrid	PSHRID
SET HLHSR MODE	psethlhsrmode	PSHRM
SET INDIVIDUAL ASF	psetindivasf	PSIASF
SET INTERIOR COLOUR INDEX	psetintcolourind	PSICI
SET INTERIOR INDEX	psetintind	PSII
SET INTERIOR REPRESENTATION	psetintrep	PSIR
SET INTERIOR STYLE	psetintstyle	PSIS
SET INTERIOR STYLE INDEX	psetintstyleind	PSISI
SET INVISIBILITY FILTER	psetinvisfilter	PSIVFT
SET LINETYPE	psetlinetype	PSLN
SET LINEWIDTH SCALE FACTOR	psetlinewidth	PSLWSC
SET LOCAL TRANSFORMATION 3	psetlocaltran3	PSLMT3
SET LOCATOR MODE	psetlocmode	PSLCM
SET MARKER SIZE SCALE FACTOR	psetmarkersize	PSMKSC
SET MARKER TYPE	psetmarkertype	PSMK
SET MODELLING CLIPPING INDICATOR	psetmodelclipindicator	PSMCLI
SET MODELLING CLIPPING VOLUME 3	psetmodelclipvolume3	PSMCV3
SET PATTERN REFERENCE POINT	psetpatrefpt	PSPAR

PHIGS function	C	Fortran
SET PATTERN REFERENCE POINT AND VECTORS	psetpatrefptvectors	PSPRPV
SET PATTERN REPRESENTATION	psetpatrep	PSPAR
SET PATTERN SIZE	psetpatsize	PSPA
SET PICK FILTER	psetpickfilter	PSPKFT
SET PICK IDENTIFIER	psetpickid	PSPKID
SET PICK MODE	psetpickmode	PSPKM
SET POLYLINE COLOUR INDEX	psetlinecolourind	PSPLCI
SET POLYLINE INDEX	psetlineind	PSPLI
SET POLYLINE REPRESENTATION	psetlinerep	PSPLR
SET POLYMARKER COLOUR INDEX	psetmarkercolourind	PSPMCI
SET POLYMARKER INDEX	psetmarkerind	PSPMI
SET POLYMARKER REPRESENTATION	psetmarkerrep	PSPMR
SET STRING MODE	psetstringmode	PSSTM
SET STROKE MODE	psetstrokemode	PSSKM
SET TEXT ALIGNMENT	psettextalign	PSTXAL
SET TEXT COLOUR INDEX	psettextcolourind	PSTXCI
SET TEXT FONT	psettextfont	PSTXFN
SET TEXT INDEX	psettextind	PSTXI
SET TEXT PATH	psettextpath	PSTXP
SET TEXT PRECISION	psettextprec	PSTXPR
SET TEXT REPRESENTATION	psettextrep	PSTXR
SET VALUATOR MODE	psetvalmode	PSVLM
SET VIEW INDEX	psetviewind	PSVWI
SET VIEW REPRESENTATION 3	psetviewrep3	PSVWR3
SET VIEW TRANSFORMATION INPUT PRIORITY	psetviewtraninputpri	PSVTIP
SET WORKSTATION VIEWPORT 3	psetwsviewport3	PSWKV3
SET WORKSTATION WINDOW 3	psetwswindow3	PSWKW3
TEXT 3	ptext3	PTX3(S)
TRANSFORM POINT 3	ptranpt3	PTP3
TRANSLATE 3	ptranslate3	PTR3
UNPOST ALL STRUCTURES	punpostallstruct	PUPAST
UNPOST STRUCTURE	punpoststruct	PUPOST
UPDATE WORKSTATION	pupdatews	PUWK
WRITE ITEM TO METAFILE	pwritemf	PWITM

E.2   PHIGS functions arranged by type

This section gives a list of PHIGS functions arranged according to their type. Functions which create structure elements are marked *.

Control

open PHIGS
close PHIGS
open workstation
close workstation

redraw all structures
update workstation
set display update state
message

Output primitives

annotation text relative 3*
cell array 3*
fill area 3*
fill area set 3*

generalized drawing primitive 3*
polyline 3*
polymarker 3*
text 3*

Attribute specifications

add names to set*
remove names from set*
set annotation style*
set annotation text alignment*
set annotation text char height*
set annotation text char up vector*
set annotation text path*
set character expansion factor*
set character height*
set character spacing*
set character up vector*
set edge colour index*
set edge flag*
set edge index*
set edge representation
set edgetype*
set edgewidth scale factor*
set highlighting filter
set HLHSR identifier*
set individual ASF*
set interior colour index*
set interior index*

set interior style*
set interior style index*
set invisibility filter
set linetype*
set linewidth scale factor*
set marker size scale factor*
set marker type*
set pattern reference point*
set pattern reference point and vectors*
set pattern size*
set pick identifier*
set polyline colour index*
set polyline index*
set polymarker colour index*
set polymarker index*
set text alignment*
set text colour index*
set text index*
set text font*
set text precision*
set text representation

Transformation and clipping

build transformation matrix 3
compose transformation matrix 3
evaluate view mapping matrix 3
evaluate view orientation matrix 3
restore modelling clipping volume*
rotate
rotate X
rotate Y
rotate Z
scale 3

set global transformation 3*
set local transformation 3*
set modelling clipping indicator*
set modelling clipping volume 3*
set view index*
set view representation 3
set workstation window 3
set workstation viewport 3
transform point 3
translate 3

Structure content

application data*
close structure
copy all elements from structure
delete element
delete element range
delete element between labels
empty structure
execute structure*

generalized structure element*
label*
offset element pointer
open structure
set edit mode
set element pointer
set element pointer at label

Structure manipulation

change structure identifier
change structure references
change structure identifier and
    references

delete all structures
delete structure
delete structure network

Structure display

post structure
unpost all structures

unpost structure

Structure archiving

archive all structures

archive structures

archive structure networks
close archive file
delete all structures from archive
delete structures from archive
delete structure networks from archive
open archive file
retrieve all structures

retrieve paths to ancestors
retrieve paths to descendants
retrieve structures
retrieve structure identifiers
retrieve structure networks
set conflict resolution

Input

await event
flush device events
get choice
get item type from metafile
get locator 3
get pick
get string
get stroke 3
get valuator
initialize choice 3
initialize locator 3
initialize pick 3
initialize string 3
initialize stroke 3
initialize valuator 3
request choice
request locator 3
request pick

request string
request stroke 3
request valuator
sample choice
sample locator 3
sample pick
sample string
sample stroke 3
sample valuator
set choice mode
set string mode
set locator mode
set pick mode
set stroke mode
set valuator mode
set pick filter
set pick identifier*

Metafiles

get item type from metafile
interpret item

read item from metafile
write item to metafile

Inquiry

all conflicting structures
annotation facilities
archive files
archive state value

choice device state 3
colour facilities
colour model

colour model facilities
colour representation
conflict resolution
conflicting structures in network
current element content
current element type and size
default choice device data 3
default display update state
default locator device data 3
default pick device data 3
default string device data 3
default stroke device data 3
default valuator device data 3
display space size 3
display update state
dynamics of structures
dynamics of workstation attributes
edge facilities
edge representation
edit mode
element content
element pointer
element type and size
error handling mode
generalized drawing primitive 3
generalized structure element facilities
highlighting filter
HLHSR facilities
HLHSR mode
input queue overflow
interior facilities
interior representation
invisibility filter
list of generalized drawing primitives 3
list of generalized structure elements
list of workstation types
list of colour indices
list of edge indices
list of interior indices
list of pattern indices
list of polyline indices
list of polymarker indices
list of text indices
list of view indices
locator device state 3

modelling clipping facilities
more simultaneous events
number of available logical input
  devices
number of display priorities supported
open structure
paths to ancestors
paths to descendants
pattern facilities
pattern representation
PHIGS facilities
pick device state 3
polyline facilities
polyline representation
polymarker facilities
polymarker representation
posted structures
predefined colour representation
predefined edge representation
predefined interior representation
predefined pattern representation
predefined polyline representation
predefined polymarker representation
predefined text representation
predefined view representation
set of open workstations
set of workstations to which posted
string device state 3
stroke device state 3
structure identifiers
structure state value
structure status
system state value
text extent
text facilities
text representation
valuator device state 3
view facilities
view representation
workstation category
workstation classification
workstation connection and type
workstation state table lengths
workstation state value
workstation transformation 3

E.3   PHIGS PLUS functions arranged by type

Functions which create structure elements are marked *

Output primitives

polyline set 3 with data*
fill area set 3 with data*
cell array 3 plus*
set of fill area set 3 with data*
triangle strip 3 with data*

quadrilateral mesh 3 with data*
non-uniform B-spline curve*
non-uniform B-spline surface with
    data*
compute fill area set geometric normal

Attribute specifications

set data mapping index*
set reflectance index*
set back interior index*
set back data mapping index*
set back reflectance index*
set parametric surface index*
set polyline colour*
set polyline shading method*
set polymarker colour*
set text colour*
set face distinguishing mode*
set face culling mode*
set interior colour*
set interior shading method*
set data mapping method*
set reflectance properties*
set reflectance characteristics*
set back interior style*
set back interior style index*
set back interior colour*
set back interior shading method*
set back data mapping method*

set back reflectance characteristics*
set light source state*
set edge colour*
set curve approximation criteria*
set surface approximation criteria*
set parametric surface characteristics*
set rendering colour model*
set depth cue index*
set colour mapping index*
set individual ASF
set polyline representation plus
set polymarker representation plus
set text representation plus
set interior representation plus
set edge representation plus
set data mapping representation
set reflectance representation
set parametric surface representation
set pattern representation plus
set light source representation
set depth cue representation
set colour mapping representation

Inquiry

polyline representation plus
polymarker representation plus

text representation plus
interior representation plus

edge representation plus
list of data mapping indices
data mapping representation
list of reflectance indices
reflectance representation
list of parametric surface indices
parametric surface representation
pattern representation plus
list of light source indices
light source representation
list of depth cue indices
depth cue representation
colour mapping state
list of colour mapping indices
colour mapping representation
direct colour model facilities
rendering colour model facilities
dynamics of workstation plus
polyline facilities plus
predefined polyline represention
   plus
predefined polymarker representation
   plus

predefined text representation plus
interior facilities plus
predefined interior representation plus
predefined edge representation plus
data mapping facilities
predefined data mapping representation
reflectance facilities
predefined reflectance representation
curve and surface facilities
predefined parametric surface
   representation
predefined pattern representation plus
light source facilities
predefined light source representation
depth cue facilities
predefined depth cue representation
colour mapping facilities
colour mapping method facilities
predefined colour mapping
   representation
workstation state table lengths plus
current element type and size
element type and size

E.4 PHIGS primitives and attributes

This is a list of all the attributes associated with output primitives. Workstation-dependent attributes are marked †.

Polyline

polyline index
linetype
linewidth scale factor
polyline colour index
linetype ASF
linewidth scale factor ASF

polyline colour index ASF
view index
HLHSR identifier
pick identifier
name set

Polymarker

polymarker index
marker type
marker size scale factor
polymarker colour index
marker type ASF
marker size factor ASF

polymarker colour index ASF
view index
HLHSR identifier
pick identifier
name set

Text

text index
text font
text precision
character expansion factor
character spacing
text colour index
text font ASF
text precision ASF
character expansion factor ASF
character spacing ASF

text colour index ASF
character height[†]
character up vector[†]
text path[†]
text alignment[†]
view index
HLHSR identifier
pick identifier
name set

Annotation text relative

Same as text, plus:
annotation text character height[†]
annotation text character up vector[†]

annotation text path[†]
annotation text alignment[†]
annotation style[†]

Fill area

interior index
interior style
interior style index
interior colour index
interior style ASF
interior style index ASF
interior colour index ASF

pattern size[†]
pattern reference point[†]
pattern reference vectors[†]
view index
HLHSR identifier
pick identifier
name set

Fill area set

Same as fill area, *plus:*

edge index

edge flag ASF

edge flag

edgetype ASF

edgetype

edgewidth scale factor ASF

edgewidth scale factor

edge colour index ASF

edge colour index

Cell array

view index

pick identifier

HLHSR identifier

name set

Generalized drawing primitive

Any of the preceding attributes, plus:

view index

pick identifier

HLHSR identifier

name set

E.5   PHIGS PLUS primitives and attributes

This is a list of all the attributes associated with PHIGS PLUS output primitives. Workstation-dependent attributes are marked [†].

Polyline set 3 with data

polyline index

pick identifier

linetype

name set

linetype ASF

polyline colour

linewidth scale factor

polyline colour ASF

linewidth scale factor ASF

polyline shading method

polyline colour index

polyline shading method ASF

polyline colour index ASF

rendering colour model

view index

depth cue index

HLHSR identifier

colour mapping index

Fill area set 3 with data, set of fill area set 3 with data, triangle strip 3 with data, quadrilateral mesh 3 with data

interior index
interior style
interior style ASF
interior style index
interior style index ASF
interior colour index
interior colour index ASF
edge index
edge flag
edge flag ASF
edgetype
edgetype ASF
edgewidth scale factor
edgewidth scale factor ASF
pattern size
pattern reference point
pattern vectors
view index
HLHSR identifier
pick identifier
name set
data mapping index
reflectance index
back interior index
back data mapping index
back reflectance index
face distinguishing mode
face culling mode
interior colour

interior colour ASF
interior shading method
interior shading method ASF
data mapping method
data mapping method ASF
reflectance properties
reflectance properties ASF
reflectance characteristics
reflectance characteristics ASF
back interior style
back interior style ASF
back interior style index
back interior style index ASF
back interior colour
back interior colour ASF
back interior shading method
back interior shading method ASF
back data mapping method
back data mapping method ASF
back reflectance properties
back reflectance properties ASF
back reflectance characteristics
back reflectance characteristics ASF
edge colour
edge colour ASF
light source state
rendering colour model
depth cue index
colour mapping index

Cell array 3 plus

view index
HLHSR identifier
pick identifier
name set
reflectance index
back reflectance index
face distinguishing mode
face culling mode
reflectance properties

reflectance properties ASF
reflectance characteristics
reflectance characteristics ASF
back reflectance properties
back reflectance properties ASF
back reflectance characteristics
back reflectance characteristics ASF
light source state

rendering colour model   colour mapping index
depth cue index

Non-uniform B-spline curve

as polyline set 3 with data plus:

curve approximation criteria   curve approximation criteria ASF

Non-uniform B-spline surface

interior index   interior shading method ASF
interior style   reflectance properties
interior style ASF   reflectance properties ASF
interior style index   reflectance characteristics
interior style index ASF   reflectance characteristics ASF
interior colour index   back interior index
interior colour index ASF   back reflectance index
data mapping index   back interior style
data mapping method   back interior style ASF
edge index   back interior style index
edge flag   back interior style index ASF
edge flag ASF   back interior colour
edgetype   back interior colour ASF
edgetype ASF   back interior shading method
edgewidth scale factor   back interior shading method ASF
edgewidth scale factor ASF   back data mapping index
pattern size   back data mapping method
pattern reference point   back reflectance properties
pattern vectors   back reflectance properties ASF
view index   back reflectance characteristics
HLHSR identifier   back reflectance characteristics ASF
pick identifier   edge colour
name set   edge colour ASF
reflectance index   light source state
parametric surface index   surface approximation criteria
face distinguishing mode   surface approximation criteria ASF
face culling mode   parametric surface characteristics
interior colour   parametric surface characteristics ASF
interior colour ASF   rendering colour model
interior shading method   depth cue index

colour mapping index

E.6   PHIGS and PHIGS PLUS errors

Errors marked * are PHIGS PLUS errors.

Implementation dependent

< 0   Implementation-dependent errors

States

001   Ignoring function, function requires state (PHCL, WSCL, STCL, ARCL)

002   Ignoring function, function requires state (PHOP, *, *, *)

003   Ignoring function, function requires state (PHOP, WSOP, *, *)

004   Ignoring function, function requires state (PHOP, WSCL, STCL, ARCL)

005   Ignoring function, function requires state (PHOP, *, STOP, *)

006   Ignoring function, function requires state (PHOP, *, STCL, *)

007   Ignoring function, function requires state (PHOP, *, *, AROP)

Workstations

050   Ignoring function, connection identifier not recognized by the implementation.

051   Ignoring function, this information is not yet available for this generic workstation type; open a workstation of this type and use the specific workstation type.

052   Ignoring function, workstation type not recognized by the implementation.

053   Ignoring function, workstation identifier already in use.

054   Ignoring function, the specified workstation is not open.

055   Ignoring function, workstation cannot be opened for an implementation dependent reason.

056   Ignoring function, specified workstation is not of category MO.

057   Ignoring function, specified workstation is of category MI.

058   Ignoring function, specified workstation is not of category MI.

059   Ignoring function, the specified workstation does not have output capability (that is, the workstation category is neither OUTPUT, OUTIN, nor MO).

060   Ignoring function, specified workstation is not of category OUTIN.

061   Ignoring function, specified workstation is neither of category INPUT nor of category OUTIN.

062   Ignoring function, this information is not available for this MO workstation type.

063   Ignoring function, opening this workstation would exceed the maximum number of simultaneously open workstations.

064   Ignoring function, the specified workstation type is not able to generate the specified generalized drawing primitive.

Output attributes

100   Ignoring function, the bundle index value is less than one.

101   Ignoring function, the specified representation has not been defined.

102   Ignoring function, the specified representation has not been predefined on this workstation.

103   Ignoring function, setting this bundle table entry would exceed the maximum number of entries allowed.

104   Ignoring function, the specified linetype is not available on the specified workstation.

105   Ignoring function, the specified marker type is not available on the specified workstation.

106   Ignoring function, the specified font is not available for the requested text precision on the specified workstation.

107   Ignoring function, the specified edgetype is not available on the specified workstation.

108   Ignoring function, the specified interior style is not available on the workstation.

109   Ignoring function, interior style PATTERN is not supported on the workstation.

110   Ignoring function, the specified colour model is not available on the workstation.

111   Ignoring function, the specified HLSHR mode is not available on the specified workstation.

112   Ignoring function, the pattern index value is less than one.

113   Ignoring function, the colour index value is less than zero.

114   Ignoring function, the view index value is less than zero.

115   Ignoring function, the view index value is less than one.

116   Ignoring function, one of the dimensions of pattern colour index array is less than one.

117   Ignoring function, one of the dimensions of the colour index array is less than zero.

118   Ignoring function, one of the components of the colour specification is out of range. The valid range is dependent on the current colour model.

119*   Ignoring function, the depth cue index is less than zero.

120*   Ignoring function, the depth cue index is less than one.

121*   Ignoring function, the colour mapping index is less than zero.

122*   Ignoring function, the specified polyline shading method is not available on the workstation.

123*   Ignoring function, the specified interior shading method is not available on the workstation.

124*   Ignoring function, the specified reflectance characteristics value is not available on the workstation.

125*   Ignoring function, the total of the colour range fields in all the table entries is too large.

126*   Ignoring function, the specified colour mapping method is not available on the specified workstation.

127*   Ignoring function, the specified approximation criteria type is not available on the specified workstation.

128*   Ignoring function, the specified parametric surface characteristics type is not available on the specified workstation.

129*   Ignoring function, the light source index is less than 1.

130*   Ignoring function, invalid reference planes; *dqmin > dqmax*.

131*   Ignoring function, the specified light source type is not available on the workstation.

132*   Ignoring function, the specified spot light spread angle is out of range.

133*   Ignoring function, one of the entries in the activation list or deactivation list is less than 1.

134*   Ignoring function, the requested entry contains a general colour specification with colour type other than INDIRECT.

135*   Ignoring function, the same entry exists in both the activation list and the deactivation list.

136*   Ignoring function, one of the components of the colour specification is out of range.

137*   Ignoring function, the specified data mapping method is not available on the specified workstation.

138*   Ignoring function, one or more of the fields in the specified data record is inconsistent with the specified type.

Transformations and viewing

150   Ignoring function, setting this view table entry would exceed the maximum number of entries allowed in the workstation's view table.

151   Ignoring function, invalid window; *xmin* ≥ *xmax*, *ymin* ≥ *ymax*, *zmin* > *zmax*, *umin* ≥ *umax* or *vmin* ≥ *vmax*.

152   Ignoring function, invalid viewport; *xmin* ≥ *xmax*, *ymin* ≥ *ymax*, *zmin* > *zmax*.

153   Ignoring function, invalid view clipping limits; $xmin \geq xmax$, $ymin \geq ymax$, $zmin > zmax$.

154   Ignoring function, the view clipping limits are not within NPC range.

155   Ignoring function, the projection viewport limits are not within NPC range.

156   Ignoring function, the workstation window limits are not within NPC range.

157   Ignoring function, the workstation viewport is not within display space.

158   Ignoring function, front plane and back plane distances are equal when z-extent of the projection viewport is non-zero.

159   Ignoring function, the view plane normal vector has length zero.

160   Ignoring function, the view up vector has length zero.

161   Ignoring function, the view up and view plane normal vectors are parallel thus the viewing coordinate system cannot be established.

162   Ignoring function, the projection reference point is between the front and back planes.

163   Ignoring function, the projection reference point cannot be positioned on the view plane.

164   Ignoring function, the back plane is in front of the view plane.

Structures

200   Warning, ignoring structures that do not exist.

201   Ignoring function, the specified structure does not exist.

202   Ignoring function, the specified element does not exist.

203   Ignoring function, specified starting path not found in CSS.

204   Ignoring function, specified search ceiling index out of range.

205   Ignoring function, the label does not exist in the open structure between the element pointer and the end of the structure.

206   Ignoring function, one or both of the labels does not exist in the open structure between the element pointer and the end of the structure.

207   Ignoring function, the specified path depth is less than zero.

208   Ignoring function, the display priority is out of range.

Input

250   Ignoring function, the specified device is not available in the specified workstation.

251   Ignoring function, the function requires the input device to be in REQUEST mode.

252   Ignoring function, the function requires the input device to be in SAMPLE mode.

253   Ignoring function, the specified prompt/echo type is not available on the specified workstation.

254   Ignoring function, invalid echo area/volume; $xmin \geq xmax$, $ymin \geq ymax$ or $zmin > zmax$.

255   Ignoring function, one of the echo area/volume boundary points is outside the range of the device.

256   Warning, the input queue has overflowed.

257   Ignoring function, input queue has not overflowed, since OPEN PHIGS or last invocation of INQUIRE INPUT QUEUE OVERFLOW.

258   Ignoring function, input queue has overflowed, but associated workstation has been closed.

259   Ignoring function, the input device class of the current input report does not match the class being requested.

260   Ignoring function, one of the fields within the input device data record is in error.

261   Ignoring function, initial value is invalid.

262   Ignoring function, number of points in the initial stroke is greater than the buffer size.

262   Ignoring function, length of the initial string is greater than the buffer size.

Metafiles

300   Ignoring function, item type is not allowed for user items.

301   Ignoring function, item length is invalid.

302   Ignoring function, no item is left in metafile input.

303   Ignoring function, metafile item is invalid.

304   Ignoring function, item type is unknown.

305   Ignoring function, content of item data record is invalid for the specified item type.

306   Ignoring function, maximum item data record length is invalid.

307   Ignoring function, user item cannot be interpreted.

Escape

350   Warning, the specified escape is not available on one or more workstations in this implementation. The escape will be processed by those workstations on which it is available.

351   Ignoring function, one of the fields within the escape data record is in error.

Archiving

400   Ignoring function, the archive file cannot be opened.

401   Ignoring function, opening this archive file would exceed the maximum number of simultaneously open archive files.

402   Ignoring function, archive file identifier already in use.

403   Ignoring function, the archive file is not a PHIGS archive file.

404   Ignoring function, the specified archive file is not open.

405   Ignoring function, name conflict occurred while conflict resolution flag has value ABANDON.

406   Warning, the archive file is full. Any structures that were archived were archived in total.

407   Warning, some of the specified structures do not exist on the archive file.

408   Warning, some of the specified structures do not exist on the archive file. PHIGS will create empty structures in their places.

Miscellaneous

450   Ignoring function, the specified error file is invalid.

PHIGS PLUS output primitives

500*   Ignoring function, the specified order is less than 1.

501*   Ignoring function, not enough control points for the specified order.

502*   Ignoring function, the specified order is inconsistent with number of knots and control points.

503*   Ignoring function, the knot sequence is not non-decreasing.

504*   Ignoring function, one or more of the vertex indices is out of range.

505*   Ignoring function, the fill area is degenerate.

506*   Ignoring function, the parameter range is inconsistent with the knots.

507*   Ignoring function, the fourth coordinate of a rational control point is less than or equal to zero.

508*   Ignoring function, a trimming curve order is less than 2.

509*   Ignoring function, a trimming curve does not contain enough control points for its specified order.

510*   Ignoring function, a trimming curve's order is inconsistent with the its number of knots and control points.

511*   Ignoring function, a trimming curve's knot sequence is not non-decreasing.

512*   Ignoring function, a trimming curve's parameter range is inconsistent with its knots.

513*   Ignoring function, inconsistent edge flag specification.

System

900   Storage overflow has occurred in PHIGS.

901   Storage overflow has occurred in CSS.

902   Input/output error has occurred while reading.

903   Input/output error has occurred while writing.

904   Input/output error has occurred while sending data to a workstation.

905   Input/output error has occurred while receiving data from a workstation.

906   Input/output error has occurred during program library management.

907   Input/output error has occurred while reading workstation description table.

908   Arithmetic error has occurred.

Appendix F
Colour models

A colour model is a method for describing colour *quantitively*, by expressing a colour as a set of coordinates in a colour space. This appendix gives a brief description of the RGB, CIE LUV, HSV and HLS colour models. Every PHIGS implementation is required to support the RGB and CIE LUV models, and the others may be optionally available.

F.1 RGB

In the RGB model (Figure F.1), a colour is represented as a triple of the form (r, g, b), where r, g and b are the magnitudes of the red, green and blue components respectively, each specified in the range 0 to 1. The RGB colour space may

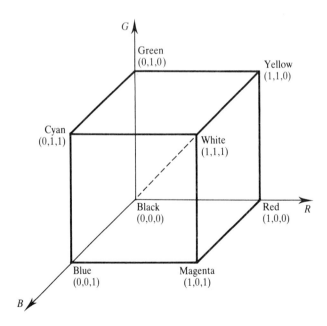

Figure F.1   The RGB colour model.

be conveniently visualized as a cube, where the 3D coordinate axes represent the red, green and blue components. A value of 0 for a primary means that it makes no contribution to the colour, and a value of 1 means it makes a maximum contribution. For example, pure red is expressed as $(1,0,0)$ (red = 1, green = 0, blue = 0), and pure blue as $(0,0,1)$. Shades of grey are found on the diagonal line connecting $(0,0,0)$ with $(1,1,1)$.

F.2   CIE LUV

The CIE colour model is an internationally accepted standard for colour specification. It was originally established by the Commission Internationale de l'Éclairage (CIE) in 1931. In 1978, a revision of the system known as the CIE LUV colour model was adopted, which removed a number of problems with the original model. Figure F.2 illustrates CIE LUV space.

One of the strengths of the CIE LUV model is that it provides a method for specifying colours in a device-independent manner. Typically, for a particular application, colours will be defined in terms of the RGB, HSV or HLS models. These are device-dependent specifications. Then, by taking into account the characteristics of the display device, the definition can be transformed to a device-independent CIE LUV specification.

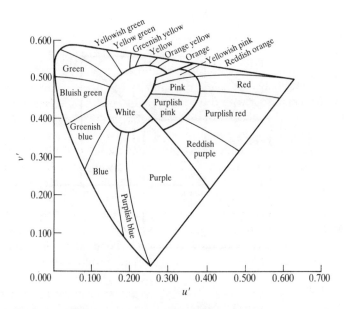

Figure F.2   The CIE LUV colour model.

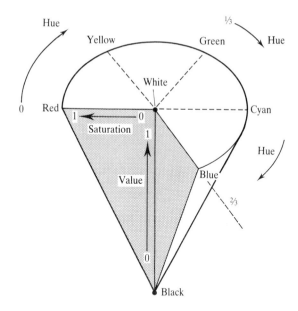

Figure F.3   The HSV colour model.

F.3   HSV

The RGB colour model is oriented towards the way in which colour is specified in cathode-ray display devices, and it is often difficult to use it in an interactive sense to specify colours you want to see. Similarly, the CIE LUV model is not particularly user friendly. We can more naturally describe a colour on the basis of three factors connected with our perception of colour: **hue, saturation** and **value**. The HSV colour model uses these ideas directly. The model is visualized as a cone, as shown in Figure F.3.

Hue is specified as an angle measured around the cross-section of the cone, with $0-360°$ expressed on a scale of $0-1$. Red is situated at $H = 0$, green at $H = 1/3$ and blue at $H = 2/3$ (red occurs again at $H = 1$). Saturation is measured along the radius of the cross-section of the cone, with 0 at the centre and 1 at the circumference. Colours around the circumference of the cross-section of the cone are fully saturated 'pure' colours. Value is measured along the vertical axis of the cone, with $V = 1$ at the base, and $V = 0$ at the apex. Points along the vertical axis of the cone represent colours which are fully desaturated ($S = 0$), which gives a range of greys, with pure white at the base of the cone, and pure black at its apex.

Because of its perceptual basis, the HSV model is much easier to manipulate than the RGB model, primarily because the specification of hue is separated from saturation and intensity.

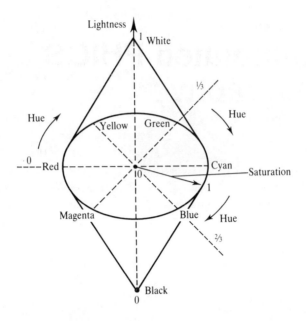

Figure F.4   The HLS colour model.

F.4   HLS

In this model, the hue and saturation parameters are measured in the range 0–1, using the same conventions as the HSV model. However, the *value* parameter is replaced by **lightness**, as shown in Figure F.4. Here, white occurs at $L = 1$, and black at $L = 0$.

Appendix G

An annotated PHIGS bibliography

This is a bibliography of publications that relate to PHIGS, arranged by subject. For the more important sources we give a precis of their contents and usefulness. The bibliography is divided into five sections, and within each section sources are arranged chronologically. Where documents have appeared in several versions, only the current versions are listed. The sections are:

- defining documents
- general sources
- technical implementation issues
- practice and experience
- PHIGS and other graphics systems

G.1 Defining documents

The following are documents published by the International Organization for Standardization which define and relate to PHIGS and PHIGS PLUS. For further details, contact the International Organization for Standardization (Case postale 56, CH-1211 Genève 20, Switzerland), or your national standardization body (for the UK, British Standards Institution (BSI), 2 Park Street, London W1A 2BS; for the USA, American National Standards Institute (ANSI), 1430 Broadway, New York NY 10018).

PHIGS: Functional description, ISO/IEC 9592-1, 1988.

PHIGS: Archive file format, ISO/IEC 9592-2, 1988.

PHIGS: Archive file clear text encoding, ISO/IEC 9592-3, 1988.

PHIGS Language Bindings: (Part 1)—Fortran, ISO/IEC DIS 9593-1, 1988.

PHIGS Language Bindings: (Part 3)—Ada, ISO/IEC DIS 9593-3, 1988.

PHIGS PLUS Committee Draft: CD 9592-4.

G.2   General sources

The following sources provide general introductions to PHIGS. The specification of PHIGS has undergone many changes in the five years it took to appear as an international standard, and while the majority of the underlying concepts have remained the same, many of these papers do not reflect the details of the finalized standard.

The PHIGS system
D.U. Cahn, E. McGinnis, R.F. Puk, C.S. Seum, *Computer Graphics World*, pages 33–40, February 1984.

A brief introduction to PHIGS
A.J. Bunshaft, in *Proceedings Computer Graphics '85*, Vol. II, pages 326–331. NCGA, April 1985.

PHIGS: The standard and the IBM implementation
J. Bettels, in *Proceedings of the SEAS Spring Meeting on Expert Systems*, pages 717–725, Nijmegen, Netherlands, April 1986, SEAS.

PHIGS in CAD
S.S. Abi-Ezzi and S.E. Kader, *Computers in Mechanical Engineering*, **5**(1):28–36, July 1986.

PHIGS
W.T. Hewitt, in *Advances in Computer Graphics I*, (G. Enderle, M. Grave, and F. Lillehage, eds), pages 227–236. Springer-Verlag, 1986.

PHIGS: A standard, dynamic, interactive graphics interface
D. Shuey, D. Bailey, T. Morrissey, *IEEE Computer Graphics & Applications*, **6**(8):50–57, August 1986. Written when PHIGS was still a draft standard proposal, this paper is still a useful introduction to the basic ideas of PHIGS as a modelling system.

Understanding PHIGS
M.D. Brown and M. Heck, Template Graphics Software, Inc., 9685 Scranton Road, San Diego, CA 92121, 1987. This book describes a version of PHIGS as it was before it was approved as an international standard. While the general description is still valid, some details are obsolete.

Three dimensional graphics standards – a critical appraisal
R.J. Hubbold, in *Proceedings Ausgraph '87*. Australasian Computer Graphics

Association, 1987. Looks at PHIGS in the general context of graphics standards, and examines implementation issues and the need for PHIGS PLUS functionality.

PHIGS tutorial notes
D. Shuey and E. McGinnis, in *Proceedings Computer Graphics '87*, Philadelphia, 1987. NCGA.

PHIGS
M. Plaehn, *Byte*, **12**(13):275–286, November 1987. A non-technical overview of PHIGS from a commercial standpoint.

PHIGS
K.M. Wyrwas, in *Computer Graphics Standards: Myth and Reality*, Eurographics UK, 1988.

GKS-3D and PHIGS – theory and practice
R.J. Hubbold and W.T. Hewitt, in *Advances in Computer Graphics IV*, Springer-Verlag, 1990. These tutorial notes approach PHIGS and GKS-3D from two points of view. The first gives a comparative overview of the facilities the two standards provide, and summarizes their interrelationship and particular differences. The second takes a look at PHIGS and GKS-3D in practice, using a number of real applications as case studies, and goes on to discuss how to evaluate and compare different commercial implementations of the two standards.

An annotated PHIGS bibliography
T.L.J. Howard, *Computer Graphics Forum*, **8**(5):262–265, December 1989. This paper is an earlier version of this appendix.

PHIGS and PHIGS PLUS tutorial notes
T.L.J. Howard, Eurographics UK, 1990.

Using PHIGS with FIGARO+
Gia Rozells-Kuhnert, Kathy Tinoco, Dan Morenus, Norbert Kuhnert, Template Graphics Software, Inc., 1990.

CAD/CAM focus report: notes on PHIGS
Albert consulting group, *The Anderson Report*, **12**(8):8–10, December 1990.

Professional CADAM's use of PHIGS
Dave Coalsworth and Gary Gaudisco, In *Proceedings Computer Graphics '87*, Volume III, pages 490–496. NCGA, March 1987.

G.3   Implementation issues

These papers cover techniques for implementing PHIGS.

An approach for a PHIGS machine
S.S. Abi-Ezzi and M.A. Milicia, in *Proceedings of the Data Structures for Raster Graphics* Workshop, Eindhoven, Netherlands, June 1985.

An implementor's view of PHIGS
S.S. Abi-Ezzi and A.J. Bunshaft, *IEEE Computer Graphics & Applications*, **6**(2): 12–23, February 1986. Describes a complete prototype Pascal implementation of PHIGS on an IBM system. There is useful discussion of the issues involved in designing the centralized structure store, the viewing pipeline, and the partitioning of the system into device-independent and device-dependent sections.

The priority tree, a HL/HSR approach for PHIGS
S.S. Abi-Ezzi, *Computer Graphics Forum*, **5**(4):282–289, December 1986. Describes techniques for incorporating hidden line and hidden surface elimination into PHIGS. The method is based on the Binary Space Partitioning (BSP) tree, and sorts primitives from a structure network in a back-to-front order for rendering. An interesting feature is that another PHIGS structure network is used for the BSP tree representation itself.

An implementation of the GKS-3D/PHIGS viewing pipeline
K.M. Singleton, in *Proceedings Eurographics '86*, (A.A.G. Requicha, ed.), pages 325–356. Eurographics, North-Holland, 1986.
also Technical Report UMCS-86-4-1, Department of Computer Science, University of Manchester, M13 9PL, UK, 1986.
also in *Computers & Graphics*, **11**(2), 1987, pages 163–184.
also in *GKS Theory and Practice*, Eurographics Seminars, (P.R. Bono and I. Herman, eds), Springer-Verlag, 1987, pages 145–183. This is the definitive paper on the technical specification and implementation of the GKS-3D and PHIGS viewing pipeline. It describes in detail how to derive the coordinate transformations required, and how to express them as homogeneous transformation matrices. It concludes with a useful discussion on how to express standard projections using the GKS-3D/PHIGS model.

A shareable centralized database for KRT^3 – a hierarchical graphics system based on PHIGS
T.L.J. Howard, in *Proceedings Eurographics '87*, (Guy Maréchal, ed.), pages 465–480. North-Holland, 1987.
also in *Computers & Graphics*, **12**(2), 1988, pages 201–211. Describes data structures and techniques for implementing the PHIGS hierarchical centralized structure store. Experience is based on the experimental KRT^3 graphics system at the University of Manchester, which served as a testbed for many of the ideas that are embodied in PHIGS.

A means to improve the GKS-3D/PHIGS viewing pipeline implementation
I. Herman and J. Reviczky, *Proceedings Eurographics '87*, (Guy Maréchal, ed.), pages 481–494, North-Holland, 1987.
also in *Computers & Graphics*, **12**(2), 1988, pages 191–199. Describes techniques for improving the efficiency of implementations of the GKS-3D/PHIGS viewing pipeline. It also considers the practicalities of filling polygons after they have been transformed by the viewing pipeline.

A special graphics system for PHIGS
S.S. Abi-Ezzi, J.F. Molina, M.A. Toelle, *Computers & Graphics*, **12**(2):155–162, 1988. Describes a pipelined architecture to support the functionality of PHIGS directly. The architecture is constructed from standard hardware modules, and a prototype implementation has proved the suitability of the design.

Some remarks on the modelling clip problem
I. Herman and J. Reviczky, *Computer Graphics Forum*, **7**(4):265–272, 1988. Gives a mathematical analysis of the PHIGS modelling clip, and describes a method for its implementation which avoids all possible singularities which can occur in the course of projective transformations.

IxPHIGS: a portable implementation of the international PHIGS standard
J. Gorog, G. Krammer, A. Vincze, in *Proceedings Eurographics '88*, (D.A. Duce and P. Jancene, eds), pages 13–19, North-Holland, 1988. Describes an object-oriented C implementation of PHIGS for an IBM PC-AT.

Notes on the mathematics of the PHIGS viewing pipeline
Gergely Krammer, *Computer Graphics Forum*, **8**(5):219–226, 1989.

Yet another remark on the modelling clip problem
Morten Zachrisen, *Computer Graphics Forum*, **8**(5):237–238, 1989.

Response to Morten's note about the modelling clip problem
Ivan Herman, *Computer Graphics Forum*, **8**(5):238, 1989.

An analysis of modelling clip
Robert M. O'Bara and Salim Abi-Ezzi, in *Proceedings Eurographics '89*, (W. Hansmann, F.R.A. Hopgood, and W. Strasser, eds), pages 367–379, Eurographics, North-Holland, 1989.

GKS, structures and formal specification
D.A. Duce, in *Proceedings Eurographics '89*, (W. Hansmann, F.R.A. Hopgood, and W. Strasser, eds), pages 271–287, North-Holland, 1989.

Highlight shading, lighting and shading in a PHIGS+/PEX-environment
J. Pöpsel and C. Hornung, in *Proceedings Eurographics '89*, (W. Hansmann, F.R.A. Hopgood, and W. Strasser, eds), pages 317–332, North-Holland, 1989.

A method for the representation, evaluation and display of CSG models in PHIGS and PHIGS+
Manjula Patel, *Computer Graphics Forum*, **8**(4):337–345, 1989.

G.4   Practice and experience

These articles describe PHIGS implementations and applications.

PHIGS: A graphics platform for CAD application development
D. Shuey, *Computer Aided Design*, **19**(8):410–416, 1987. This paper looks at PHIGS through the eyes of a CAD programmer. It gives an overview of what PHIGS can do, and how its functionality relates to common requirements in CAD.

A PHIGS-based graphics input interface for spatial-mechanism design
B.R. Thatch and A. Myklebust, *IEEE Computer Graphics & Applications*, **8**(2): 26–38, February 1988. Describes the design and implementation of a sophisticated system for interactively designing spatial mechanisms. Primarily to achieve device independence, the system is based on IBM's graPHIGS implementation, although the paper does not discuss in detail the way the application has been mapped onto the PHIGS model. Interestingly, much of the application's data is stored outside the centralized structure store.

A survey of GKS and PHIGS implementations
K.M. Wyrwas and W.T. Hewitt, *Computer Graphics Forum*, **8**(1):49–59, 1989. Surveys the GKS, GKS-3D and PHIGS implementations available worldwide. Each product is described in terms of its relationship to the respective standard, its hardware support, availability and price.

Visual design: programming with SunPHIGS
Ingrid Van Den Hoogen, *SunTech Journal*, **2**(4):62–74, Autumn 1989.

TopDraw: an interactive structure network visualizer for PHIGS
T.L.J. Howard, *Computer Graphics Forum*, **9**(2):139–147, 1990. Describes a portable application tool for automatically creating diagrams showing the topologies of structure networks.

An Interactive Debugger for PHIGS
T.L.J. Howard, W.T. Hewitt and S. Larkin, in *Proceedings Eurographics '90*, (C.E. Vandoni and D.A. Duce, eds), pages 177–193. Eurographics, North-Holland, 1990. Describes an application tool for interactively debugging PHIGS programs.

G.5   PHIGS and other graphics systems

These papers discuss PHIGS in relation to other computer graphics standards. A recurring topic – now mainly of historical interest – is the relationship between GKS-3D and PHIGS, and although many of the issues of PHIGS/GKS-3D compatibility have since been resolved, one area that is likely to assume major importance in practice is the integration of PHIGS and GKS/GKS-3D into a single programming environment.

GKS programming in a PHIGS environment
D.B. Arnold, G. Hall, G.J. Reynolds, *Computer Graphics Forum*, **4**(4):349–358, 1985. This paper discusses in detail the implications of running GKS and GKS-3D programs in a PHIGS environment, by introducing a 'shell' between the two. It is based on preliminary versions of both GKS-3D and PHIGS.

Degree of PHIGS/GKS compatibility still hotly debated
T. Williams, *Computer Design*, **24**(17):38–9, December 1985. Written at a time when the PHIGS/GKS-3D debate was in full swing, when many issues were still unresolved.

A GKS shell for PHIGS implementations
P.J.W. ten Hagen, B.P. Rouwhorst, L.R.A. Kessener, Technical Report ISO TC97/SC21/WG2 N541, 1987. The first detailed proposal for a GKS 'shell' to enable GKS and GKS-3D programs to be run 'on top of' a PHIGS implementation. Based on preliminary versions of GKS-3D and PHIGS.

Are PHIGS and GKS necessarily incompatible?
J. Schoenhut, *IEEE Computer Graphics & Applications*, **6**(7):51–53, July 1986. A short discussion of the compatibility issues under discussion at the time.

Approach to solving the compatibility problem between GKS and PHIGS
S. Noll, J. Poller, J. Rix, *Computer Aided Design*, **19**(8):456-463, October 1987. Describes a proposal for the Programmer's Hierarchical Interactive Graphics Kernel System (PHI-GKS), a system which does not use the 'shell' approach for running GKS/GKS-3D 'on top of' PHIGS, but instead incorporates features from GKS-3D and PHIGS into a new single system. The development of PHI-GKS was not taken forward within the standardization process.

Issues raised by the PHI-GKS approach
B. Shephard, J. Rix, *Computer Aided Design*, **19**(8):464, October 1987. A short exchange on issues raised in the paper 'Approach to solving the compatibility problem between GKS and PHIGS'.

PHI-GKS: An implementation to support GKS-3D and PHIGS
S. Noll and J. Poller, *Computers & Graphics*, **12**(2):163–172, 1988. This paper presents in detail a proposal for the Programmer's Hierarchical Interactive

Graphics Kernel System (PHI-GKS). This was an attempt to incorporate features of GKS-3D and PHIGS into a single system. The development of PHI-GKS was not taken forward within the standardization process.

Guidelines for determining when to use GKS and when to use PHIGS
J. Bettels, P. Bono, E. McGinnis, J. Rix, *Computers & Graphics*, **13**(1):91–98, 1989. Given a particular application, which is the most applicable graphics standard to use: GKS, GKS-3D or PHIGS? This paper discusses the pros and cons involved in making the decision.

The development of PEX, a 3D graphics extension to X11
W.H. Clifford, J.I. McConnell, J.S. Saltz, in *Proceedings Eurographics '88*, (D.A. Duce and P. Jancene, eds), pages 21–30, North-Holland, 1988. Describes the need for 3D extensions to the X11 protocol, and the technical basis of the PEX approach.

Migration of GKS/GKS-3D and PHIGS
J. Poller, S. Noll and J. Rix, *Computer Graphics Forum*, **8**(5):239–248, 1989.

Components, frameworks and GKS input
D.A. Duce, P.J.W. ten Hagen, R. van Liere, In *Proceedings Eurographics '89*, (W. Hansmann, F.R.A. Hopgood, and W. Strasser, eds), pages 87–106. North-Holland, 1989.

Bibliography

[Abi-Ezzi, 1986] S.S. Abi-Ezzi. The priority tree, a HL/HSR approach for PHIGS. *Computer Graphics Forum*, 5(4):282–289, December 1986.

[Abi-Ezzi and Bunshaft, 1986] S.S. Abi-Ezzi and A.J. Bunshaft. An implementor's view of PHIGS. *IEEE Computer Graphics & Applications*, 6(2):12–23, February 1986.

[Abi-Ezzi and Kader, 1986] S.S. Abi-Ezzi and S.E. Kader. PHIGS in CAD. *Computers in Mechanical Engineering*, 5(1):28–36, July 1986.

[Abi-Ezzi and Milicia, 1985] S.S. Abi-Ezzi and M.A. Milicia. An approach for a PHIGS machine. In *Proceedings of the Data Structures for Raster Graphics Workshop*, Eindhoven, Netherlands, June 1985.

[Abi-Ezzi et al., 1988] S.S. Abi-Ezzi, J.F. Molina, and M.A. Toelle. A special graphics system for PHIGS. *Computers & Graphics*, 12(2):155–162, 1988.

[Albert Consulting Group, 1990] Albert Consulting Group. CAD/CAM focus report: Notes on PHIGS. *The Anderson Report*, 12(8):8–10, December 1990.

[Arnold and Duce, 1990] D.B. Arnold and D.A. Duce. *ISO Standards for Computer Graphics*. Computer Graphics Standards. Butterworths, London, 1990.

[Arnold et al., 1985] D.B. Arnold, G. Hall, and G.J. Reynolds. GKS programming in a PHIGS environment. *Computer Graphics Forum*, 4(4):349–358, 1985.

[Bakker, 1990] Miente Bakker. Parametric surfaces in PHIGS PLUS: a new chance for patterning and hatching? *Computer Graphics Forum*, 9(1):3–8, March 1990.

[Bartels et al., 1987] Richard H. Bartels, John C. Beatty, and Brian A. Barsky. *An Introduction to Splines for use in Computer Graphics*. Morgan Kauffman, Los Altos, California, 1987.

[Bettels, 1986] J. Bettels. PHIGS: The standard and the IBM implementation. In *Proceedings of the SEAS Spring Meeting on Expert Systems*, pages 717–725, Nijmegen, Netherlands, April 1986. SEAS.

[Bettels et al., 1989] J. Bettels, P. Bono, E. McGinnis, and J. Rix. Guidelines for determining when to use GKS and when to use PHIGS. *Computers & Graphics*, 13(1):91–98, 1989.

[Brown and Heck, 1987] M.D. Brown and M. Heck. *Understanding PHIGS.* Template Graphics Software, Inc., 9685 Scranton Road, San Diego, CA 92121, 1987.

[Bunshaft, 1985] A.J. Bunshaft. A brief introduction to PHIGS. In *Proceedings Computer Graphics*, volume II, pages 326–331. NCGA, April 1985.

[Cahn *et al.*, 1984] D.U. Cahn, E. McGinnis, R.F. Puk, and C.S. Seum. The PHIGS system. *Computer Graphics World*, pages 33–40, February 1984.

[Clifford *et al.*, 1988] W.H. Clifford, J.I. McConnell, and J.S. Saltz. The development of PEX, a 3D graphics extension to X11. In D.A. Duce and P. Jancene, editors, *Proceedings Eurographics '88*, pages 21–30. North-Holland, Amsterdam, 1988.

[Coalsworth and Gaudisco, 1987] Dave Coalsworth and Gary Gaudisco. Professional CADAM's use of PHIGS. In *Proceedings NCGA, Volume III*, pages 490–496, March 1987.

[Duce *et al.*, 1989] D.A. Duce, P.J.W. ten Hagen, and R. van Liere. Components, frameworks and GKS input. In W. Hansmann, F.R.A. Hopgood, and W. Strasser, editors, *Proceedings Eurographics '89*, pages 87–106. North-Holland, Amsterdam, 1989.

[Duce, 1989] D.A. Duce. GKS, structures and formal specification. In W. Hansmann, F.R.A. Hopgood, and W. Strasser, editors, *Proceedings Eurographics '89*, pages 271–287. North-Holland, Amsterdam, 1989.

[Farin, 1990] Gerald Farin. *Curves and Surfaces for Computer Aided Geometric Design: A Practical Guide.* Academic Press, London, 1990.

[Foley *et al.*, 1990] J. D. Foley, A. Van Dam, S.K. Feiner, and J.F. Hughes. *Computer Graphics: Principles and Practice.* Addison-Wesley, Reading MA, 1990.

[Gorog *et al.*, 1988] J. Gorog, G. Krammer, and A. Vincze. IxPHIGS: a portable implementation of the international PHIGS standard. In D.A. Duce and P. Jancene, editors, *Proceedings Eurographics '88*, pages 13–19. North-Holland, Amsterdam, 1988.

[Guedj and Tucker, 1979] R.A. Guedj and H.A. Tucker, editors. *Methodology in Computer Graphics.* North-Holland, Amsterdam, 1979.

[Hearn and Baker, 1986] D. Hearn and M.P Baker. *Computer Graphics.* Addison-Wesley, Reading MA, 1986.

[Henderson and Mumford, 1990] L.R. Henderson and A.M. Mumford. *The Computer Graphics Metafile.* Butterworths, London, 1990.

[Herman and Reviczky, 1987] I. Herman and J. Reviczky. A means to improve the GKS-3D/PHIGS viewing pipeline implementation. In Guy Maréchal, editor, *Proceedings Eurographics '87*, pages 481–494. North-Holland, Amsterdam, 1987.

[Herman and Reviczky, 1988] I. Herman and J. Reviczky. Some remarks on the modelling clip problem. *Computer Graphics Forum*, 7(4):265–272, 1988. Errata to this paper were published in *Computer Graphics Forum*, 9(2), 1990, page 170.

[Herman, 1989] Ivan Herman. Response to Morten's note about the modelling clip problem. *Computer Graphics Forum*, 8(5):238, 1989.

[Hewitt *et al.*, 1988] W.T. Hewitt, T. Howard, and Y.W. Lau. *A PHIGS Demonstrator*. Technical report, Computer Graphics Unit, University of Manchester, 1988. Final report for SERC Grant N2A 9M 0051.

[Hewitt, 1986] W.T. Hewitt. PHIGS. In G. Enderle, M. Grave, and F. Lillehage, editors, *Advances in Computer Graphics I*, pages 227–236. Springer-Verlag, 1986.

[Hoogen, 1989] Ingrid Van Den Hoogen. Visual design: programming with Sun-PHIGS. *SunTech Journal*, 2(4):62–74, Autumn 1989.

[Hopgood *et al.*, 1983] F. R. A. Hopgood, D. A. Duce, J. R. Gallop, and D. C. Sutcliffe. *Introduction to the Graphical Kernel System GKS*. APIC Studies in Data Processing No 19. Academic Press, 1983.

[Howard, 1987] T.L.J. Howard. A shareable centralised database for KRT^3 – a hierarchical graphics system based on PHIGS. In Guy Maréchal, editor, *Proceedings Eurographics '87*, pages 465–480. North-Holland, Amsterdam, 1987.

[Howard, 1989] T.L.J. Howard. An annotated PHIGS bibliography. *Computer Graphics Forum*, 8(5):262–265, December 1989.

[Howard, 1990a] T.L.J. Howard. *An Introductory Guide to PHIGS*. Advisory Group on Computer Graphics, 1990.

[Howard, 1990b] T.L.J. Howard. *PHIGS and PHIGS PLUS Tutorial Notes*. Eurographics UK, 1990.

[Howard, 1990c] T.L.J. Howard. *TopDraw*: An interactive structure network visualiser for PHIGS. *Computer Graphics Forum*, 9(2):139–147, 1990.

[Howard and Larkin, 1988] T.L.J. Howard and S. Larkin. *HashStrings: A General Purpose Naming Tool for PHIGS and other Applications*. Project Report KRT^3/83, Computer Graphics Unit, Department of Computer Science, University of Manchester, 1988.

[Howard *et al.*, 1990a] T.L.J. Howard, W.T. Hewitt, and S. Larkin. An interactive debugger for PHIGS. In C.E. Vandoni and D.A. Duce, editors, *Proceedings Eurographics '90*, pages 177–193. North-Holland, Amsterdam, 1990.

[Howard *et al.*, 1990b] T.L.J. Howard, W.T. Hewitt, J.G. Williams, and S. Larkin. *A Portable Applications Toolkit for PHIGS*. Technical Report PTK/1, Department of Computer Science, University of Manchester, November 1990.

[Howard *et al.*, 1990c] T.L.J. Howard, W.T. Hewitt, K.M. Wyrwas, and S. Larkin. *A Toolkit for PHIGS Applications*, 1990. In preparation.

[Hubbold, 1987] R.J. Hubbold. Three dimensional graphics standards – a critical appraisal. In *Proceedings Ausgraph '87*. Australasian Computer Graphics Association, 1987.

[Hubbold *et al.*, 1987] R.J. Hubbold, W.T. Hewitt, T.L.J. Howard, and K.M. Wyrwas. Parameterisation mechanisms for KRT^3. Project reports KRT3/40, KRT3/42, KRT3/43, KRT3/45, KRT3/47, Manchester Computing Centre Computer Graphics Unit, 1987.

[Hubbold and Hewitt, 1990] R.J. Hubbold and W.T. Hewitt. GKS-3D and PHIGS – theory and practice. In *Advances in Computer Graphics IV*. Springer-Verlag, 1990.

[Hübl and Herman, 1990] Oosef Hübl and Ivan Herman. Modelling clip: some more results. *Computer Graphics Forum*, 9(2):101–107, 1990.

[IBM, 1988] IBM. *The graPHIGS Programming Interface: Tutorial User's Guide*, 1988. SC33-8119-0.

[ISO, 1985] International Organization for Standardization. *ISO 7942 Information Processing Systems – Computer Graphics – Graphical Kernel System (GKS)*, 1985.

[ISO, 1987] International Organization for Standardization. *ISO 8805 Information Processing Systems – Computer Graphics – Graphical Kernel System for Three Dimensions (GKS–3D) Functional Description*, 1987.

[ISO, 1989a] International Organization for Standardization. *ISO 9592 Information Processing Systems – Computer Graphics – Programmer's Hierarchical Interactive Graphics System (PHIGS)*, 1989.

[ISO, 1989b] International Organization for Standardization. *ISO 9592 Information Processing Systems – Computer Graphics – Programmer's Hierarchical Interactive Graphics System (PHIGS: Archive File Format)*, 1989.

[ISO, 1989c] International Organization for Standardization. *ISO 9592 Information Processing Systems – Computer Graphics – Programmer's Hierarchical Interactive Graphics System (PHIGS: Archive file clear text encoding)*, 1989.

[ISO, 1989d] International Organization for Standardization. *ISO 9593 Information Processing Systems – Computer Graphics – Programmer's Hierarchical Interactive Graphics System (PHIGS: Language Bindings (Part 1) – Fortran)*, 1989.

[ISO, 1989e] International Organization for Standardization. *ISO 9593 Information Processing Systems – Computer Graphics – Programmer's Hierarchical Interactive Graphics System (PHIGS: Language Bindings (Part 3) – Ada)*, 1989.

[ISO, 1989f] International Organization for Standardization. *ISO Information Processing Systems – Computer Graphics – Programmer's Hierarchical Interactive Graphics System (PHIGS PLUS)*, 1989.

[Krammer, 1989] Gergely Krammer. Notes on the mathematics of the PHIGS viewing pipeline. *Computer Graphics Forum*, 8(5):219–226, 1989.

[Noll and Poller, 1988] S. Noll and J. Poller. PHI-GKS: An implementation to support GKS-3D and PHIGS. *Computers & Graphics*, 12(2):163–172, 1988.

[Noll *et al.*, 1987] S. Noll, J. Poller, and J. Rix. Approach to solving the compatibility problem between GKS and PHIGS. *Computer Aided Design*, 19(8):456–463, October 1987.

[O'Bara and Abi-Ezzi, 1989] Robert M. O'Bara and Salim Abi-Ezzi. An analysis of modeling clip. In W. Hansmann, F.R.A. Hopgood, and W. Strasser, editors, *Proceedings Eurographics '89*, pages 367–379. North-Holland, Amsterdam, 1989.

[Patel, 1989] Manjula Patel. A method for the representation, evaluation and display of CSG models in PHIGS and PHIGS+. *Computer Graphics Forum*, 8(4):337–345, 1989.

[Plaehn, 1987] M. Plaehn. PHIGS. *Byte*, 12(13):275–286, November 1987.

[Poller *et al.*, 1989] J. Poller, S. Noll, and J. Rix. Migration of GKS/GKS-3D and PHIGS. *Computer Graphics Forum*, 8(5):239–248, 1989.

[Pöpsel and Hornung, 1989] J. Pöpsel and C. Hornung. Highlight shading, lighting and shading in a PHIGS+/PEX-environment. In W. Hansmann, F.R.A. Hopgood, and W. Strasser, editors, *Proceedings Eurographics '89*, pages 317–332. North-Holland, Amsterdam, 1989.

[Rozells-Kuhnert *et al.*, 1990] Gia Rozells-Kuhnert, Kathy Tinoco, and Norbert Kuhnert. *Using PHIGS with Figaro+*. Template Graphics Software, Inc., 1990.

[Schoenhut, 1986] J. Schoenhut. Are PHIGS and GKS necessarily incompatible? *IEEE Computer Graphics & Applications*, 6(7):51–53, July 1986.

[Shephard and Rix, 1987] B. Shephard and J. Rix. Issues raised by the PHI-GKS approach. *Computer Aided Design*, 19(8):464, October 1987.

[Shuey, 1987] D. Shuey. PHIGS: A graphics platform for CAD application development. *Computer Aided Design*, 19(8):410–416, 1987.

[Shuey and McGinnis, 1987] D. Shuey and E. McGinnis. PHIGS tutorial notes. In *Proceedings Computer Graphics 1987*, Philadelphia, 1987. NCGA.

[Shuey et al., 1986] D. Shuey, D. Bailey, and T. Morrissey. PHIGS: A standard, dynamic, interactive graphics interface. *IEEE Computer Graphics & Applications*, 6(8):50–57, August 1986.

[Singleton, 1986] K.M. Singleton. An implementation of the GKS-3D/PHIGS viewing pipeline. In A.A.G. Requicha, editor, *Proceedings Eurographics '86*, pages 325–356. North-Holland, Amsterdam, 1986.

[ten Hagen et al., 1987] P.J.W. ten Hagen, B.P. Rouwhorst, and L.R.A. Kessener. *A GKS Shell for PHIGS Implementations.* Technical Report ISO TC97/SC21/WG2 N541, ISO, 1987.

[Thatch and Myklebust, 1988] B.R. Thatch and A. Myklebust. A PHIGS-based graphics input interface for spatial-mechanism design. *IEEE Computer Graphics & Applications*, 8(2):26–38, February 1988.

[Watt, 1989] Alan Watt. *Fundamentals of Three-Dimensional Computer Graphics*. Addison-Wesley, Wokingham, 1989.

[Williams, 1985] T. Williams. Degree of PHIGS/GKS compatibility still hotly debated. *Computer Design*, 24(17):38–9, December 1985.

[Wyrwas, 1988] K.M. Wyrwas. PHIGS. In *Computer Graphics Standards: Myth and Reality*. Eurographics UK, 1988.

[Wyrwas and Hewitt, 1989] K.M. Wyrwas and W.T. Hewitt. A survey of GKS and PHIGS implementations. *Computer Graphics Forum*, 8(1):49–59, 1989.

[Zachrisen, 1989] Morten Zachrisen. Yet another remark on the modelling clip problem. *Computer Graphics Forum*, 8(5):237–238, 1989.

Glossary

Cross-references to other definitions in the glossary are shown in italics.

ambient light A type of *light source* which is independent of the orientation of the area being illuminated or the location of the *eye point*.

ambient reflection coefficient The fraction of incident *ambient light* which is reflected from an area.

ancestor structure A *parent* of another *structure*, or one of its parents.

annotation text relative An *output primitive* comprising a text string, intended specifically for annotating pictures; it is always drawn parallel to the display screen, and is therefore always legible.

application data Data stored in a *structure* which is meaningful to a particular application. *PHIGS* provides a special element type for the storage of application data, and it is up to the application to manage its use. Application data *structure elements* have no effect during *traversal*.

archive file A file external to *PHIGS* in which *structure elements* and *structure networks* may be stored and subsequently restored.

area defining primitive Any of the *output primitives*: *fill area, fill area set, cell array, fill area set with data, cell array plus, set of fill area set with data, triangle strip with data, quadrilateral mesh with data* and *non-uniform B-spline surface*.

ASF See *aspect source flag*.

aspect A property of an *output primitive* which determines its visual appearance. There are two sorts of aspect: global (also called geometric, or workstation independent) and workstation dependent (also called non-geometric). Each aspect is controlled by an *attribute*.

aspect ratio The ratio of width to height of an image.

aspect source flag (ASF) A flag which determines whether a workstation-dependent (non-geometric) *aspect* of a primitive is set using an *individual attribute* or a *bundled attribute*. There is one aspect source flag associated with each kind of workstation-dependent aspect.

attenuation coefficient A parameter which models the decrease in intensity of light as a function of the distance from a light source to an illuminated object. It is often used to simulate the light-attenuating effects of different media, such as mist.

attribute Attributes control the properties of *output primitive*s. There are four kinds: geometric (or workstation independent), workstation dependent, viewing and identification.

back face A *facet* of an *area defining primitive* whose *geometric normal* when transformed to *NPC* has a negative *z* component.

back plane In *viewing*, a plane parallel to the *view plane* specified as an *N* coordinate in the *view reference coordinate system*. *Output primitive*s placed behind the back plane lie outside the *view volume*.

break action A special action performed by an *operator* which causes a graphical input operation to be interrupted, and control to be returned to the application program. The way in which the break action is realized is implementation-dependent; for example, breaking an input operation which uses a mouse may involve pressing CONTROL-C on the keyboard. The particular techniques used to break input at your installation will be described in your *Local Guide*.

bundle A collection of all the workstation-dependent *aspect*s of an *output primitive*, stored in a *bundle table* on a *workstation*.

bundled attribute An *attribute* which controls an *aspect* by selecting an entry in a *bundle table*. For an *attribute* to control an *aspect* in this way the corresponding *aspect source flag* must be set to BUNDLED.

bundle table A table in the *workstation state list* of a *workstation* which contains a fixed number of *bundle*s.

bundle table index An *attribute* used to select a particular *bundle* for an *output primitive*. The *aspect*s contained in the bundle then control the appearance of the output primitive.

cell array An *output primitive* comprising a parallelogram of equally sized cells, each of which is a parallelogram and has a colour.

centralized structure store (CSS) The storage area in *PHIGS* in which *structure network*s are stored. The centralized structure store is independent of *workstation*s.

CGM See *Computer Graphics Metafile*.

character expansion factor An *aspect* of *text* which determines the deviation from the nominal *character width* for a particular *font* on a given *workstation*.

character height An *aspect* of *text* which determines the height of an upper-case character.

character spacing An *aspect* of *text* which determines the spacing between characters in a *string*. It is specified as a fraction of *character height*.

character up vector An *aspect* of *text* which determines the 'up direction' of a *string*. It is a 2D vector in the *text plane* of a *text output primitive*.

character width An *aspect* of *text* which determines the nominal value of the width of a character. This quantity is fixed for a particular *font* on a particular *workstation*.

child structure A *structure* specified in an *execute structure element*. The structure containing the execute element is called the parent of the child.

choice device A type of *logical input device* which provides a selection (expressed as a non-negative integer) from a number of alternatives.

CIE An abbreviation for the Commission Internationale de l'Eclairage *colour model*.

clipping The process, performed by *PHIGS*, of removing those parts of an *output primitive* which lie outside a specified volume.

CMT See *composite modelling transformation*.

colour index An integer index used to select an entry from a *colour table*.

colour mapping In the *rendering pipeline*, the conversion of direct colours to workstation-dependent colours before they are displayed on the *workstation*.

colour model A method for quantitatively describing a colour. Examples of colour models are *RGB, HSV,* and *CIE*.

colour table A table on a *workstation*, each entry of which defines a colour in terms of a *colour model*.

composite modelling transformation (CMT) The transformation applied to *output primitive*s produced during *traversal*. It is derived from the concatenation of the *local modelling transformation* and the *global modelling transformation*, such that the local modelling transformation takes effect first. It is also commonly called the *current transformation matrix*, or *CTM*.

Computer Graphics Metafile (CGM) A standard definition of a *metafile* for the capture of static picture definitions (ISO 8632).

concentration exponent A measure of the intensity of light from a *spot light source* as the light deviates from the centreline of the light source's *cone of influence*.

cone of influence A conceptual cone that represents the influence of light from a *spot light source*. Only portions of primitives within the cone are affected by the light from the spot light source. The cone of influence is defined by the light source's position, direction and spread angle.

conflict resolution flag A flag which determines the action taken during *structure archiving* or *structure retrieval* when conflicts are detected between the names of structures in the *CSS* and an *archive file*.

connection identifier A implementation-dependent means of defining the correspondence between a *workstation* and a particular set of physical devices. It is used in the OPEN WORKSTATION function – see your *Local Guide* for details of your installation.

CSS See *centralized structure store.*

CTM See *composite modelling transformation.*

current transformation matrix (CTM) See *composite modelling transformation.*

data mapping The conversion of application-specific data to a colour.

data record A data type used to specify additional implementation-dependent information in *PHIGS* functions such as input device initializations.

DC See *device coordinates.*

deferral mode A property of a *workstation* which is part of its *display update state* and which enables the application to specify the times at which changes to posted *structure networks* and the *workstation state list* are reflected in the displayed image.

depth cue mode A field in each entry of the *depth cue table* of the *workstation state list* that indicates whether or not *depth cueing* should be performed.

depth cue plane A reference plane in *NPC*, parallel to the *xy* plane. There are two depth cue planes which together define the limits of the effects of *depth cueing.*

depth cue scale factors Weights, specified at each *depth cue plane*, that indicate the proportion of the depth cue colour to combine with the colours of primitives falling within the depth cue planes.

depth cue table A table in the *workstation state list* that controls *depth cueing.*

depth cueing An effect in which the colour of a primitive is combined with a specified depth cue colour such that a colour variation over the primitive is achieved between two reference planes (in *NPC*). Depth cueing is often used to make portions of primitives that are farther away from the viewer appear darker.

descendant structure A *child structure*, or a child of one of its children.

device coordinates (DC) A device-dependent coordinate system. For a device which can produce a precisely scaled image, such as a pen-plotter, DC units are metres; otherwise, DC units are workstation dependent, such as pixels.

diffuse reflection The reflection of light equally in all directions from a surface. Diffusely reflected light gives a surface a dull, matt appearance that is independent of the viewing direction.

diffuse reflection coefficient The fraction of light from non-ambient light sources diffusely reflecting from a surface.

direct colour specification A method of specifying colour using a set of coordinates in a colour space, together with the colour model in which they are expressed.

directional light A *light source* that enters into the *reflectance calculation*, which is dependent on the orientation of the area being illuminated, but independent of the area's distance from the light source. Directional light sources are used to simulate light sources relatively far from the area being lit.

display device A graphics device which can display images. A display device is one possible component of a *workstation*.

display priority The priority assigned by an application to a *structure network* when it is *posted* to a *workstation*. It is used to distinguish between *output primitives* which are drawn at the same location on a *display device*.

display space The part of a *workstation* on which images are displayed.

display update state A property of a *workstation* which determines how and when the displayed image is modified to reflect changes in the *centralized structure store* and the *workstation state list*. It has two components: *deferral mode* and *modification mode*. An application can set the display update state of a workstation to make best use of the capabilities of the workstation.

echo An indication to an *operator* of the current *measure* of a *logical input device*. For example, for a *locator device* this might be the appearance of crosshairs on the display of a *workstation*.

echo area/volume An area or volume expressed in *device coordinates* in which the *prompt* and *echo* are displayed.

edge The boundary of a polygon defined as part of a *fill area set output primitive*.

edge flag An *aspect* of *fill area set* which enables or disables the display of *edges*.

edge visibility flag An indicator, part of the specification of some *output primitives*, such as *fill area set with data*, which controls whether an individual *edge* is visible. This indicator is only used during *traversal* when the edge flag aspect is ON.

edgetype An *aspect* of *fill area set* which determines the visual style in which its *edges* are displayed.

edgewidth scale factor An *aspect* of *fill area set* which determines the displayed width of *edges*. It is expressed as a multiple of a nominal edge width.

edit mode During *structure editing*, the edit mode determines whether a new *structure element* replaces the structure element at the element pointer, or is inserted after the *element pointer*, which will then be updated to point to the new *element*.

element See *structure element*.

element pointer A pointer used during *structure editing* which specifies a position within the open *structure* at which the creation and deletion of *structure elements* will take place.

element type   The nature of a *structure element*. *PHIGS* defines 71 different types of element; some examples are *polyline*, *text*, *label*, *set linetype* and *add names to set*. Additional types of element are defined by *PHIGS PLUS*.

empty interior style   One possible representation of the *interior* of a *fill area* or *fill area set output primitive*. If the *edges* are not displayed, the image of fill area set with *interior style* empty will be invisible. The image of a fill area with interior style empty is always invisible.

escape   A function which provides access to implementation-dependent facilities, the nature of which are not specified by *PHIGS*. Escape functions must not produce graphical output nor create *structure elements*.

even–odd rule   The rule used by *PHIGS* to determine whether a point is part of the interior of a *fill area* of *fill area set*.

event mode   An operating mode for a *logical input device* in which the *operator* may generate input data at any time. The input data is placed as an *event report* on an *event queue*, which the application may interrogate at its convenience.

event queue   A time-ordered collection of *event reports* generated by *logical input devices* in *event mode*.

event report   An entry on an *event queue* which comprises a value obtained from a *logical input device*, together with the identification of the *logical input device* responsible.

exclusion set   The part of a *filter* which defines a set of *names* which are not eligible for a particular operation.

execute element   A type of *structure element* which enables *structures* to be arranged hierarchically. An execute element specifies the name of a structure to be referenced.

eye point   A point in *WC* that transforms to infinite positive *z* in *NPC* (the homogeneous point $(0, 0, 1, 0)$). This point is used in the *reflectance calculation* for determining viewing-position-dependent effects of lighting.

face culling   The process of removing back-facing or front-facing portions of *output primitives* from the *rendering pipeline*, and thus from being displayed.

facet   A portion of an *area defining primitive*. Facets may be defined by vertices that constitute a subset of the primitive's set of vertices. The following primitives comprise one or more facets: *fill area, fill area set, cell array, fill area set with data, cell array plus, set of fill area set with data, triangle strip with data, quadrilateral mesh with data*. Any subprimitives produced from the tessellation of parametric surfaces are also considered to be facets.

facet normal   A normal vector supplied with an *area defining primitive* and associated with a *facet* of such a primitive. A facet normal is typically used for determining the geometric normal of a facet, and in some cases for determining the *reflectance normal*.

fill area   An *output primitive* comprising a single polygon defined in *modelling coordinates*.

fill area set   An *output primitive* comprising a collection of *fill area*s with or without *edge*s.

fill area set with data   An *output primitive* comprising a set of coplanar polygons. The corresponding *structure element* may include other information such as colours or normals that may be used to colour, light and shade the primitive.

filter   The combination of an *inclusion set* and an *exclusion set* used to identify *output primitives* as eligible or ineligible for a particular operation. Each *workstation* has three filters for controlling *picking*, *highlighting* and *invisibility* of output primitives. A filter is also used in *incremental spatial search*.

font   A collection of characters which share a particular set of visual characteristics.

front face   Any *facet* of an *area defining primitive* whose *geometric normal* when transformed to *NPC* has a non-negative z component.

front plane   In *viewing*, a plane parallel to the *view plane* specified as an *N* coordinate in the *view reference coordinate system*. *Output primitives* placed in front of the front plane lie outside the *view volume*.

frustum   A geometrical figure, defined by two parallel planes and projectors joining each corresponding corners of each plane.

G   See *global modelling transformation*.

GDP   See *generalized drawing primitive*.

general colour   An abstraction that allows both the direct and indirect specification of colour. General colour specifies a colour type and colour values. The colour type can either indicate a *colour model*, in which case the colour values are coordinates in the colour space corresponding to that model, or it can indicate that the colour is being specified indirectly, in which case the single colour value is an index into the workstation-dependent colour table.

generalized drawing primitive (GDP)   An *output primitive* used to access special implementation-dependent graphical facilities, not defined by *PHIGS*. Typically, these might include curve or surface drawing.

generalized structure element (GSE)   A *structure element* used to access special implementation-dependent facilities, not defined by *PHIGS*, with the proviso that *output primitives* are not created.

geometric normal   A unit vector used to determine the front-facing or back-facing orientation of portions of area defining *output primitives*.

GKS   See *Graphical Kernel System*.

global modelling transformation (G)   A transformation which exists during *traversal*, and which is one component of the *composite modelling trans-*

formation. When traversal of a *structure* begins, the value of the global modelling transformation is set to the composite modelling transformation of the *parent structure*, or if the structure being traversed is the *posted structure*, to the default value in the *PHIGS description table*, which is the *identity transformation.*

Graphical Kernel System (GKS)   An international standard for 2D graphical input and output (ISO 7942).

GSE   See *generalized structure element.*

half-space   An infinite plane defined by a point and a *normal vector.*

hatch interior style   One possible representation of the *interior* of a *fill area* or *fill area set output primitive*. The interior is filled with a pattern of parallel and/or crossing hatch lines, selected from the *workstation*'s *hatch table.*

hatch table   A table of hatch specifications stored on a *workstation.*

hidden line/hidden surface removal (HLHSR)   The process of removing those parts of *output primitive*s which are obscured by other output primitives.

highlighting   Emphasizing an *output primitive* by modifying its visual appearance in some workstation-dependent manner. For example, an output primitive might be highlighted by making it flash on and off rapidly, or by drawing it in a special highlighting colour.

highlighting filter   A *filter* on a *workstation* comprising two *name set*s, the highlighting *inclusion set* and the highlighting *exclusion set*, which together are used to select *output primitive*s for *highlighting.*

HLHSR   See *hidden line/hidden surface removal.*

HLS   An abbreviation for the 'Hue, Lightness and Saturation' *colour model.*

hollow interior style   One possible representation of the *interior* of a *fill area* or *fill area set output primitive*. The image of the output primitive is the boundary line only, including any extra boundaries produced by *clipping.*

HSV   An abbreviation for the 'Hue, Saturation and Value' *colour model.*

identity transformation   A coordinate transformation which maps a point onto itself. An identity transformation is commonly known as the 'unit matrix'.

implicit regeneration   The complete recreation of the image on a *workstation* such that it represents exactly the description of the model. This may occur when changes to the posted *structure network*s or *workstation state list* cause the displayed image to be out of date.

inclusion set   The part of a *filter* which defines a set of *name*s which are eligible for a particular operation, such as *highlighting* or *picking.*

incremental spatial search   A *PHIGS* function which enables the application to search within the *centralized structure store* for a graphical output *structure element* which lies within a specified *world coordinate* region.

indirect colour specification   A method of specifying colour via an index into a workstation-dependent *colour table*.

individual attribute   An *attribute* which controls an *aspect* directly, instead of selecting an entry in a *bundle table*. For an *attribute* to control an *aspect* directly, the corresponding *aspect source flag* must be set to INDIVIDUAL.

inheritance   The mechanism by which *child structures* obtain their initial *attribute* settings from their *ancestor structures*, or in the case of the posted *structure*, from the *PHIGS description table*.

input class   The classification of a *logical input device*. *PHIGS* has six input classes: *locator, stroke, valuator, choice, pick* and *string*.

input mode   The operating method used to obtain input from a *logical input device*. There are three input modes: *request, sample* and *event*.

interior   The region which lies inside a *fill area* or *fill area set*. *PHIGS* uses the *even–odd rule* to determine whether a point is in the interior of a fill area or fill area set.

interior style   An *aspect* which determines the style used to render the *interior* of a *fill area* or *fill area set*.

intrinsic colour   The colour of an *output primitive* that is independent of *lighting*, *depth cueing* and *colour mapping*. This colour is used as input to the *reflectance calculations* for *area defining primitives*.

invisibility   The state of an *output primitive* being not visible even though it lies on the display surface of a *workstation*, and it is not hidden by other output primitives.

invisibility filter   A *filter* on a *workstation* comprising two *name sets*, the invisibility *inclusion set* and the invisibility *exclusion set*, which together are used to determine whether *output primitives* are visible or invisible.

ISO   International Organization for Standardization.

isoparametric curve   A curve on a parametric surface produced by evaluating the surface over the range of one of its independent variables while keeping its other independent variable constant.

knot vector   A non-decreasing sequence of real numbers that is part of the definition of *non-uniform B-splines*. This vector comprises values for the independent variables of the primitive and is used in computing the B-spline basis polynomials.

L   See *local modelling transformation*.

label   A *structure element* comprising an identifier which may be used as a placemarker in a *structure* to help with *structure editing*. Label elements have no effect during *traversal*.

language binding   The way in which the functionality of *PHIGS* is expressed in a particular programming language. For example, the POLYLINE 3 function will appear in the standard C binding as `ppolyline3`, and in the standard Fortran binding as `PPL3`.

light source   An entry in a *workstation* light source table used to simulate a source of light. All light sources have a colour. Some light source types have aspects such as position, direction, concentration exponent, spread angle and attenuation.

light source direction   A unit vector that defines the orientation of a *light source*.

light source state   A field in the *traversal state list* that selects which *light source*s in a *workstation light source* table are active.

lighting   The calculation of the effect of *light source*s on an *area defining primitive*.

linetype   An *aspect* of *polyline* which determines the style in which it is drawn. For example, solid, dashed or dotted.

linewidth scale factor   An *aspect* of *polyline* which determines the width of displayed lines. It is expressed as a multiple of a nominal line width.

local modelling transformation (L)   A transformation which exists during *traversal*, and which is one component of the *composite modelling transformation*. When traversal of a *structure* begins, the value of the local modelling transformation is set to the *identity transformation*.

locator device   A type of *logical input device* which provides a position in *world coordinates* and an associated *view index*.

logical input device   A device, part of a *workstation*, which is an abstraction of one or more physical devices (such as a mouse) which an *operator* may use to provide input data to a *PHIGS* program.

marker   A symbol used by the *polymarker output primitive* to mark a location on a *display device*. The shape of a marker is not subject to transformation.

marker size scale factor   An *aspect* which determines the relative size of the image of a *marker*. It is expressed as a multiple of a nominal marker size on a *workstation*.

marker type   An *aspect* which selects the type of symbol used to display a *marker*. *PHIGS* specifies that a number of standard types of symbol should always be available, such as dot, star and plus symbols.

MC   See *modelling coordinates*.

measure   The value returned to an application program by a *logical input device*. For example, the measure of a *locator* comprises a position in *world coordinates* and an associated *view index*.

message   A character string sent by an application program to a *workstation*. It is intended for communication with the *operator*.

metafile   A file external to *PHIGS* intended for the storage and transportation of graphical and other information. A metafile contains a device-independent description of one or more pictures. Hierarchical information is not necessarily stored.

modelling clip   A clip against a *modelling clipping volume* optionally performed after the application of the *composite modelling transformation*. It is commonly used to reveal the internal structure of objects.

modelling clipping volume   A volume in *world coordinates* defined by the intersection of a collection of *half-spaces*.

modelling coordinates   A device-independent 3D right-handed Cartesian coordinate system in which an application specifies graphical information using *output primitives*.

modification mode   Part of the *display update state* of a *workstation*. The modification mode determines what category of visual effects shall be immediately achieved, and how the effects are achieved.

name set   An *output primitive* identification *attribute* comprising a number of names, used to define the eligibility of output primitives for *highlighting*, *invisibility* and *picking*.

non-uniform B-spline curve   A curve defined by a number of control points, a set of B-spline basis functions, an order and a *knot vector*.

non-uniform B-spline surface   A surface specified by two orders, two *knot vectors*, and a 2D array of control points. The basis functions are the B-spline basis functions.

normal vector   A unit vector, typically used to indicate the orientation of a *facet*.

normalized projection coordinates (NPC)   In *viewing*, a device-independent 3D right-handed Cartesian coordinate system in which images are composited. The *view clipping limits* and *workstation window* are specified in *NPC*.

NPC   See *normalized projection coordinates*.

NURB   A term sometimes used to describe *non-uniform B-spline curve* and *non-uniform B-spline surface*.

operator   A person manipulating a *logical input device*.

output primitive   A fundamental graphical entity provided by PHIGS for the definition of geometric shapes. There are eight kinds: *polyline, polymarker, text, annotation text relative, fill area, fill area set, cell array* and *generalized drawing primitive*. *PHIGS PLUS* defines several extra primitives: *polyline set with data, fill area with data, fill area set with data, set of fill area set with data, triangle strip with data, quadrilateral mesh with data, non-uniform B-spline curve, non-uniform B-spline surface* and *cell array plus*.

parameter range limits   Minimum and maximum parameter values that limit the parameter range over which parametric curves and surfaces are generated.

parameter space   The coordinate system of the independent variable(s) of para-metric curves and surfaces, one-dimensional for curves and two-dimensional for surfaces. The curve and surface primitives are defined via a mapping from parameter space to *modelling coordinates*.

parameter space boundaries   The extreme values of the *parameter space* of a parametric primitive. For *non-uniform B-spline* curves and surfaces the par-ameter space boundaries are the extreme values of the knots in the associated *knot vectors*.

parametric primitive   *Output primitives* defined as a mapping from a *param-eter space* to *modelling coordinates*. Parametric primitives defined in *PHIGS PLUS* are *non-uniform B-spline curve* and *non-uniform B-spline surface*.

parallel transformation   The transformation of an object in which parallel lines in the object appear parallel in the image regardless of their relative distance.

parent structure   A *structure* which contains *execute elements*.

pattern interior style   One possible representation of the *interior* of a *fill area* or *fill area set output primitive*. The interior is filled with a 2D pixel pattern selected from a *workstation*'s *pattern table*.

pattern table   A table on a *workstation* which defines a number of patterns.

PDT   See *PHIGS description table*.

PET   See *prompt and echo type*.

perspective transformation   The transformation of an object in which parallel lines in the object which intersect the view plane appear to converge in the image.

PHIGS   Programmer's Hierarchical Interactive Graphics System (ISO 9592).

PHIGS description table (PDT)   A set of static workstation-independent data stored in a *PHIGS* implementation. It contains implementation-specific information, such as a list of available *workstation* types, as well as a number of default values, such as whether *attributes* are initially bundled or individ-ual.

PHIGS PLUS   A set of proposed extensions to *PHIGS* to cater for more com-plex geometry and lighting and shading.

pick device   A type of *logical input device* which provides a *pick path*.

pick filter   A *filter* on a *workstation* comprising two *name sets*, the pick *inclu-sion set* and the pick *exclusion set*, which together are used to select whether *output primitives* are eligible for *picking*.

pick identifier   A name associated with an *output primitive*, which is returned by a *pick device* as part of the *pick path*. Pick identifiers are set using *structure elements*.

pick path   A list of information returned by a *pick device*, which represents the hierarchical path to a picked *output primitive* from its posted *structure*.

Each entry in the pick path comprises a *structure identifier*, *pick identifier* and *element* number.

picking   Identifying an *output primitive* by 'pointing' at it on the display using an input device such as a mouse.

polyline   An *output primitive* comprising a connected sequence of straight lines between specified points defined in *modelling coordinates*.

polyline set with data   An *output primitive* comprising an unconnected set of *polyline*s. The corresponding *structure element* may include colour information that may be used to shade the primitive.

polymarker   An *output primitive* comprising a set of locations, each identified by a *marker* of the same type.

positional light   A *light source* that enters into the *reflectance calculation* dependent on the orientation and position of an area being illuminated relative to the light source.

post   To identify a *structure network* for display on a *workstation*. When a structure network is posted, *PHIGS* traverses it.

projection reference point (PRP)   In *viewing*, a point (expressed in *view reference coordinates*) which for parallel *projection type* determines the direction of *projector*s and for perspective projection type determines the point from which all projectors emanate.

projection type   In *viewing*, the type of transformation to be used in *view mapping*. PHIGS specifies two types: parallel, where all *projector*s are parallel, and perspective, where projectors emanate from a single point.

projection viewport   In *viewing*, a *rectangular parallelepiped* in *normalized projection coordinate*. The *view mapping* transformation maps the contents of the *view volume* into the projection viewport.

projector   In *viewing*, a conceptual line which passes through a point on an *output primitive* and intersects the *view plane*.

prompt   An indication to the *operator* that a particular *logical input device* is available for use. For example, for a *locator device* a special cursor may appear on the display.

prompt and echo type   Part of a *logical input device* which specifies the nature of the *prompt* and *echo* used during graphical input operations.

PRP   See *projection reference point*.

pseudo-colour mapping   A *colour mapping* method that uses a weighted average of the colour coordinates to produce an index into a table of colours.

pseudo-N colour mapping   A *colour mapping* method that uses each coordinate of a colour as an index into one of a number of separate lists of colour components. The combination of these components defines the colour used for display.

quadrilateral mesh   An *output primitive* in which an array of quadrilaterals is specified by a 2D array of points.

rectangular parallelepiped   A geometrical figure bounded by six parallelograms, such that opposite pairs are equal and parallel, and adjacent pairs are at right angles.

reflectance calculation   The computation of the effect of *light source*s on a portion of an *output primitive*.

reflectance characteristics   An *aspect* that controls the complexity of the *reflectance calculation* and the *lighting* effects it considers.

reflectance formulae   Formulae that model the light reflected by an *area defining primitive*.

reflectance normal   A vector, conceptually perpendicular to some portion of an *area defining primitive*, that indicates the orientation of that portion. It typically influences the *reflectance calculation* and is derived from *vertex normal*s or other geometry of the primitive.

reflectance properties   An *aspect* of *area defining primitive*s that indicates how a primitive reflects light. Reflectance properties include *ambient reflection coefficient*, *diffuse reflection coefficient*, *specular reflection coefficient*, *specular colour* and *specular exponent*.

rendering colour model   The *colour model* used for performing colour interpolation within the *rendering pipeline*.

rendering pipeline   A sequence of operations that performs *data mapping*, *lighting*, *shading*, *depth cueing* and *colour mapping* of *output primitive*s. Each of these operations is considered a stage in the pipeline.

request mode   An operating mode for a *logical input device* in which *PHIGS* waits until the *operator* signals that input is ready by activating the *trigger* of the logical input device. The *measure* of the the logical input device is then returned to the application program, and *PHIGS* continues.

RGB   An abbreviation for the 'Red, Green and Blue' colour model.

sample mode   An operating mode for a *logical input device* in which the current *measure* of the logical input device is returned to *PHIGS* without the need for the *operator* to activate any *trigger*.

set of fill area set with data   An *output primitive* in which a number of possibly non-coplanar *fill area set*s are defined by indices into a single vertex list. The fill area sets are not required to form a closed or connected surface.

shading   The interpolation portion of the *rendering pipeline*.

solid interior style   One possible representation of the *interior* of a *fill area* or *fill area set output primitive*. The interior is filled with a uniform colour.

specular colour   The colour of specular highlights on an *area defining primitive*.

specular exponent A number indicating the shininess of an area; the higher the specular exponent, the shinier the area.

specular reflection The unequal reflection of light in different directions from an *area defining primitive*. The intensity of specular reflections, unlike *diffuse reflection*s, is dependent on the viewing angle of the observer.

specular reflection coefficient The fraction of non-*ambient light* contributing to *specular reflection*.

spot light A *light source* that enters into the *reflectance calculation* dependent on the orientation and relative position of the area being illuminated. Light from such a source is restricted to a cone of influence and its intensity is possibly modified as it deviates from the centreline of this cone.

spread angle An angle that determines the *cone of influence* of a *spot light source*. Only portions of primitives that intersect this cone are affected by the light source.

string A collection of characters.

string device A type of *logical input device* which provides a *string*.

stroke device A type of *logical input device* which provides a sequence of points in *world coordinates*, and an associated *view index* which applies to all the points.

structure A named sequence of *structure element*s. Each structure element in a structure is numbered, starting at 1.

structure archiving The process of copying specified *structure*s and *structure network*s to an *archive file*, for subsequent *structure retrieval*. If a conflict should occur (when the same names are present in the *centralized structure store* and in the archive file), PHIGS consults the *conflict resolution flag* to decide what to do.

structure editing The process of modifying a *structure*, for example by inserting, replacing or deleting *structure element*s.

structure element The fundamental unit of data in the *centralized structure store*. A *structure* comprises a named sequence of structure elements, each of which is numbered. A structure element belongs to only one structure, and may not exist outside a structure. *PHIGS* has many different types of element; some examples are *polyline*, *text*, *label*, *set polyline index* and *add names to set*.

structure identifier The unique name used by an application to reference a *structure*. The name is attached to the structure when it is created, and may be subsequently changed.

structure network A collection of *structure*s arranged with the topology of a directed acyclic graph, commonly referred to as a hierarchy. The structures form the nodes of the graph, and references between structures (created by *execute element*s) the arcs between nodes.

structure reference   The invocation of one *structure* from within another, using an *execute element*.

structure retrieval   The process of copying *structure* and *structure networks* from an *archive file* into the *centralized structure store*. If a conflict should occur (when the same names are present in the centralized structure store and in the archive file), PHIGS consults the *conflict resolution flag* to decide what to do.

tessellate   To subdivide a parametric curve or surface into segments that approximate the original curve or surface.

text   An *output primitive* comprising a character string drawn at a specified location in *modelling coordinates* (the *text position*) on a specified *text plane*, specified by two vectors.

text alignment   An *aspect* of *text* which specifies how a *string* is to be aligned with the *text position*. It has two components: horizontal and vertical.

text direction vectors   Two vectors, specified as part of the *text structure element*, which, together with the *text position* define the *text plane* on which text is drawn.

text font   An *aspect* of *text* which determines which *font* is used to draw characters.

text path   An *aspect* of *text* which determines the relative positioning of successive character in a string. For example, HELLO (text path = RIGHT) and OLLEH (text path = LEFT).

text plane   A plane in *modelling coordinates* on which a *text output primitive* is displayed.

text position   A point in *modelling coordinates*, specified as part of the *text output primitive*, which, together with the *text direction vectors*, determines the *text plane*. It also determines the location of the first character in the text *string*.

text precision   An *aspect* of *text* which selects the fidelity with which it is rendered on the display. There are three precisions of text defined by *PHIGS*. In order of increasing fidelity they are: string, character, and stroke.

traversal   The process, performed by *PHIGS*, of processing a *structure network* for display on a *workstation*. PHIGS traverses a structure network by stepping through its *elements* in order starting with element 1, processing each one in turn. When an *execute element* is encountered, traversal of the current structure is temporarily halted, and the referenced structure network is completely traversed; traversal of the original *structure* then resumes.

traversal state list (TSL)   A set of information maintained by *PHIGS* during *traversal*, including the current values of all the *attributes* used to render *output primitives*, the *local modelling transformation* and the *global modelling transformation*. Because it exists only during traversal, the TSL may not be inquired by the application.

triangle strip An *output primitive* in which *n* points define *n* − 1 triangles.

trigger The mechanism by which the *operator* indicates to *PHIGS* that an input value has been generated. For example, if a *locator logical input device* is realized as a mouse, pressing one of the mouse buttons might be used as the trigger.

trimmed surface A *non-uniform B-spline surface* whose specification contains a set of *trimming loop*s that limit the range of the independent variables over which the surface is evaluated.

trimming curve A parametric curve defined in the *parameter space* of the surface to which it applies. Trimming curves are combined to form *trimming loop*s which limit the parameter range over which a parametric surface is evaluated.

trimming loop A sequence of non-intersecting, connected and similarly oriented *trimming curve*s that form a closed loop. These loops are used to limit the parameter range over which a parametric surface is evaluated.

TSL See *traversal state list*.

unpost To remove a *structure network* from display on a *workstation*.

UVN In *viewing*, the names given to the axes in the *view reference coordinate system*. *U, V, N* correspond to *x, y, z* respectively.

valuator device A type of *logical input device* which provides a single real number.

vertex colour A *general colour* associated with each vertex of some types of *output primitive*s. Examples of such primitives are *polyline set with data* and *fill area set with data*. This colour may be used within the *rendering pipeline* to colour and shade the primitive.

vertex data Geometric, colour or other data specified at vertices of certain *output primitive*s. This data specifies the geometry of a primitive and, depending on various *attribute* settings, is used to influence the appearance of a primitive.

vertex normal A unit *normal vector* optionally supplied with *area defining primitive*s and associated with vertices of such primitives. Vertex normals are typically used for determining *reflectance normal*s. For example, an application can approximate a smooth surface using *fill area set with data* primitives, and supply vertex normals to allow *PHIGS PLUS* to produce a smooth appearing visual representation. In this case, the normals are not necessarily perpendicular to the plane of the *fill area set*.

view index An *output primitive attribute* which selects the *view representation* on a *workstation* used to transform *output primitive*s during *traversal*. View index is an integer.

view mapping   In *viewing*, the process of transforming points from *view reference coordinates* to *normalized projection coordinates*.

view orientation   In *viewing*, the process of transforming points from *world coordinates* to *view reference coordinates*.

view plane   In *viewing*, a plane parallel to the *UV* plane in *view reference coordinates*, specified as an *N* coordinate in *VRC*. Note that the *view plane* is not the same as the *view reference plane*.

view plane normal   In *viewing*, a vector in *world coordinates*, relative to the *view reference point*, which defines the *N* axis of the *view reference coordinate system*.

view reference coordinate system (VRC)   In *viewing*, a device-independent 3D right-handed Cartesian coordinate system in which the parameters of *view mapping* are specified. VRC is defined relative to *world coordinates*, and is used to simplify the specification of viewing parameters. The position and orientation of VRC are determined by three quantities: *view reference point*, *view plane normal* and *view up vector*. The *x, y, z* axes of VRC are referred to as *U, V, N* respectively.

view reference plane   A plane used to assist the definition of the *view reference coordinate system*. It is a plane perpendicular to the *view plane normal* which contains the *view reference point*. The orthogonal projection of the *view up vector* onto this plane defines the *V* axis of *VRC*. Note that the *view reference plane* is not the same as the *view plane*.

view reference point   A point in *world coordinates* which defines the origin of the *view reference coordinate system*.

view representation   An entry in the *view table* on a *workstation* which determines *viewing* parameters. It comprises a *view orientation* matrix, a *view mapping* matrix, view *clipping* limits and a set of clipping indicators.

view table   A *workstation* table comprising a list of *view representations*. Its entries are referenced using the *view index attribute*.

view transformation input priority   In *viewing*, a parameter which determines the order in which *view table* entries are tested when selecting the inverse view transformation to be applied to *locator* and *stroke* input.

view up vector   In *viewing*, one of the parameters used to define the *view reference coordinate system*. The view up vector is expressed in *world coordinates*, and its orthogonal projection onto the *view reference plane* defines the *V* axis of VRC. Vectors in world coordinates which are parallel to the view up vector will appear upright in the displayed image.

view volume   In *viewing*, a 3D volume determined by the *view window* defined in the *view plane*, the *front plane*, the *back plane*, and *projectors* which pass through the corners of the view window. If the projection type is perspective, the view volume is a *frustum*; if the projection type is parallel, the view volume is a *rectangular parallelepiped*. In 2D viewing, the view volume reduces to the view window.

view window   A rectangle defined in the *view plane*.

viewing   The process of producing an image of a 3D scene, involving the definition of a number of parameters including a *projection type*, a *view volume*, *clipping* specifications, and so on.

VRC   See *view reference coordinates*.

WC   See *world coordinates*.

WDT   See *workstation description table*.

workstation   A workstation is an abstraction of one or more physical input devices. It comprises zero or one *display device*s, and zero or more *logical input device*s. The association between a workstation and a set of real devices is achieved using the OPEN WORKSTATION function.

workstation category   A property of a *workstation* which specifies whether it can perform graphical output, graphical input, or both.

workstation description table (WDT)   A static set of read-only data which defines the capabilities of a particular *workstation type*.

workstation identifier   A name chosen by the application to refer to a particular *workstation*. It is associated with a workstation using the OPEN WORKSTATION function.

workstation state list (WSL)   A set of data which represents dynamic operational information about a *workstation*.

workstation transformation   A transformation which maps the contents of the *workstation window* into the *workstation viewport*. This transformation is guaranteed to preserve the aspect ratio in x and y, but not necessarily in z.

workstation type   The nature of a *workstation* which determines its overall capabilities. Workstations of the same type share a common *workstation description table*.

workstation viewport   A *rectangular parallelepiped* defined in *device coordinate space*. All graphical output appears in this volume.

workstation window   A *rectangular parallelepiped* defined in *normalized projection coordinate space*. Its contents are mapped into the *workstation viewport* by the *workstation transformation*.

world coordinates   A device-independent 3D right-handed Cartesian coordinate system in which an application organizes graphical information for display. *Output primitive*s expressed in *modelling coordinates* and defined by *structure element*s are mapped to world coordinates when the *composite modelling transformation* is applied during *traversal*.

WSL   See *workstation state list*.

Index

The names of PHIGS functions are shown in SMALL CAPITALS, and only their 3D forms are listed (the names of the 2D forms are obtained by removing the suffix '3'). Small capitals are also used for the values of enumerated types. Concise definitions of many of the entries may be found in the Glossary (pages 309–327).